The Cutting Garden

GROWING AND ARRANGING GARDEN FLOWERS

Sarah Raven

Photographs by

Pia Tryde

Reader's Digest

THE READER'S DIGEST ASSOCIATION, INC.

Pleasantville, New York/Montreal

for Adam, Rosie, Molly, and Louise

A READER'S DIGEST BOOK

Conceived, edited, and designed by
Frances Lincoln Limited, London

Copyright © 1996 Frances Lincoln Limited
Text copyright © 1996 Sarah Raven
Planting plans copyright © 1996 Frances Lincoln Limited
Photographs by Pia Tryde copyright © 1996 Frances Lincoln Limited
Photographs on pages 10, 22, 26, 27, 31 copyright © 1996 Andrew Lawson

Library of Congress Cataloging in Publication Data

Raven. Sarah.
    The cutting garden : growing and arranging garden flowers /
Sarah Raven ; foreword by Penelope Hobhouse
        p.   cm.
    Includes index.
    ISBN 0-89577-884-X
    1. Flower gardening. 2. Cut flowers. 3. Flowers
4. Flower arrangement. I. Title.
SB405.R27 1996
635.9'66—dc20   96-15547

Reader's Digest and the Pegasus logo are registered trademarks of
The Reader's Digest Association, Inc.

Printed in Hong Kong by Kwong Fat Offset Printing Co. Ltd

9 8 7 6 5 4 3 2 1

Half-title page: The chartreuse-green double Zinnia 'Envy' is one of my favorite flowers for cutting (see page 73).

Frontispiece: In early fall the cutting garden is full of hot colors, luxurious textures, and interesting shapes. Buckets of freshly picked crabapples and white phlox rest among pink zinnias, gloriosa daisies, amaranthus tassels, and white cosmos.

Title page: Tithonia rotundifolia 'Torch' and Viburnum opulus.

Right: Early flowers such as hellebores, hyacinths, and snowdrops stapled to a cheese-cloth curtain make a simple but unusual winter decoration (see page 92).

Foreword: One or two precious late-winter or early-spring gems, such as these aconites and gold-laced polyanthus, a few sprigs of winter cherry blossom, and some lichened witch hazel, bring a bright glow to your desk on even the dullest morning.

Contents

Foreword

The Cutting Garden is a beautiful, stimulating, and practical book. Sarah Raven's descriptions of how to grow flowers and leaves are not only very useful, they also make the cutting garden itself a desirable object. She designs a totally seasonal garden, producing flowers to display together in vases just as they grow and flower together in the garden. Having told the reader how to grow them in beautifully simple ways, she then suggests how to pick, prepare, and arrange them. Each daily or weekly harvest from the garden reflects that exact gardening moment. Sometimes her displays are luxuriant with clashing colors or subtle harmonies; at other times a single flower and stem provides a simple statement. This is why her approach works so well: it takes the garden and intensifies it, enriching what the moment gives her.

Professional flower arrangers can be intimidating. Often they seem rigidly controlled by an elaborate assembly of rules concerning choice of flowers as well as methods of arrangement. The rules seem designed to make the task difficult. But Sarah Raven is a talented and innovative flower arranger who uses real garden flowers in simple, natural ways. She encourages a break with the stale formula of the commonplace (and often exotic) flowers usually found in the florist's shop – flown in from all over the world and therefore in no way reflecting the natural seasons. For her, branches from home-grown cherries, sprigs of scented viburnum or daphne, acid-green euphorbias and lady's mantle, wine-colored perennials and summer-flowering annuals – some quite unusual – replace artificial-looking tropicals or the more mundane "everlastings" and spray chrysanthemums. Plants such as old man's beard and honeysuckle extend her range beyond the boundaries of the cultivated flower garden. For the actual arranging she recommends a full range of schemes, from a cottage garden style to sumptuous colored globes you might have found in the background of a Titian. While her guidelines emphasize a simplicity of approach, and an escape from elaborate rules and flower show marking, her goal is often the rich and luxurious, with both color harmonies and clashes matched to nature's seasonal hues and shades.

But this is not just a romantic book. It is also eminently practical. Planning the cutting garden, growing from seed, choosing vases, preparation of stems and flowers, all have careful explanations.

Sarah Raven is knowledgeable and inspiring. Her writing is alive and modern. Some of the book's charm comes from its evocative recommendations which, in their simplicity, seem old-fashioned. But there is a vitality to it which sets it apart. This is flower arranging for people who understand that flowers are living things, the crowning glories of the natural world. She gardens and writes for the craftsman – in a 1990's interpretation of Arts and Crafts in which real flowers, including almost forgotten favorites, grown and displayed with skill and sensitivity, replace the mass-produced forced artifacts to which we have become accustomed.

Penelope Hobhouse

Introduction

There's nothing like going out into the garden and picking flowers for the house. It's the gardener's equivalent of collecting new-laid eggs from nesting boxes. It's a personal harvest, a gathering of good and life-enhancing things that you have nurtured yourself. Gardening, as anyone knows who has ever really got their hands dirty, involves a good deal more than pretty things and lovely effects. There is a lot of planning, preparation, patience, and sheer hard work necessary if that final moment is to be as glorious as you know it can be. So, in a funny way, this harvesting feels earthy as well as beautiful. You know the whole history of the flower that you are picking, you know what has gone into producing it. It is the culmination of a long haul which may well have begun the year before. The picking, in that sense, puts you in touch with nature in a way that simply looking at a flower that is growing in a garden could not.

Many people discover this pleasure and pride through growing vegetables, but for me it is an even richer experience to grow flowers for cutting. You pick a vegetable, peel it, cook it, eat it, and it is gone. Cut flowers, however, can be installed in pride of place all over the house and, as you go from room to room, you can walk through the beauty and scent of your harvest.

Of course, there is more to growing your own flowers than these rare and intense moments. The question of money comes into it. To fill the house with flowers from a shop would be enormously expensive. That kind of cost simply doesn't need to apply if you produce your own. There obviously will be some expense, but you can be sure that it will be a fraction of what you would have spent at the flower shop to get the same effect. And you can control that expense yourself: perhaps decide to grow just a few of the easy recommendations in a line or two in the vegetable patch to begin with, but then, as the habit grips, as the pleasure becomes addictive, expand. One year when you have a wedding or party planned, or just decide you would like more flowers in the house, you can try a few more. And then you will find yourself hooked!

Far more important, you can always tell garden-grown flowers from their commercially grown and store-bought equivalents. The flowers that you produce yourself are so much more generous, so much more scented, so much more relaxed in habit, and often so much more intense and interesting in color than those that you can buy from a florist. It is like the difference between meeting someone in an office in a bland business suit and meeting that same person on vacation, radiant with sun and *joie de vivre*. Commercial flowers are bred for their regularity and reliability, not for their relaxed, blowzy, open look, scent, and character. A bunch of bought sweet peas may have straighter stems and a more uniform color, but they won't fill your room with scent. An ebullient, heavily scented, double deep-magenta rose like *R.* 'Nuits de Young' or *R.* 'Souvenir du Docteur Jamain' has no equivalent among its straight-stemmed cultivated cousins, whose heads stand with parade-ground precision in the wrap when you buy them and, once released, droop with just as boring a regularity.

Another wonderful thing about flowers that you grow yourself is that you won't find yourself stuck inside the straitjacket that restricts many florists – a narrow selection of only the most reliable flowers, the stocks, the alstroemerias, the chrysanthemums, and the carnations. These hard and buttony flowers last well and don't usually offend. They are, in fact, the lowest common denominator of cut flowers, the ones that the florist can rely on not to die before they are sold.

This whole problem with florists' flowers comes into focus over the question of scale. Most things you find in most flower shops are smack in the middle of the mid-range, right only for the average-sized bunch. But one of the great things about your own cut flowers is the way they can swoop up and down the scale, from the boughs of whole trees dressing an entire room with their curving-over, leafy arches, and the intense sappy smell of newly cut wood, through the flamboyance of a fountain of lilies or agapanthus, right down to the jewellike, enameled beauty of a single zinnia, or the simplicity of a few wood anemones floating in a bowl. Bunches are more fun if they are wildly over the top, more touching, if they are miniature. If these are flowers from your own garden, then that full choice is there. It is like a piano with a full keyboard. What florists can usually provide is no more than a single octave based firmly on middle C. They won't commonly supply boughs of sweet chestnut or dramatic plants like acanthus, teasels, and bulrushes, which are invaluable for a spectacular showpiece. Nor will they have the small and delicate plants which can be arranged simply on their own, like *Pulsatilla vulgaris*, a sprig of *Magnolia stellata*, or the autumn chocolate flower, *Cosmos atrosanguineus*. Only you can provide those for yourself.

You might well say that your garden already provides all of these things, and indeed pages 28–31 show how to integrate a cutting garden with growing herbs, fruit, and salads in a family garden. So what need is there to have something called a cutting garden, or even a cutting patch? There is a great deal to be said for using your main garden as a source of flowers for the house, but if that is the path you decide to follow, you will inevitably make some compromises. You won't pick enough fritillaries to fill a vase, because your patch of orchard grass would look denuded without them. Later in the year you will hold back from cutting the most regal of plants, tall irises, lilies, agapanthus, and eremurus, because they are so grand and so stately where they are in the garden, so essential to the effects that you want to achieve there, that to remove them would feel like wanton damage, a piece of vandalism in your own back yard. So they stay where they are, and all the pleasures from having these flowers in the house will be lost. It is a double luxury to be able to have both.

With a cutting garden, or patch, arranged in a way that allows you to see the flowers as a growing crop, that reluctance to pick will evaporate. What would have felt untouchable in the main part of the garden can be guiltlessly harvested here. Not to pick a flower, when that so obviously is what it has been grown for, even feels like wastage, allowing it, as Thomas Gray said, "to blush unseen, And waste its sweetness on the desert air."

A cutting garden is a place for picking, part of the garden that is in service to the house. More than that, a cutting garden provides a means of integrating house and garden, of pulling inside and outside together. You can see the cutting garden as another of the house's rooms, where things are carefully prepared to make the house as a whole more beautiful and welcoming. Bringing the garden inside you dissolve the walls of the house, making way for a flood of life and beauty that flows between inner and outer, domesticating the garden, naturalizing the home. A house filled with flowers seems to come alive. A flowery house will wear a smile on its face.

But there is something else here, too: picking flowers makes you look at them. A picked flower is seen for longer and more closely than one that lives and dies in the flower bed. This is partly because there is so much else going on in the garden that you don't look at flowers in isolation, but partly it is that out of context, maintained artificially, the details of these living things become apparent almost for the first time. You will stop, amazed at something like the huge yellow tulip called the 'Jewel of Spring', whose giant, thin, but perfectly formed yellow petals are lined with the narrowest of red eye-liner touches along their outer rim, applied with a precision that any catwalk model would be proud of; or at the bosomy richness of a peony; or at the dark snakeskin netting on the hanging head of a meadow fritillary. These things, glanced at or swept past in the garden, come into dazzlingly sharp focus if held and displayed in a vase on your desk top. Cutting flowers provides a whole new, intense way of looking at them.

So this is what a cutting garden is for: bringing the natural into the house, providing flowers that you can pick without censorship, flowers in abundance, flowers with all their foibles and their glories, flowers with the quirk of the real.

In harvesting flowers you have grown yourself, you will be experiencing one of the closest relationships with the natural world that you can have. I honestly don't know what life would be like if I didn't have a garden for cutting now. It has, in a way that surprises me, become central to my life.

Planning and Stocking the Garden

Once you decide to start growing your own flowers for cutting, you need to resolve how much space you are going to devote to them, and this will depend above all on the size of your garden.

If you have a big garden with lots of underused space, the choice is wide open: you could opt for a small patch and cram it full of annuals (see pages 24–27), or you could go the distance and make a large self-contained cutting garden (see pages 14–23). If, on the other hand, you are bursting at the seams and want to incorporate vegetables, children's swings and slides, a lawn, and pretty herbaceous borders and flowers for cutting, the options are more limited: you could sacrifice one area to make a cutting patch, or you could integrate plants that are good for cutting into a mixed garden (see pages 28–31).

You will probably think next about your budget, which is an important, individual decision, but just as crucial is the question of time: the size of your cutting area must be geared to the amount of time you are prepared to give to it. There is no point pretending that stocking and maintaining a garden can be done in an instant. From the moment that the days lengthen in spring, you will be mulching, pruning, sowing, dividing, weeding, and watering. Remember, even a tiny cutting patch requires some commitment.

In late summer the cutting garden overflows with late-flowering annuals such as flowering tobacco and cosmos, and tubers or perennials like dahlias, crocosmia, phlox, ornamental thistles, and tall Verbena bonariensis.

Planning a Cutting Garden

Before you put pen to paper in designing a cutting patch or garden, you need to work out its exact size and where to place it. These, with some other considerations such as adjacent structures and planting, determine the form the garden takes, and what plants you can grow there.

Choosing a Site

Try to pick a prime site in a sunny spot with good soil because much will be demanded of this area. Check that it does not have any fundamental problems, such as a frost pocket that reduces your possible growing season, or a rain shadow from a nearby building that increases the already considerable amount of watering that a cutting garden demands. You need a convenient water source and, ideally, you should consider installing some form of irrigation system. Even something as basic as a leaky hose laid along the beds is a useful device.

Surveying the ground and drawing a plan

Once you decide on your site, you should draw up a reasonably accurate plan to scale. Do a detailed survey of the plot, seeing how it relates to other areas of the garden and to nearby structures. Any noticeably dry or damp areas should be marked on your drawing. Keep in mind that hedges and trees tend to suck up nutrients and water from a large surrounding area; trees are the same size below ground as they are above it. Note the shady areas and those in full sun. Try to draw in the shadows thrown from surrounding buildings, shrubs, and trees at different times of day. In an ideal world you would allow enough time to observe the plot through each season, taking rainfall measurements at different points in the garden, and observing how frost and prevailing winds affect existing planting. Most of us are too impatient to wait that long before starting to plant, but a year of observation should be your aim. Finally, dig a good spade deep to check your soil structure. Take a sample for pH testing. All these things have a direct influence on what you plant and where.

Once you incorporate this preliminary information on your ground plan, you can draw up your design for the beds and permanent structural planting, such as new hedges and trees, and hard structures such as paths and fences. Apart from matters of personal taste and finance, there are a few points worth noting.

Beds and paths

Straight lines and clean geometric shapes are easier to work with than curving ones, and they divide more naturally into smaller sections. You need paths to give you easy access to all the beds. The paths should have generous proportions, too, since this is high-intensity gardening and you need wheelbarrow access to each area. For the same reason, it is best to avoid steps in the cutting garden or plot. Paths of brick, gravel, or stone might initially seem an extravagance, but will prove worthwhile in the long run because grass requires far more maintenance.

Walls, hedges, and fences

It is well worth using part of your budget to provide some form of windbreak. Plants grow better and quicker in a sheltered site. In the long term consider building a wall, or the cheaper alternative of growing a hedge, to protect the whole area. As a temporary measure, the most attractive alternatives are hazel fencing, made from a frame of stakes interwoven with flexible split branches (see pages 24–27), or closely spaced picket fencing. For areas with particularly high-density annuals, you might consider fencing around the beds as well, so that you do not have to worry endlessly about staking and support, both of which are time-consuming.

Choosing a Planting Design

Once you have made all the structural decisions, it is time to start planning the planting design. One of the most fundamental questions you must ask yourself is whether you want shrubs, perennials, and annuals all mixed together, or whether you would prefer to concentrate on one of these groups? If your site and funds are limited, then consider stocking the whole patch with annuals. They require more work, but with minimal capital outlay. They provide flowers in summer and fall only, but you can always extend the picking season with spring bulbs. Remember, though, that if your plot is stocked mainly with annuals, it is important to keep picking them, for they stop flowering if the plants go to seed. So if you are away for a long spell in summer, then perennials and shrubs would be more suitable, since most continue to flower without picking.

Another way to spread the cost of making a productive cutting garden is to invest the majority of your planting budget in shrubs during the first year or two, temporarily filling the area you have allocated to herbaceous plants with annuals. Then add perennial plants as you can afford them. It is always cheaper to grow them yourself from seed if you have the space to do so.

One of the best reasons for growing your own flowers is the range of possibilities it opens to you. My own favorites appear in Flowers and Foliage through the Seasons (see pages 94–163). But, of course, there is no reason for you to be limited by my preferences. If you see a flower that appeals to you, check its soil and sun requirements, and if they suit your site, try it.

It is always worth keeping a note of the plants you particularly like and those you dislike whenever you see them in garden centers and other gardens. And if you especially want particular groups of plants, such as those that are scented or those that will give you huge, statuesque arrangements, then note them as you find them. One of the chief joys of having a special cutting garden is that you can grow plants such as flamboyant, raspberry-ripple Parrot tulips, multicolored zinnias, and bright, zingy-colored dahlias, that are fantastic in a vase but might be considered too gaudy for the general garden.

Plant lots of foliage plants as well as flowers. It is easy to forget the importance of beautiful foliage in completing an arrangement. Architectural plants, too, should figure large in any list. These immediately make a group of flowers more dramatic. Acanthus, thistles, teasels, cattails, globe artichokes, and – in winter – dogwood stems, and branches of catkins and pussy willow will add an extra dimension.

Before you make any final decisions about plants, you must make sure that the plants will survive in your garden. The type of soil, amount of sun, and temperature extremes all have a bearing on your choice. Don't expect, for example, a silver-leaved, sun-loving, drought-tolerant artemisia to thrive in boggy shade. For the same reason, it is useful to list all your chosen plants in their site groups: those that do best in sun or in shade, in damp or dry conditions.

Armed with all this information, you can start to place the plants on the plan of your proposed cutting garden.

Balance of plants and color

If you decide to include a full range of colors in your garden, group the colors carefully to work well with each other. Concentrate the stronger colors in the foreground, with the whites and pale colors fading off into the distance. Don't try to have too many effects in one enclosed area. It is worth it to draw and roughly color how this will look for every month of the year. You may find that at certain times there are some large gaps in the planting or that there is a violent pink flower right next to a scar-

let one in the same month. Check your plan and concentrate on achieving a good balance between foliage and flowers at all times of the year.

Go from the plan to the ground and back again, time and time again. If you fail to do this, it is all too easy to over- or underestimate the actual scale of your garden and err on the side of planting too much or too little for your site.

Placing permanent planting

Except for the largest shrubs, always plant in groups. Esthetically, this gives a more uniform and less dotted effect. Practically, if there are many flower heads, rather than just two or three, picking won't leave holes. Buy the larger herbaceous plants in threes, and the smaller ones in groups of five or seven.

Plan to position plants closer together than you would in your normal garden. Particularly with shrubs, if you pick regularly and with attention to the shape and overall look of the plant, then you can use species which you may have considered too large for your garden because the plants will always be well clipped. Even in a small patch you could think of including, for example, both a viburnum and a smokebush. Look up heights and spreads as you plan what to plant, and simply space the plants slightly closer than their estimated span. Having said all this, a common mistake made by people new to gardening is to underestimate the ultimate size a plant will grow to in a few years. Another mistake is to plant a tall, vigorous plant next to a much smaller, more delicate one, which will be swamped and die in a year or two. So always check sizes and also try to group together those of a similar habit.

Note on buying plants

Don't be tempted to buy large pot-grown shrubs at enormous expense. You may believe that this will give you an instant garden, allowing you to start harvesting right away. In fact, mature shrubs tend to resent disturbance and may add almost no new growth for a year or two. In this time a smaller and much cheaper plant may well have caught up in size. The same is true for herbaceous plants; a much more expensive 2ft (60cm) plant is often less than a year older than a far smaller, cheaper one and may just have been placed into a larger pot by the retailer for the new season. For a few months the larger plant will look more imposing, but the younger one will soon catch up.

The Cutting Garden

If you decide to devote a part of your garden solely to cut flower production, ideally you should think about an area large enough to contain a mix of flowering trees, shrubs, climbers, perennials, annuals, and bulbs. This will guarantee that there is something to pick all through the year. My own cutting garden, which is illustrated on the following pages, measures 40ft × 80ft (12m × 24m).

The design

The rectangular plot is divided by brick paths into eight planting areas: four beds in the center and four L-shaped peripheral borders. It is contained by evergreen hedges on two sides, hazel fencing on another, and, at the sunniest end, by a valuable heat-retaining wall that supports a variety of wall shrubs and climbers. The center beds are generously proportioned; you should allow just enough space between plants to enable you to squeeze through them to pick from the middle. Evergreen planting includes four yews clipped into cones at the crossing, and lavender hedges lining the paths that run down the center. The trees also contribute a sense of permanence and vertical structure. Flowering cherries, an apple, and a crabapple produce blossom and decorative fruit, an amelanchier brings spring blossoms and good fall leaf color, and a sorbus provides bright, silvery foliage.

The planting

The center beds are used for plants that change through the seasons. Bulbs are followed by annuals and biennials, which are simply planted between the lines of bulbs in blocks with irregular edges. A line of string with permanent labels at each end indicates where the now-invisible bulbs are when their leaves have died down, so that they are not constantly dug up.

The L-shaped beds contain more permanent plantings of shrubs, climbers, and herbaceous perennials. These include winter-flowering shrubs underplanted with bulbs that flower in early spring and a few evergreen plants to provide winter foliage.

Maintenance

Maintenance is minimized by adding a thick mulch of garden compost or well-rotted manure as soon as temperatures begin to rise in spring and annual weeds start to germinate (see page 37). Mulching helps reduce the need for watering, but regular watering and fertilizing is crucial, since high demands are made on plants and soil. The borders are hoed regularly to keep them weed-free.

The Cutting Garden in Spring

Top and center: These two Lily-flowered tulips – scarlet Tulipa 'Dyanito' (top) and yellow T. 'West Point' (center) – have the pointed curving petals that give them the typical silhouette characteristic of this group of tulips. Each one is tall, svelte, and elegant, like the slimmest 1950's model. It is a shape that always adds flair and is very useful in breaking up a too-neat dome in any spring arrangement (see page 62).

Bottom: The Large-cupped Narcissus 'Professor Einstein' is a good one for arranging on its own or trimming short to mix with blue grape hyacinths.

Opposite: My cutting garden in spring in its first year. The center beds are filling up with colorful rows of tulips, daffodils, and anemones, interspersed with yellow euphorbias, all ready for cutting.

At the center of each section, not yet in flower, are tall and stately bulbs such as lilies; they will later provide height. Lining the outer edges of the beds are wallflowers and forget-me-nots, which can be mixed with any of the bulbs.

In the shady bed against the back hedge, hellebores, pulmonarias, and early-flowering primulas are planted for winter and spring flowering, while later in the season Solomon's seal and scillas will fill any patches around rose bushes and newly planted perennials.

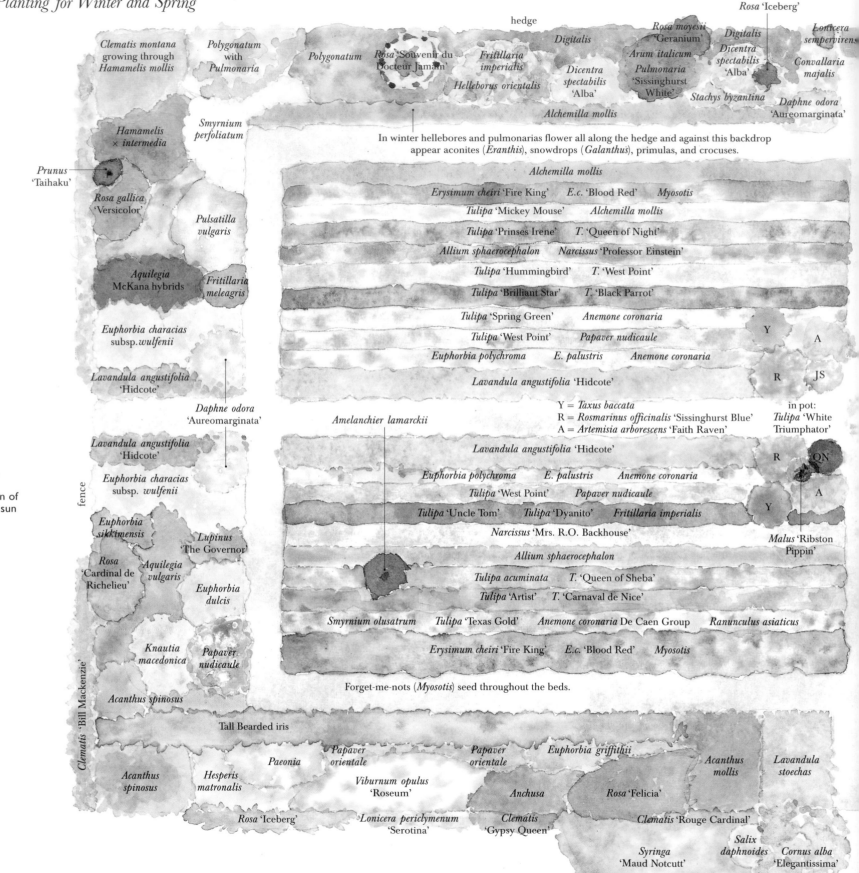

Clematis montana growing through Hamamelis mollis

Polygonatum with Pulmonaria

hedge

Rosa 'Iceberg'

Rosa moyesii 'Geranium'

Polygonatum

Rosa 'Souvenir du Docteur Jamain'

Fritillaria imperialis

Digitalis

Digitalis

Lonicera sempervirens

Arum italicum

Dicentra spectabilis 'Alba'

Dicentra spectabilis 'Alba'

Convallaria majalis

Helleborus orientalis

Pulmonaria 'Sissinghurst White'

Stachys byzantina

Daphne odora 'Aureomarginata'

Smyrnium perfoliatum

Alchemilla mollis

Hamamelis × intermedia

In winter hellebores and pulmonarias flower all along the hedge and against this backdrop appear aconites (*Eranthis*), snowdrops (*Galanthus*), primulas, and crocuses.

Prunus 'Taihaku'

Rosa gallica 'Versicolor'

Pulsatilla vulgaris

Alchemilla mollis

Erysimum cheiri 'Fire King' *E.c.* 'Blood Red' *Myosotis*

Tulipa 'Mickey Mouse' *Alchemilla mollis*

Tulipa 'Prinses Irene' *T.* 'Queen of Night'

Allium sphaerocephalon *Narcissus* 'Professor Einstein'

Aquilegia McKana hybrids

Fritillaria meleagris

Tulipa 'Hummingbird' *T.* 'West Point'

Tulipa 'Brilliant Star' *T.* 'Black Parrot'

Tulipa 'Spring Green' *Anemone coronaria*

Y

A

Euphorbia characias subsp. *wulfenii*

Tulipa 'West Point' *Papaver nudicaule*

Euphorbia polychroma *E. palustris* *Anemone coronaria*

R

JS

Lavandula angustifolia 'Hidcote'

Lavandula angustifolia 'Hidcote'

Y = *Taxus baccata*
R = *Rosmarinus officinalis* 'Sissinghurst Blue'
A = *Artemisia arborescens* 'Faith Raven'

in pot:
Tulipa 'White Triumphator'

Daphne odora 'Aureomarginata'

Amelanchier lamarckii

Lavandula angustifolia 'Hidcote'

R

QN

Lavandula angustifolia 'Hidcote'

Euphorbia polychroma *E. palustris* *Anemone coronaria*

A

direction of midday sun

fence

Euphorbia characias subsp. *wulfenii*

Tulipa 'West Point' *Papaver nudicaule*

Tulipa 'Uncle Tom' *Tulipa* 'Dyanito' *Fritillaria imperialis*

Y

Euphorbia sikkimensis

Lupinus 'The Governor'

Narcissus 'Mrs. R.O. Backhouse'

Malus 'Ribston Pippin'

Rosa 'Cardinal de Richelieu'

Aquilegia vulgaris

Allium sphaerocephalon

Euphorbia dulcis

Tulipa acuminata *T.* 'Queen of Sheba'

Tulipa 'Artist' *T.* 'Carnaval de Nice'

Knautia macedonica

Papaver nudicaule

Smyrnium olusatrum *Tulipa* 'Texas Gold' *Anemone coronaria* De Caen Group *Ranunculus asiaticus*

Erysimum cheiri 'Fire King' *E.c.* 'Blood Red' *Myosotis*

Acanthus spinosus

Forget-me-nots (*Myosotis*) seed throughout the beds.

Clematis 'Bill Mackenzie'

Tall Bearded iris

Papaver orientale

Papaver orientale

Euphorbia griffithii

Acanthus mollis

Lavandula stoechas

Paeonia

Acanthus spinosus

Hesperis matronalis

Viburnum opulus 'Roseum'

Anchusa

Rosa 'Felicia'

Rosa 'Iceberg'

Lonicera periclymenum 'Serotina'

Clematis 'Gypsy Queen'

Clematis 'Rouge Cardinal'

Syringa 'Maud Notcutt'

Salix daphnoides

Cornus alba 'Elegantissima'

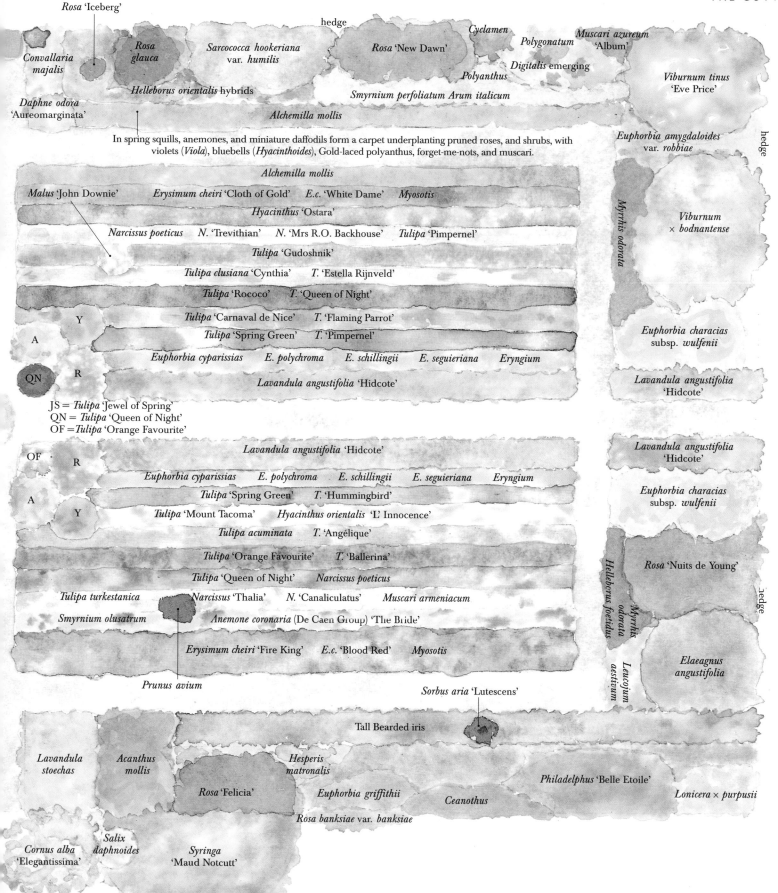

In spring squills, anemones, and miniature daffodils form a carpet underplanting pruned roses, and shrubs, with violets (*Viola*), bluebells (*Hyacinthoides*), Gold-laced polyanthus, forget-me-nots, and muscari.

Planting for Summer and Fall

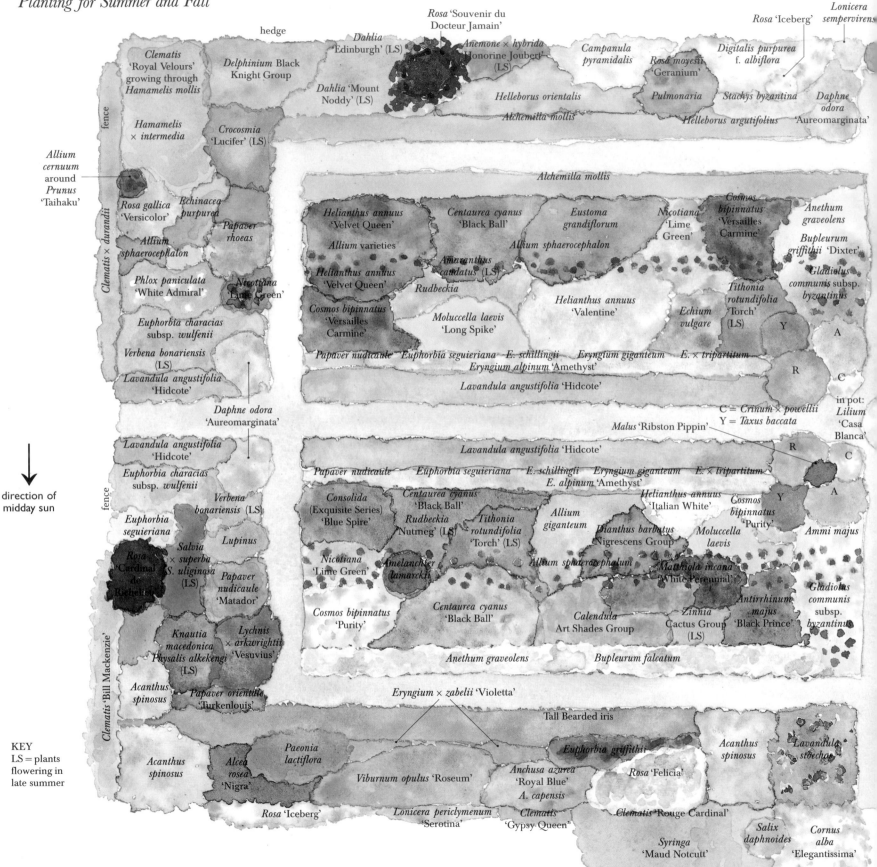

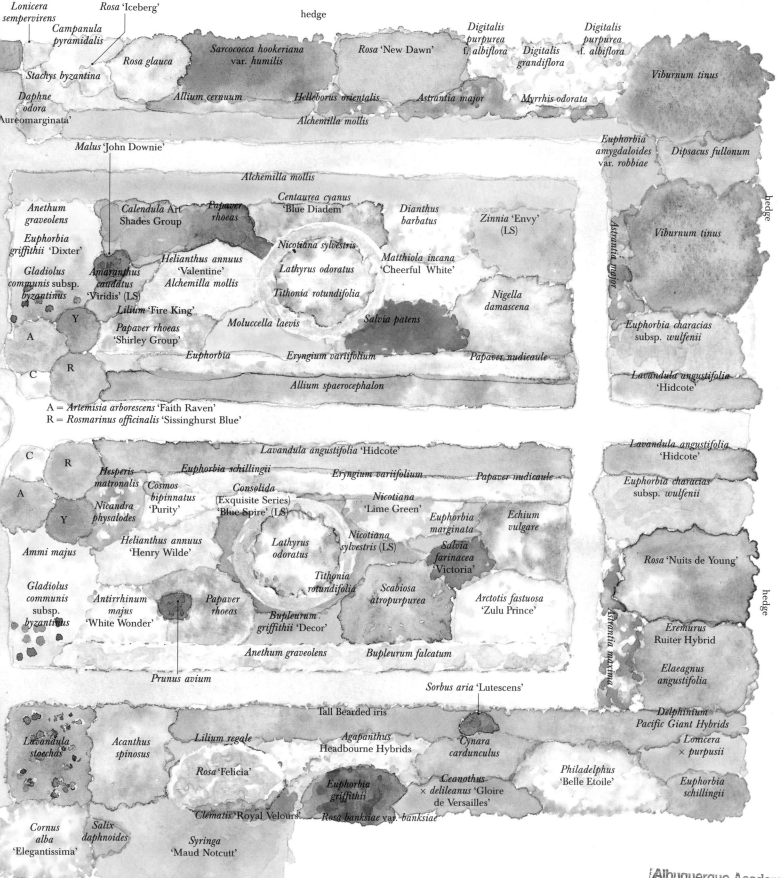

hedge

Lonicera sempervirens

Campanula pyramidalis

Rosa 'Iceberg'

Stachys byzantina

Rosa glauca

Sarcococca hookeriana var. humilis

Rosa 'New Dawn'

Digitalis purpurea f. *albiflora*

Digitalis grandiflora

Digitalis purpurea f. *albiflora*

Viburnum tinus

Daphne odora 'Aureomarginata'

Allium cernuum

Helleborus orientalis

Astrantia major

Myrrhis odorata

Alchemilla mollis

Malus 'John Downie'

Euphorbia amygdaloides var. robbiae

Dipsacus fullonum

Alchemilla mollis

Anethum graveolens

Calendula Art Shades Group

Papaver rhoeas

Centaurea cyanus 'Blue Diadem'

Dianthus barbatus

Zinnia 'Envy' (LS)

Viburnum tinus

Euphorbia griffithii 'Dixter'

Nicotiana sylvestris

Matthiola incana 'Cheerful White'

Gladiolus communis subsp. *byzantinus*

Amaranthus caudatus 'Viridis' (LS)

Helianthus annuus 'Valentine'

Alchemilla mollis

Lathyrus odoratus

Tithonia rotundifolia

Nigella damascena

A

Y

Lilium 'Fire King'

Papaver rhoeas 'Shirley Group'

Moluccella laevis

Salvia patens

Euphorbia characias subsp. *wulfenii*

C

R

Euphorbia

Eryngium variifolium

Papaver nudicaule

Astrantia major

Allium spaerocephalon

Lavandula angustifolia 'Hidcote'

A = *Artemisia arborescens* 'Faith Raven'
R = *Rosmarinus officinalis* 'Sissinghurst Blue'

C

R

Lavandula angustifolia 'Hidcote'

Lavandula angustifolia 'Hidcote'

A

Y

Hesperis matronalis

Cosmos bipinnatus 'Purity'

Euphorbia schillingii

Consolida (Exquisite Series) 'Blue Spire' (LS)

Eryngium variifolium

Nicotiana 'Lime Green'

Papaver nudicaule

Euphorbia characias subsp. *wulfenii*

Nicandra physalodes

Euphorbia marginata

Echium vulgare

Ammi majus

Helianthus annuus 'Henry Wilde'

Lathyrus odoratus

Nicotiana sylvestris (LS)

Salvia farinacea 'Victoria'

Rosa 'Nuits de Young'

Gladiolus communis subsp. *byzantinus*

Antirrhinum majus 'White Wonder'

Papaver rhoeas

Tithonia rotundifolia

Bupleurum griffithii 'Decor'

Scabiosa atropurpurea

Arctotis fastuosa 'Zulu Prince'

Astrantia maxima

Anethum graveolens

Bupleurum falcatum

Eremurus Ruiter Hybrid

Prunus avium

Elaeagnus angustifolia

Sorbus aria 'Lutescens'

Delphinium Pacific Giant Hybrids

Tall Bearded iris

Lavandula stoechas

Acanthus spinosus

Lilium regale

Agapanthus Headbourne Hybrids

Cynara cardunculus

Lonicera × *purpusii*

Rosa 'Felicia'

Euphorbia griffithii

Ceanothus × *delileanus* 'Gloire de Versailles'

Philadelphus 'Belle Etoile'

Euphorbia schillingii

Cornus alba 'Elegantissima'

Salix daphnoides

Syringa 'Maud Notcutt'

Clematis 'Royal Velours'

Rosa banksiae var. *banksiae*

hedge

hedge

direction of midday sun

The Cutting Garden in Summer

A view of the cutting garden showing the planting plan on the previous two pages. In high summer the garden is a mass of flower color. Banks of herbaceous perennials provide a sumptuous summer harvest, supplemented by the center beds that are now brimming over with annuals. A wealth of foliage – shrubs, perennials, and annuals – provides greenery to play a supporting role to the flowers.

Structural foliage

Large shrubs planted for architectural and background foliage during the summer months include the silver-leaved *Elaeagnus angustifolia* and *Sorbus aria* 'Lutescens', the white-and-green-dappled leaves of *Cornus alba* 'Elegantissima' with its striking red branches, and the spiky, silver leaves of the cardoon *Cynara cardunculus*.

Foliage fillers and flowers

The sunny bed in the near fore-ground has a gray-green European guelder rose (*Viburnum opulus* 'Roseum'), which provides glamorous early-summer foliage. Near it are spikes of acanthus (*A. spinosus*). Across the garden the shadier L-shaped bed contains lady's mantle (*Alchemilla mollis*), while stachys (*S. byzantina*) spreads out beside the arbor seat.

All over the garden the euphorbias provide a brilliant succession of yellow and green and, in the case of *E. griffithii* varieties, red, for mixing with greens, other orange-reds, and blacks. Among the eryngiums are the steely silver giant sea holly (*E. giganteum*) and the rich indigo-blue *E.* × *zabelii* 'Violetta'.

As the season progresses, the annual bells of Ireland (*Moluccella laevis*), dill (*Anethum graveolens*), and a late sowing of bupleurum (*B. griffithii*) supply armfuls of pretty and useful apple-green foliage well into fall.

Shady perennial beds

Tall blue spikes of delphinium and Campanula pyramidalis *are flowering between* Rosa *'Souvenir du Docteur Jamain' and* Rosa moyesii *'Geranium', both of which tolerate some shade.*

Center annual beds

*These two beds contain many of my favorite annuals: the black cornflower (*Centaurea cyanus *'Black Ball'), snapdragons (*Antirrhinum*), green flowering tobacco (*Nicotiana *'Lime Green'), larkspur (*Consolida *Exquisite Series), and sunflowers (*Helianthus annuus*). The sumptuous, green-tasseled love-lies-bleeding (*Amaranthus caudatus *'Viridis'), zinnias, Mexican sunflower (* Tithonia rotundi-folia*), and prairie gentian (* Eustoma grandiflorum*) mature and flower in high summer and fall, continuing the harvest.*

9 ft
3 m

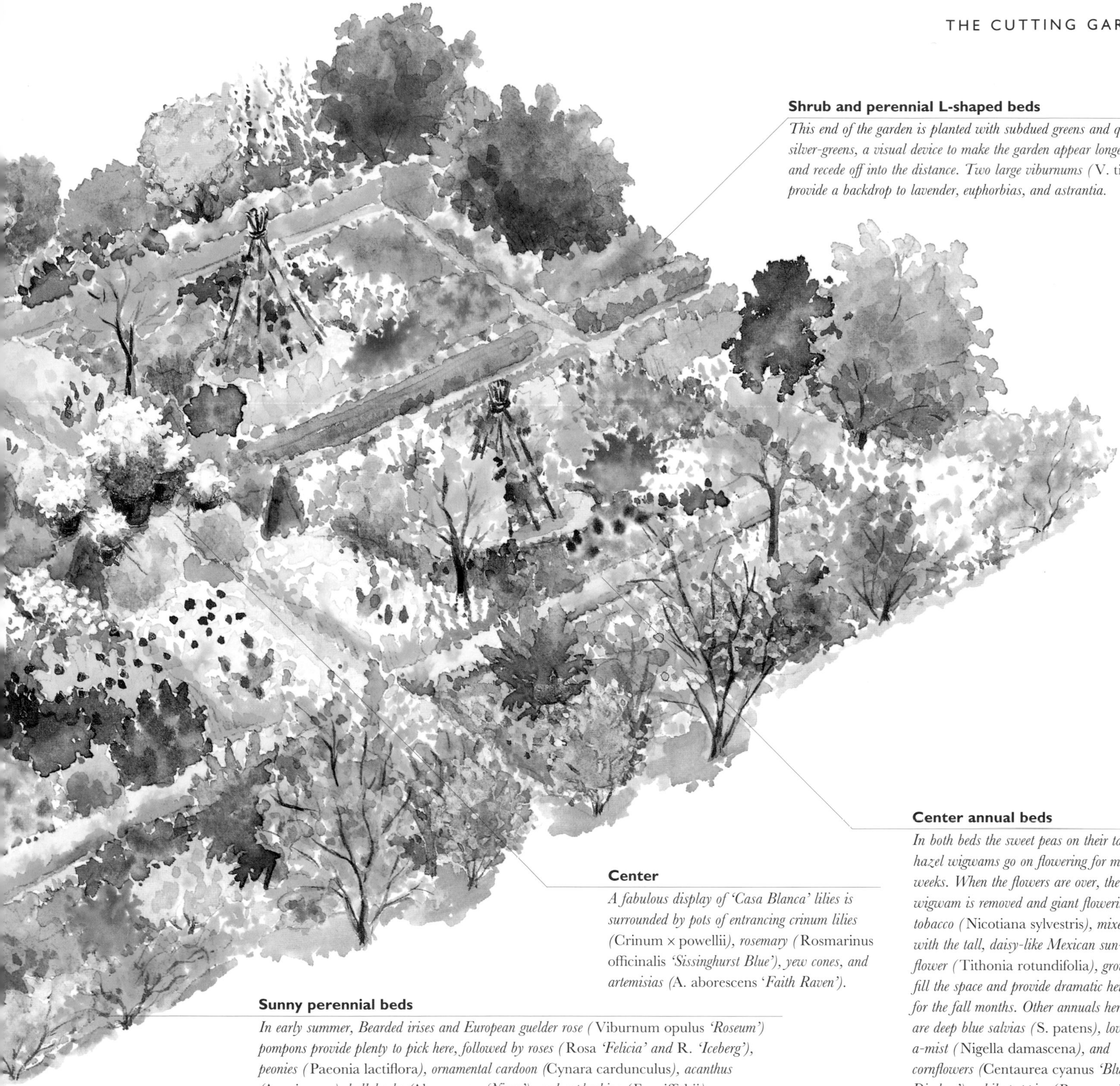

Shrub and perennial L-shaped beds

*This end of the garden is planted with subdued greens and quiet silver-greens, a visual device to make the garden appear longer and recede off into the distance. Two large viburnums (*V. tinus*) provide a backdrop to lavender, euphorbias, and astrantia.*

Center annual beds

*In both beds the sweet peas on their tall hazel wigwams go on flowering for many weeks. When the flowers are over, the wigwam is removed and giant flowering tobacco (*Nicotiana sylvestris*), mixed with the tall, daisy-like Mexican sun-flower (*Tithonia rotundifolia*), grow to fill the space and provide dramatic height for the fall months. Other annuals here are deep blue salvias (*S. patens*), love-in-a-mist (*Nigella damascena*), and cornflowers (*Centaurea cyanus 'Blue Diadem'*), while poppies (*Papaver rhoeas and P. nudicaule*) add splashes of red, pink, and white.*

Center

*A fabulous display of 'Casa Blanca' lilies is surrounded by pots of entrancing crinum lilies (*Crinum × powellii*), rosemary (*Rosmarinus officinalis 'Sissinghurst Blue'*), yew cones, and artemisias (*A. aborescens 'Faith Raven'*).*

Sunny perennial beds

*In early summer, Bearded irises and European guelder rose (*Viburnum opulus 'Roseum'*) pompons provide plenty to pick here, followed by roses (*Rosa 'Felicia' and R. 'Iceberg'*), peonies (*Paeonia lactiflora*), ornamental cardoon (*Cynara cardunculus*), acanthus (*A. spinosus*), hollyhocks (*Alcea rosea 'Nigra'*), and euphorbias (*E. griffithii*).*

The Cutting Garden in Early Fall

Left: Though the season is late, there are still plenty of flowers to pick. Orange Lilium *'Fire King' and drumstick chives (*Allium sphaerocephalon*), with their great purple heads, go on flowering. Beyond a scattering of white cosmos (*C. bipinnatus *'Purity'), late-sown sweet peas (*Lathyrus odoratus*) still give color on their hazel wigwam.*

Above: The sumptuous velvety rudbeckias and amaranthus, either red-tasseled as shown here or with tassels of green, are a bonus to harvest through the fall in the cutting garden. Rudbeckias last only three or four days in water, but the flowers are produced so prolifically that you can keep on picking more to replace spent stems.

The Cutting Garden in Winter

*Far left: Dewy snowdrops (*Galanthus*).*
*Left: Frosted winter aconites (*Eranthis hyemalis*).*

Below: In winter the garden's structure is most clearly seen. Bright blue posts marking rows of bulbs give color interest when little is in flower. In the outer perennial and shrub borders, winter aconiies and snowdrops appear first.

The Cutting Patch

This small cutting patch, measuring 10ft × 15ft (3m × 4.5m), could be placed in any sunny position. It is stocked with annuals and biennials. The colors and textures of the plants guarantee a balanced arrangement from almost any combination.

The design

The plan is straightforward: a series of rectangles with a central diamond-shaped bed and a sweet-pea wigwam as the focal point. Woven hazel fencing, 18in (45cm) high, surrounds the beds and contains and supports the plants. Alternatively, the beds could be edged with low, wooden picket fences. All parts of the beds are easily reached either from the center paths or from outside.

The plants

As long as they are cut or picked regularly, the plants provide a continuous supply of foliage and flowers from late spring until the first frosts. They are easily grown from seed, but for those who prefer to buy in plants, most are available as seedlings from nurseries and garden centers. All are planted 8–10in (20–25cm) apart. Cornflowers and scabious do not transplant well so they are sown directly into the ground and the seedlings are thinned.

Preparation and maintenance

Prepare the area in fall. Seedlings should be planted out in spring as soon as there is little risk of frost. Dense planting in blocks gives a lovely mosaic appearance and helps keep the weeds under control. When the plants are still small, fill gaps with a mulch of well-rotted manure to inhibit weed seedlings and retain moisture. Fertilize and water regularly. Keep cutting to stop the plants from going to seed.

Extending the picking season

After clearing the cutting patch in fall, plant it with bulbs for harvesting from early spring through to the beginning of summer, when the annuals take over. Choose hyacinths, scillas, tulips, and narcissi from the sections on spring and winter flowers and foliage on pages 96–113 and 148–159. Lift the bulbs after picking. Also, make effective use of the ground by doubling up the planting of the patch. For example, replace the early flowerers like sweet Williams, which tend to be over by mid-summer, with a selection of pot-reared dahlias and penstemons. These will give you richly colored flowers right through to the first frost.

bupleurum and **bells of Ireland** (*B. griffithii* and *Moluccella laevis*)

Plant alternating blocks of bupleurum and bells of Ireland seedlings. These two plants provide essential lime-green foliage to contrast perfectly with brightly colored flowers or bunches of whites, pinks, and blues.

cosmos and **snapdragons**

(*C. bipinnatus* 'Purity' and *Antirrhinum majus* 'White Wonder')

Plant a mixture of cosmos and snapdragon seedlings. This cosmos grows to 3–4ft (90cm–1.2m), an impressive sight in both garden and vase: white flowers are always pretty on their own or useful in mixed color arrangements.

bishop's flower (*Ammi majus*)

Plant seedlings in rows 10in (25cm) apart. Sown as an annual in spring, this is a beautiful plant with its filigree flower heads, but if you sow the seed in fall, you will get bumper-sized plants reaching 3–4ft (90cm–1.2m). The flowers will be over by mid-summer, when they can be replaced by a planting of zinnias for fall picking.

annual scabious

(*Scabiosa atropurpurea*)

Sow seed in rows 10in (25cm) apart where they are to flower, and thin them to 8–10in (20–25cm) apart. These pink, mauve, deep red, blue, and white pompons are good mixed together. Alternatively, separate the colors and combine them with other flowers from the patch. The paler shades mixed with love-in-a-mist, sweet peas, bupleurum, and bishop's flower make a fresh-looking bunch.

sweet Williams and **flowering tobacco**

(*Dianthus barbatus* and *Nicotiana* 'Lime Green')

Transplant sweet William seedlings in early spring, placing them 8in (20cm) apart in a zigzag. After the last frost, fill in around the lines with flowering tobacco. These will flower until late fall, but the sweet Williams can be replaced with dahlias and penstemons.

cosmos and **dill** (*C. bipinnatus* 'Versailles Carmine' and *Anethum graveolens*)

*Plant cosmos seedlings 10in (25cm) apart in a zigzag or wavy line. Fill in each triangle with plants of dill 8in (20cm) apart or grow them here direct from seed and then thin. With strong stems, feathery foliage, and vivid lime-green umbels, dill is a good foil to deep carmine-pink cosmos. The cosmos will flower for months, but you may want to repeat the sowing of dill. Fennel (*Foeniculum vulgare*) is an alternative to dill, but do not grow both since the two can cross-fertilize.*

snapdragons and **arctotis**

(*Antirrhinum majus* 'Black Prince' and *Arctotis fastuosa*)

Plant snapdragon seedlings 8in (20cm) apart and in a U-shaped line. Fill the spaces in between with arctotis. After the arctotis has finished flowering, you could fill in with Rudbeckia *'Nutmeg', whose rich orange-browns mix well with the snapdragons.*

black cornflowers and **marigolds**

(*Centaurea cyanus* 'Black Ball' and *Calendula* Art Shades Group)

*Sow both plants directly in position and thin to 4–6in (10–15cm) apart. Marigolds and dill are also a successful pairing, and they both mix well with gentian sage (*Salvia patens*). When the cornflowers are over, remove the plants and replace with seedlings of summer icicle (*Euphorbia marginata*).*

euphorbias and **Iceland poppies**

(*E. palustris* and *Papaver nudicaule*)

Plant Iceland poppies in a V-shape with euphorbia seedlings in the blocks between. When you pull out the finished annuals in late fall, transplant the euphorbias to the main garden.

blue cornflowers (*Centaurea cyanus* 'Blue Diadem')

*Sow cornflowers in spring and thin the seedlings to 4–6in (10–15cm) apart. We all love cornflowers. Mix them with orange marigolds and poppies or have them on their own. After flowering, you can replace them with gentian sage (*Salvia patens*) seedlings or another flowering annual.*

sweet peas (*Lathyrus odoratus*)

Plant two sweet peas at the bottom of each of the 12 sticks that form the wigwam. A simple bunch of sweet peas, freshly picked every other day, provides a delicious scent to wake up to.

poppies and **love-in-a-mist**

(*Papaver rhoeas* 'Shirley Group' and *Nigella*)

Sow poppy seed in a curving U-shaped line and love-in-a-mist in three roughly triangular blocks. Thin them to 4–6in (10–15cm) apart. The flowers and seed cases of love-in-a-mist are excellent when used as foliage for a bunch into which you can push any color, and the poppy seed heads are also lovely for late-summer and fall picking.

larkspur (*Consolida* Exquisite Series)

Plant out 8–10in (20–25cm) apart or sow directly and thin. This rich royal blue flower with its tall, airy spikes is lovely next to the carmine cosmos and will go on flowering until the first frosts.

3 ft

1 m

The Cutting Patch in Summer

*Left: A rich, intense arrangement can be made from flowering tobacco (*Nicotiana *'Lime Green'), the deep blue larkspur (*Consolida Exquisite Series *'Blue Spire'), and sumptuous* Cosmos bipinnatus *'Versailles Carmine'. This cosmos – one of my favorite plants for cutting – is perfect for the cutting patch since it earns its keep many times over, flowering from late spring until the end of fall. Mix it, too, with green dill, both in the cutting patch and in the vase.*

*Opposite, top: When you plant an annual cutting patch, think of arranging the colors as you might in a bunch of flowers. Here, sweet peas, cornflowers, and poppies make good partners to pincushion flower (*Scabiosa atropurpurea*), while the black cornflower* Centurea cyanus *'Black Ball' provides a brilliant contrast to marigolds (*Calendula Art Shades Group*).*

*Opposite, bottom: Nearby, rich crimson snap-dragons (*Antirrhinum majus *'Black Prince') are interplanted with burnt-orange* Arctotis fastuosa *(which is nearly over).* Antirrhinum majus *'White Wonder' mixes with anything, in the garden or in an arrangement, and bupleurum,* Euphorbia palustris, *bells of Ireland (*Moluccella laevis*), and globe artichokes (*Cynara cardunculus Scolymus Group*) provide interesting foliage.*

The Mixed Garden

If you don't have a separate area to devote to cut flowers, think of making some space in different parts of your garden so that you can grow a range of plants for cutting. You need, at the least, several spots in full sun, a few in shadier positions, an area for climbers, and somewhere to grow tall and small plants. If you are starting from scratch with an average-sized rectangular urban or small suburban garden that is always in view from the house, here is a design that is both productive and decorative for much of the year. This garden, measuring 30ft × 40ft (9m × 12m), has a brick-paved terrace leading to french windows and the kitchen door. To maximize use, the planting plan focuses on salads, herbs, a few vegetables, and flowers and foliage for the house.

The design

This layout can be adapted to a variety of needs. For example, if you wanted to include grass, the center bed could be a small lawn. The brick paths are wide enough to allow a wheelbarrow to pass, and the beds and borders allow easy picking of the plants. The mass of plants is given order and coherence by the low clipped boxwood hedges at the edges, the rounded boxwood balls, and pairs of mophead bay in pots that punctuate the design.

The plants through the year

Although the garden is seen here in high summer, there are lots of spring flowers planted among the shrub and perennial borders: hyacinths, tulips, and anemones grouped in panels down the path, with biennial forget-me-nots and wallflowers, scillas, and minia-ture narcissi under the old apple tree; crown imperials and Solomon's seal combine in the shady border.

The summer annuals – including marigolds, violets, love-in-a-mist, and snapdragons – can be mixed with euphorbias, bupleurum, bells of Ireland, and dill for your foliage. There are deep crimson scented roses and pink 'New Dawn' and white 'Iceberg', which flower until severe frost. Among the perennials are lupines, anchusas, peonies, and echinops, and white and spotted foxgloves are massed beside the hedge. As long as you pick them, many of the annuals such as sunflowers will flower through the fall.

The summer vegetables are selected for dwarf or ornamental characteristics that integrate well with the flowers. There are miniature fava beans, green and crimson lettuces, rocket, eggplants, tomatoes, beans climbing with the sweet peas, and nasturtiums and violet flowers for adding to salads.

Shrub and perennial beds

Scrambling all along the fence are clematis, including the richly colored 'Etoile Violette' and 'Royal Velours'. Other climbers include the purple-flowered Akebia quinata *as backdrop to a group of deep crimson* Rosa *'Tuscany Superb', while* Lonicera × brownii *and* Solanum crispum *'Glasnevin' are behind a ceanothus. The highly scented honeysuckle* Lonicera periclymenum *'Serotina' climbs through* Salix daphnoides *in the corner farthest from the house.*

Sunny beds

The beautiful deep purple-blue flowers of the agapanthus growing all along this bed will later produce elegant seed heads. Deep purple-black eggplants are grown along the low wall, and there is a splash of red from cherry tomatoes. The blue-purple color theme continues into fall with alliums and various salvias, and in winter with Iris reticulata *and* I. unguicularis. *Green and crimson lettuces flank a large clump of lady's mantle along the path, and the lady's mantle is repeated on both sides of the foreground steps. The small bed here has soft pink* Rosa *'New Dawn' growing with tall drumstick chives.*

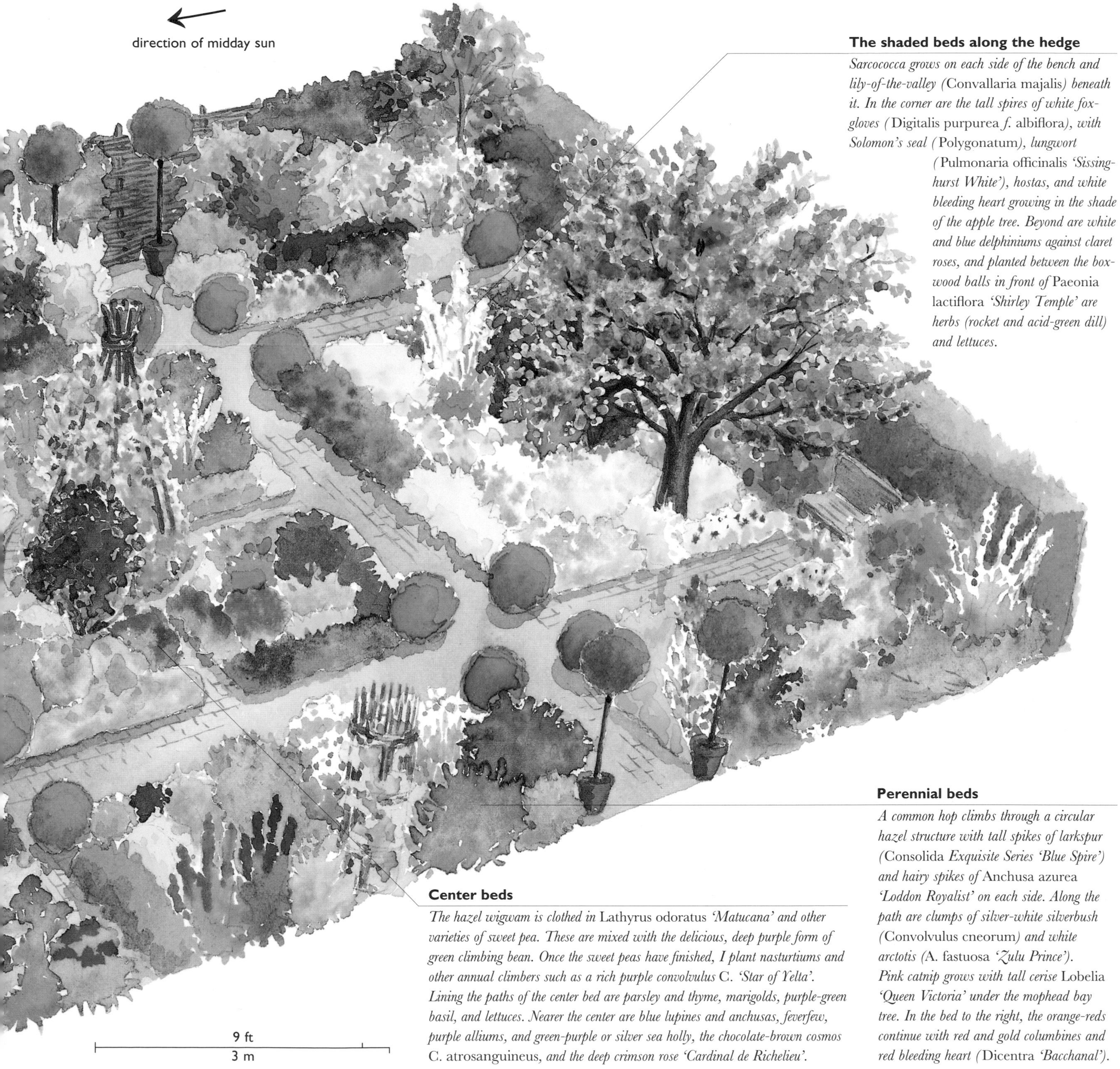

direction of midday sun

The shaded beds along the hedge

*Sarcococca grows on each side of the bench and lily-of-the-valley (*Convallaria majalis*) beneath it. In the corner are the tall spires of white foxgloves (*Digitalis purpurea *f.* albiflora*), with Solomon's seal (*Polygonatum*), lungwort (*Pulmonaria officinalis 'Sissing-hurst White'*), hostas, and white bleeding heart growing in the shade of the apple tree. Beyond are white and blue delphiniums against claret roses, and planted between the box-wood balls in front of *Paeonia lactiflora *'Shirley Temple' *are herbs (rocket and acid-green dill) and lettuces.*

Perennial beds

*A common hop climbs through a circular hazel structure with tall spikes of larkspur (*Consolida *Exquisite Series 'Blue Spire') and hairy spikes of *Anchusa azurea 'Loddon Royalist' *on each side. Along the path are clumps of silver-white silverbush (*Convolvulus cneorum*) and white arctotis (*A. fastuosa *'Zulu Prince'). Pink catnip grows with tall cerise *Lobelia 'Queen Victoria' *under the mophead bay tree. In the bed to the right, the orange-reds continue with red and gold columbines and red bleeding heart (*Dicentra *'Bacchanal').*

Center beds

*The hazel wigwam is clothed in *Lathyrus odoratus *'Matucana' and other varieties of sweet pea. These are mixed with the delicious, deep purple form of green climbing bean. Once the sweet peas have finished, I plant nasturtiums and other annual climbers such as a rich purple convolvulus *C. *'Star of Yelta'. Lining the paths of the center bed are parsley and thyme, marigolds, purple-green basil, and lettuces. Nearer the center are blue lupines and anchusas, feverfew, purple alliums, and green-purple or silver sea holly, the chocolate-brown cosmos *C. atrosanguineus*, and the deep crimson rose 'Cardinal de Richelieu'.*

9 ft

3 m

The Mixed Garden in Summer

Far left: The resonant blue Delphinium Black Knight Group flowers from mid-summer on into fall. Pick the main stem, and the laterals will then develop and flower.

Left: Sow annuals which are good for cutting, like these sunflowers, in any gaps between the perennials and herbs.

*Left: Broad clumps of decorative silverbush (*Convolvulus cneorum*) with catnip just behind are echoed in the shape of the corner boxwood ball. All around are flowers that are excellent for picking over long flowering seasons:* Arctotis fastuosa *'Zulu Prince',* Antirrhinum majus *'Black Prince', and bronze-claret violets with yellow-dot centers.*

Opposite: This garden integrates vegetables and salad herbs with flowers and foliage for cutting, mixing them throughout the beds. The rectangular beds, the central sweet-pea wigwam, the hazel frames along the boundary fence, and pairs of standard bay trees give this productive jungle some order and formality. I do not weed out my bolted oak-leaf lettuces since I love their curvy-leaved, acid-green spikes – they make most unusual garden foliage. The foreground pots contain crimson flowering tobacco and pink ivy-leaved pelargoniums, with a red-flowered abutilon in the large pot to the right.

Cultivating Plants: Tips for Success

Stocking and maintaining a cutting garden that is both productive and beautiful involves a little work a lot of the time. Jobs are best done for an hour here and there on a regular basis: an occasional manic splurge for a weekend every few months is not as effective. Try to gear the size of your garden to the amount of time you have to give it. If you can't find the time to do regular watering or weeding, beds and borders that are full of plants and promise in spring will look like a wasteland or a weed jungle by summer. It's most depressing. I know, because I've done it; or, rather, not done it.

Growing your own plants from seed or cuttings or from rootstock division is time-consuming, but opens up huge possibilities barred to those who garden only out of a nursery or garden center. Growing your own, adding to what you already have from the vast and tantalizing choice of plants in the seed catalogs, also costs a fraction of the price of nursery plants. Moreover, you will become involved in one of the most rewarding of pastimes. As a final bonus, you will inevitably grow plants surplus to your needs, which you can present to your friends.

If you can, buy a plant incubator, which, in addition to any spare sunny windowsills, will allow you plenty of space for growing seeds and cuttings under cover. When you really get going, you might invest in a greenhouse and install a propagator bench with heated cables.

Spring

This is the busiest time of year in the cutting garden. On a crisp, clear day you will be out there mulching, pruning, and tidying. When it rains or it is freezing cold, you can take refuge in the potting shed or greenhouse and get on with jobs such as sowing, thinning, and potting.

As the season continues, picking in earnest will start. It is not obligatory to pick the spring flowers. Unlike the summer annuals, spring bulbs and herbaceous perennials will be perfectly happy if you leave them where they are. You can either pick to your heart's content, and adorn the house with your harvest, or allow your prize blooms to flourish in the garden.

General tips for sowing seed

• Sort your seeds into groups according to whether they are for sowing under cover or direct sowing into the ground, the month of sowing, the temperature needed for germination, and any special requirements.

• Always follow directions on the seed pack – for example, some seeds, like lupines and sweet peas, have a hard, protective coat and germinate much more quickly if they are soaked overnight before sowing. And be sure to sow at the recommended time. Overtaken by beginner's enthusiasm the first year I attempted to grow plants from seed, I began sowing in the depths of winter, and my seeds under cover produced pale leggy plants that never did well. Meanwhile, many of the seeds I had sown in open ground simply rotted before they could germinate at all. With a few exceptions, mostly seeds that are slow to germinate (see page 43), it is worth waiting for the days to lengthen so the seedlings have more light hours in which to grow.

• Mark all seeds as you sow them with a permanent label giving the name of the plant and the date it was sown.

• Use the finest spray on your hose or watering can when you water seeds. Large drips or dribbles will dislodge soil and seeds, clumping them together or exposing them to the air.

• You don't have to sow the whole pack. Just sow what you want for that year and store the rest for next. The germination rate may be slightly lower but will almost certainly be adequate. Fold the inner pack, label it clearly, and store in a cool, dry place.

• Remove slugs, snails, and caterpillars using pellets, or by hand if you dislike insecticide. Otherwise these garden pests can munch through your whole crop in a matter of days.

Sowing seeds under cover

• Develop a routine for watering, thinning, and potting, making it as easy as possible, so that it is all done with regularity.

• Good-quality plastic seed flats are easier to clean than wooden ones, and unlike cheap plastic they will not twist and snap if you pick them up at one end when they are full of potting mix. Wash them well at the end of the season and store them in the dark for next year. They become brittle if left out in the sun or light.

• For sowing and potting, use the best seed starter mix – a good mix of loam, peat, sand, and a slow-release fertilizer. You do not want a soggy peat bog to form, so check that the brand you are using is good and friable, or add some grit. Use a coarse metal riddle and a wooden spoon to get rid of any lumps. As a seedling tries to unfurl and grow, a lump may hold it back.

2 *Fill your flats with seed starter mix to ½in (1cm) below the top of the flat. Compress the mix gently with a block of wood the same width as the seed flat.*

3 *To moisten the seed starter mix, float your mix-filled flats in water until the air bubbles stop. Allow the flats to drain; the mix should be moist but not dripping.*

Sowing seeds under cover

1 *Gather all your equipment together on a bench at a good working height. You need seeds sorted in batches, seed starter mix, seed flats, single-cell insets, tall narrow tree pots, a soil compressor, labels and a soft pencil, a coarse sieve, a wooden spoon, and masonry sand.*

4 *Tiny seeds such as poppies are difficult to sow finely so mix them with masonry sand in a ratio of about 1 to 6 to give a better dispersion and more even distribution.*

5 *Sprinkle fine seed over the flats. Large seeds like sea hollies are best sown in rows, spaced so they can develop without competition. Plants with a long root run, such as sweet peas, need more depth: sow them in tree pots.*

6 *Cover seeds with a layer of sifted seed starter mix to the depth shown on the seed pack. Some seeds, like flowering tobacco, do not need covering. Label with the plant name and date of sowing.*

7 *Place the flats or pots on a windowsill, in a plant incubator, or on a propagator bench. Water with a fine mist spray, and cover with a styrofoam tile or with glass covered in newspaper, to cut down the light.*

• Before sowing seed, gently compress the seed starter mix with a piece of wood to remove any large air pockets. Tiny rootlets are deprived of nutrients and water in air pockets.

• Whether you use a windowsill, a plant incubator, or a propagator bench in a greenhouse, you will fit more in a small area if you use square rather than round pots.

• Single-cell insets are most often used for thinning and potting, but they are also useful for sowing large seeds such as hollyhocks, or for those that resent root disturbance, such as lupines, gentian sage, and cow parsley. Seedlings can be transferred directly from the inset to the garden, without an intermediate stage. Peat pots are an alternative.

• Always moisten seed starter mix before sowing. If you leave watering until after sowing, you may wash seeds to the edges and corners of the flats, where they will grow less well.

• Never let your flats dry out or you will destroy the network of delicate rootlets.

• Covering the sown seeds with a styrofoam tile or glass wrapped in newspaper cuts down the light, and so helps many seeds to germinate. It also reduces water loss and insulates.

• Check every day for signs of germination. As soon as there is any sign of life, remove the styrofoam tile or piece of glass and move the seed flat to a position of maximum light.

Thinning

• At first, germinating seeds will grow an atypical pair of leaves. Once there are one or two pairs of true leaves (miniature versions of those on the mature plant), it is time to thin the seedlings or move them into a richer growing mix in a tray of individual cells. Hold onto the leaves, not the stems, at all times. If you bruise the stem, the seedling will die.

• Have a minimum and maximum thermometer on the wall to check your night-time lows and day-time peaks. You must neither allow the temperature to fall below freezing nor let your plants bake in spring sunshine, although you do need the maximum amount of light. Ideally, avoid extremes in the greenhouse by having a thermostatically controlled heater and temperature-sensitive window vents, which will open and ventilate the greenhouse as soon as temperatures begin to rise. At the very least, keep a soil thermometer in the sand on your bench or make regular checks in your plant incubator or on your windowsill.

• Acclimatize seedlings gradually to the outdoors. If you are using cold frames, gradually increase the amount of time during the day that the frames are left open, and leave them open on cloudy nights when frost is not predicted. If you don't have cold frames, put the plants outside in a sheltered corner each day, bringing them in at night. Don't let the wind batter them – wind burn can be as bad as frost – and beware, too, of the heat of the midday sun. Start leaving them out all night when you are sure there is only minimal risk of frost.

Planting out

• Always rake the ground to a fine finish and apply a slow-release, granular, organic fertilizer a few days before you intend to plant the seedlings.

• Once there is little risk of frost, soak your seed flats in water, remove each plant with its root ball, and plant it out with its label.

• Space your plants at slightly less than the recommended planting distance. A little competition for light produces long, straight stems that are perfect for picking, and you can also pick without leaving great gaps in the borders.

Direct sowing of seeds

• Many hardy annuals can be sown directly in the garden. Some, like most poppies and lupines, resent root disturbance, so are best sown where they are to flower. Others, such as dill, bishop's flower, larkspur, marigolds, annual scabious, cornflowers, sunflowers, and annual bupleurum, do just as well from direct sowing, which is, of course, far less time-consuming.

• If possible, start preparing the soil several weeks before sowing. Dig it over, weed, and top-dress or add organic fertilizer. Avoid mulching the area or you will then have to clear any mulch to one side to sow straight into the soil. When you are ready to sow, create a fine finish by breaking up any clods of earth with the back of a strong rake or a hoe.

• Sow seeds in short straight, zigzag, or wavy lines. Seedlings in lines are easier to distinguish from weeds.

• Always keep the area free of weeds, which compete with the seedlings for light, moisture, and nutrients.

• Thin seedlings to just less than the distance recommended on the packet. Although the plants will bulk out and compete with their neighbors, with the amount of picking you will do you can afford to plant them slightly closer together.

Taking basal cuttings

• Cutting a young side shoot from a parent plant is a rewarding and easy way to build up stock. Now is the time to take cuttings from the base of herbaceous perennials, such as bellflowers,

Thinning

1 *Use a pencil or dibble to ease out a clump of seedlings from the rest. Split the clump carefully by hand into single plants, trying to keep a bit of soil attached to the fragile rootlets. With your pencil, make a hole in the seed starter mix in the single cell and place the seedling's root ball in this hole.*

2 *Firm the mix around the seedlings and water them to dislodge any air pockets. Label each tray with plant name and date. Place the seedlings back on the windowsill or propagator bench, where they can recover for a week or two. After this disturbance their roots are at a delicate stage.*

3 *The seedlings are now ready to move to a cooler place where there is frost protection but minimal heat. If you have cold frames, put them there. If not, put them in a sheltered corner of the garden each day and bring them in at night.*

Planting

Dig a generous hole with a hand trowel, mix in some organic matter with the soil at the bottom, and place the young plant in this hole. Firm the ground around the plants gently with your hands and water well.

Direct sowing of seeds

1 *Using sand that contrasts in color to the soil, mark out lines (or areas) where you will sow your seed. With a hand trowel or the back of a rake, or a hoe, make a shallow seed trench to the depth recommended on the seed packet. Line the base of the shallow trench with sand to maximize drainage. Sow your seed into the base of the trench.*

2 *Replace the soil but do not firm. Cover with more of the contrasting sand to remind you exactly where the seeds are for watering and weeding, and label with the name and date of sowing. Water the seeds using a watering can with a fine spray.*

delphiniums, and phlox. Use a clean, sharp blade to remove healthy shoots from the base of the plant. Thereafter, the routine for these basal cuttings is as for semi-ripe cuttings (see page 39).
• Provide a warm, moist atmosphere with light but not direct sunlight, to ensure that the cutting does not wilt and has time – two to three weeks – to root properly.

Bringing tubers into growth and taking basal cuttings
• Never leave tubers in a plastic bag when you buy them. Even with air holes in the bag, the tubers may rot.
• Feel for any soft, diseased areas in the tuber, particularly around the stem, and look closely for mildew and scab. If only limited areas are affected, cut them out; otherwise, you should discard the whole tuber.
• For early flowering, start tender tubers, such as dahlias and *Cosmos atrosanguineus,* into growth under cover about six weeks before you expect the last ground frost. Place the tubers in pots and cover with 4–6in (10–15cm) of moist potting mix. Plant them in the garden once there is little risk of frost.
• If you want to take basal cuttings, place the tubers in a shallow flat and cover with a thin layer of moist potting mix so you can see when the new basal shoots reach 2in (5cm) and the leaves start to form. If you put them in deeper mix, the shoots will be too long to be useful for propagating by the time they show.
• Remove the smaller shoots from the tuber – these will root more quickly than larger, more robust shoots. Cut away the lowest leaves and insert each new shoot in a pot of moist potting mix. Put in a plant incubator or cover with a plastic bag until roots have formed and the new tuber can be potted.

Spring planting
• Start planting fall-flowering bulbs and corms, new herbaceous perennials, and tender shrubs.
• Plant gladioli, colchicums, and nerines in mid-spring (for the techniques, see page 41). The more time they have in the ground, the better they will form adequate roots to sustain a good crop of flowers for fall picking.
• Make successive plantings of gladioli corms every two weeks to get a longer summer- and fall-flowering season.
• Snowdrops and aconites will establish and spread more quickly if planted immediately after flowering, while they still have their leaves – "in the green."
• Plant herbaceous perennials by mid-spring to give them time to form new roots before the rigors of flowering are on them.

• Plant frost-vulnerable shrubs such as rosemary in late spring so that they are well established before next winter's hard frosts. You are likely to lose some if you plant them too early in spring, or in fall before a hard winter (see also page 40 for tips on planting).

Pruning and care of clematis, shrubs, and roses
• Reshape plants that have become wild and unruly, congested in the middle, or insensitively or overpicked, by careful pruning.
• Cut out any dead, damaged, or diseased wood that threatens the health of the plant. Taking branches and stems back to about one-third their length concentrates the energies of the plant, enabling it to produce strong new growth.
• Use a pruning saw for large branches and sharp pruners for anything else. Blunt pruners crush the stems and invite disease.
• Cut back late-flowering clematis at the very beginning of spring. Prune to two buds. If you leave it any later, you will delay the flowering.
• Hard-prune shrubs that tend to get woody and bare at the base. Shrubby artemisias and rosemary, for example, benefit from a spring prune. They will almost immediately produce new shoots on the hard old wood and will make a better-shaped shrub as a result. Many people prune lavender now but it is best to tidy the plant as you pick, or just after flowering. Never cut back into the old wood of lavender, or the plant will not regenerate.
• Cut back the side shoots of winter- and early-spring-flowering shrubs, such as chaenomeles, to two or three buds, as soon as possible after flowering has ended.
• When pruning cluster-flowered and other bush roses, start by removing any frost-damaged shoots. You may have to take more at the end of spring if there is any late frost. Remove suckers at the same time, slicing them off cleanly as near the original root-stock as possible.
• Always make cuts on rose branches at an angle. This allows rain to run off immediately rather than sitting on the wound, where it may encourage disease and rot.
• Make your cut just above an outward-facing bud, so the new branch is encouraged to grow outward and not create a congested mess at the center. Choose a bud with two or three buds below it, so that if your chosen bud isn't healthy, there are others below that may be.
• Sadly, for those of us who like to garden organically, it is often necessary to spray roses and other plants prone to aphids, black-spot, and mildew, such as dahlias and *Euphorbia characias,* every two to three weeks from late spring onward.

Dividing herbaceous perennials

After two or three years, most herbaceous perennials have grown enough both above and below ground to make it possible to cut the plant apart into sections, each of which will make a viable whole (except for the old center section, which may die off, or need discarding). Most perennials actually benefit from division. When the clumps get too big, adequate light is prevented from reaching the leaves in the middle, or, in the case of irises, the sun is prevented from baking the center rhizomes (for Bearded irises, see page 38). Flowering in undivided herbaceous perennials is much less prolific.

• Dig up the whole clump, not just the outer sections, using a fork. Lift enough of the surrounding soil to avoid damaging the roots.
• Divide a woody crown with a spade. Take off small, healthy pieces from the outside of the clump, each with a few new shoots, and discard the old central part of the crown.
• Insert two forks back-to-back to divide fibrous-rooted clumps, pushing the handles of the forks apart to separate the matted roots.
• Have holes waiting for the new plants so you can replant immediately. Plant them using soil mixed with slow-release fertilizer. Minimize the time they are out of the ground and there will then be hardly a hiccup in growth. (See also page 41.)

Mulching, staking, and tidying

As the weather warms up and you see your plants sprouting from the base, the time has come to give the annual mulch, support any plants that may flop, and generally spring clean the garden.

• Spread an organic mulch as soon as the soil begins to warm up. Do not mulch after a hard frost, because you may trap any frost that is still in the ground. You can use forest bark, well-rotted farmyard manure, garden compost, or spent mushroom compost, spreading it to a depth of 2in (5cm). The garden will look immaculate at once! Mulching improves the structure of the soil as well as adding invaluable nutrients. Water evaporation will be reduced – crucial in the heat of the summer to help meet the water demands of fast-growing annuals. Mulching also cuts down on annual weeds. The seeds of weeds from last year will have to push their way through this extra layer, and most will peter out. Also, new weed seeds deposited on the coarse mulch will find it harder to germinate.
• Avoid mulching plants that thrive in poor soil, such as dill and Algerian iris, or they will produce lots of lovely, healthy-looking leaves and no flowers.
• Stake tall plants, such as delphiniums and eremurus, making a rough circle of dry sticks or hazel branches around each clump, about half the ultimate height of the clump. As taller flower spikes grow, put in longer stakes to support these, too. Tie garden twine or fisherman's nylon from stick to stick, making an almost invisible web of support.
• Heavy-headed plants, such as peonies, alstroemerias, and phlox, are better supported with a framework of dry sticks. Push these into the ground to leave a structure about half the plant's ultimate height. They soon grow up through this web to hide it.
• Cut back any seed heads left for winter decoration, or dead growth left for frost protection, once there is minimal risk of frost.

Summer

On the whole, you can now sit back and enjoy your garden. Most of the time, the summer jobs in your cutting garden are simply everyday maintenance. However, you are demanding a lot from a small area, picking flowers again and again, persuading the plants to perform repeated miracles, so you must keep on top of the watering, staking, weeding, fertilizing, and picking. Do these jobs as you see they are needed; do not allow them to pile up.

Watering and fertilizing

• Regular and generous watering and fertilizing is a must in an intensively planted and productive cutting garden.
• Water at the beginning or the end of the day, or you will lose a lot of the benefit through evaporation.
• Water plants that are prone to mildew, such as delphiniums, asters, phlox, and roses, in the morning. If you water them in the evening, the foliage will remain damp overnight and this will encourage mildew.
• Give your garden a good drenching three times a week, rather than a half-hearted sprinkle every day. With a light watering, much of the water will evaporate. What remains will encourage the development of fine, vulnerable roots near the surface. If you give the garden a good periodic drenching, the water will reach a deeper level and plant roots will grow deep to seek out the water. These longer, stronger roots will sustain the plant through dry times, tapping into a safer water source and ultimately producing a bigger and better plant.
• Help your annuals along with regular top-fertilizing. I keep a burlap sack of manure hanging in my water barrel. It makes a rich, smelly, organic top-fertilizer. Give a regular dose of a fertilizer as rich as this and your plants should be happy.

Weeding

• Weed often: in early summer, with everything growing for all it's worth, weeds left for a week or two can easily get the better of a cutting garden.

• Deal with any perennial weeds like twitch grass, bindweed, and ground elder by spot treatment. Choose a dry, calm, windless day and spray each weed individually with a contact herbicide. Mask nearby plants using two boards of wood, plastic, or metal. Wait six hours before watering so the chemical is properly absorbed. After a week or two, see if there is any new growth. If so, repeat.

• If there is serious colonization by perennial weeds, dig up every plant in the affected area. Wash the plants' roots to remove any weed roots, then spray the entire area. This is a drastic solution for a drastic problem. I've only had to do it once and it is not a pleasant experience. Far better to sort out the perennial weed problem before you plant your cutting garden.

• Remove annuals like groundsel, chickweed, and lamb's quarters, as soon as you see them. Don't think you will go back and do it later. They will have flowered, set, and distributed seed before you know it. It is worth remembering that one plant of lamb's quarters (*Chenopodium album*) can produce 70,000 seeds in a year.

Staking

• Stake tall-growing annuals and biennials, and any herbaceous plants that you did not stake in spring. Sunflowers, tithonia, onopordum, dill, moluccella, and bishop's flower are among those that need staking with a dry stick or bamboo cane, or a stick and string framework. The rule is simple: if it looks floppy or vulnerable, stake it.

Picking and deadheading

• Keep picking, deadheading, and removing seed cases to prolong the flowering season. Delphiniums, foxgloves, and other perennials develop lateral flower buds when you remove the leader, and violets flower for many months if their seed cases are removed. Repeat-flowering roses such as 'New Dawn', 'Felicia', and 'Iceberg' produce new flowering shoots if you cut stems back to a vigorous, shooting bud.

Taking semi-ripe cuttings

If you want to build up a good clump of a favorite plant, or if you are thinking of lining a path in the garden with lavender or rosemary, late summer is the time to take your semi-ripe cuttings.

• Pamper a strong, healthy plant to use for taking cuttings. It is worth giving a chosen plant plenty of fertilizer and water so that it is ready, with lots of new growth, when you want to take cuttings.

• Remove the whole shoot from the parent plant by pulling or cutting it off at the junction with the main branch.

• Take more cuttings than you need and store them immediately in a closed plastic bag to minimize water loss. Pot them as soon as possible, taking no more than two at a time out of the bag.

• Label each pot with the name of the plant and the date.

• You can fit several cuttings in a pot as long as they don't touch.

• Cover each pot with a plastic bag, to retain moisture. But do not let the cuttings come into contact with the plastic. If this happens, mildew may set in.

• Check cuttings and water regularly. Remove any cuttings that show signs of wilt, disease, or mildew. They will infect others.

Sowing and planting out biennials

• Biennials such as sweet rocket, wallflowers, and Iceland poppies like to be sown direct into the open ground in summer. Sow as described on pages 34 and 35.

• Plant out spring-sown biennials like sweet Williams and white foxgloves in lines in a prepared bed to mature during summer.

Planting bulbs, corms, and iris rhizomes

• You can still plant fall-flowering bulbs and corms in the early part of summer.

• Plant spring-flowering bulbs, such as narcissi, cyclamen, erythroniums, scillas, and chionodoxas, so they can benefit from an extra two or three months in the ground. They will establish more extensive root systems and flower more prolifically. For the planting technique, see pages 40 and 41.

• Divide and replant Bearded iris. This queen of the cutting garden is unusual in preferring a summer division. After flowering, dig up the rhizomes and discard the leafless center. Trim the ends, roots, and leaves and replant the new rhizome on or just below the surface, facing the sun so that it ripens to flower the following summer (see also page 159).

Planting late-flowering annuals

• As your wallflowers, Iceland poppies, sweet Williams, and sweet peas come to an end, fill the gaps with later flowers nurtured in the cold frame or bought from a nursery or garden center. *Nicotiana sylvestris*, rudbeckias, zinnias, tithonia, amaranthus, and summer icicle are all good for cutting. Remove the spent plants, fertilize the soil, and plant, as on pages 34 and 35.

Taking semi-ripe cuttings

1 *Set out the equipment you need: labels, 3–4in (8–10cm) square plastic pots, rooting hormone powder, a bowl of water, pruners, a sharp knife, a dibble, plastic bags, short sticks, rubber bands, and a watering can. Have one pail of cutting starter mix (loam, peat, and sand mixed with a slow-release fertilizer) and one of vermiculite or sharp sand. In a third pail, add one-third vermiculite to two-thirds cutting starter mix. Fill the pots with this mixture.*

2 *Cut or pull nonflowering, 3–4in (8–10cm) long side shoots from the parent plant – rosemary cuttings are shown here. Gather the cuttings in a plastic bag. At the workbench, remove leaves and side shoots from the lower two-thirds of the stem. Pinch out the soft tip. Make a neat cut at an angle just beneath this year's new wood. Dip the stem end in water, then into the rooting hormone powder. Use a dibble to make a hole in the vermiculite/cutting mix and push the cutting in to about one-third its length. Firm the mix and water well.*

3 *Place sticks in each corner of the pot and stretch a plastic bag over them, securing it with a rubber band, to make a moisture-retaining tent. Place the cuttings on a propagator bench or on a warm windowsill, but out of bright sunlight. Alternatively, place the pots in a mist plant incubator.*

4 *After two weeks to a month, turn one pot over. If strong roots have formed – here you can see good roots on daphne cuttings – it is time to pot the cuttings individually in fresh, moist vermiculite/cutting mix. Make a hole in the fresh rooting medium with your fingers. Plant the rooted cuttings and firm in. Water to dislodge any air pockets.*

5 *Replace the cuttings on the propagator bench or windowsill without plastic bags for another two to three weeks. Then move to a cold frame or a cooler spot until you are ready to plant them in spring.*

Fall

Fall, like spring, is a very busy time of year in the cutting garden. There is plenty of planting of bulbs, shrubs, and perennials still to do, and the garden must be prepared for the onslaught of winter. There are many other jobs to do in spare half hours. You can wrap up a tender ceanothus or young abutilon, transplant a patch of biennials, or plant a bag of bulbs. Get as much done as you can while it is still a pleasure to be outside.

Fall planting

For many plants the demands of flowering are over in fall, but they have not yet reached a dormant stage. This means that newly planted herbaceous perennials, shrubs, and trees can put on some root growth before winter cold sets in. Fall planting is most suited to truly hardy plants such as alchemilla, stachys, and astrantia that, even when young, can survive hard frosts.

• Plant well before frost is forecast. Frost endangers the tiny, fragile rootlets that are so important for water uptake.

• Give each plant a good soaking before you plant it by immersing the pot in a wheelbarrow filled with water. When the air bubbles stop, all the potting mix is wet. Water it very thoroughly once it is in the ground, too.

• Always dig generous holes so there is plenty of room to spread out the roots of each plant. Never cram the root ball into a confined space, or you will at best delay growth and at worst kill the plant. Mix some organic fertilizer into the bottom of the hole and spread some over the soil you replace around the new plant.

• For a large plant, firm the soil around the plant with your shoe, to get rid of large air pockets. For a smaller plant, it is best to use your hands.

• Move biennials that were sown during summer to their final flowering positions in early fall. This allows them to settle into their new site and put on some more growth before the cold weather starts in earnest. Dig them up individually, trying to dislodge as little soil as possible from their roots to preserve the smallest, fragile rootlets. Water them and keep moist.

Bulb care and planting

Bulbs provide a sequence of irises, snowdrops, aconites, crocuses, narcissi, scillas, tulips, and hyacinths and are the mainstay of the cutting garden from late winter and throughout spring. Some people dig their bulbs up every year and ripen them out of the ground, while others treat them as annuals and throw them away after flowering. Both of these involve what seems to me unnecessary work and expense, so I leave my bulbs in the ground, replenishing them every couple of years by planting new ones on either side of the original line.

• Select and plant your bulbs with their flowering dates in mind. You can then have a continuous flow of bright and brilliant flowers for many months commencing at the beginning of the year.

• Prepare the soil before planting. Bulbs mostly like humus-rich and very well-drained soil. Add organic matter and grit or coarse sand, according to your soil type. Mine is heavy clay, so I spread several inches of sharp sand followed by well-rotted manure over the planting area and dig them in.

• Position tall, wooden, gloss-painted markers in the ground before planting bulbs in the cutting garden. Put one at each end of the planned row where they will stay from one year to the next, marking exactly where your bulbs are.

• Try to plant your bulbs as soon as they arrive. With the exception of tulips (see below), the sooner they get in the ground the better. If you cannot plant them immediately, remove them from their bags so they do not get mildewy, and keep them in a cool, dark place. Roll them in a fungicidal powder if you have to store them for a while.

• Look for signs of old roots on cyclamen corms. This will tell you which way to plant them.

• Plant anemone corms preferably with their flat axis horizontal – although they do not have an obvious bottom or top and it does not seem to matter which way up you plant them. If you have room, plant them in big blocks, which makes a more colorful and impressive effect than scattering them. Dig a wide trench and place three or four bulbs next to each other.

• Delay planting tulips until the really cold weather starts. This avoids the problem of fire blight, which will rot the bulb. Plant them with the pointed end upright.

• Do not walk on the soil after planting, because this may break off the growing point of the bulb; just firm it gently with the flat of your hand. If it is dry or dries out in the next couple of weeks, give it a good soaking.

• To naturalize bulbs in grass, cut and remove a circle of turf and use a bulb planter to remove a core of soil 2–3in (5–8cm) deep. Place your bulb in the hole and replace the soil and the sod. If you want the bulbs to flower in a more random and natural pattern, collect a handful of pale stones or use marbles. Cast the whole handful over the area and plant a bulb where each stone or marble lands.

Forcing bulbs

It is a great treat to have lots of bulbs around the house in pots and vases to cheer you in the depths of winter. To do this you must force them into flower early. Many spring bulbs, such as the sumptuous purple *Iris reticulata* and buttercup-yellow *I. danfordiae*, the highly scented *Narcissus* 'Paper White' and 'Soleil d'Or', and many different hyacinths, tulips, and the delicate, pretty scillas, and grape hyacinths, are all well suited to this treatment. Start successive plantings in early fall and you can have flowers through-out winter and well into spring when the cutting garden gets going again.

• Pot the bulbs in plastic pots that will fit into a terracotta or ceramic flower pot. When one potful dies you can just remove it and replace it with a fresh one.

• Once potted, store bulbs in moist potting mix in a cold, dark place. Traditionally bulbs were buried beneath a sunless wall, but a cold store or darkened cold frame will do. This will encourage strong root growth before the leaves and flowers develop. Narcissi, an exception, need cold but not dark for strong growth.

• Pot your bulbs in several different batches so that the flowering season is extended. You can ask the bulb companies to send them at different times. Or you can store them in a cool, dark, frost-free place and lay them out, not touching, like apples on a storage rack.

Digging up and dividing herbaceous perennials

• You can divide herbaceous perennials as successfully in fall as in spring. The hardier perennials can be planted out straight away. With the more delicate plants, it is best to play safe and nurture the new offspring for a while, potting them and putting them in a cold frame or a cool greenhouse for protection until spring (see page 37 for tips on division).

• Dig up your tender perennials, such as salvias and penstemons, and overwinter them in a frost-free cold frame or greenhouse.

Planting bulbs

1 *You will need: bulbs, wooden markers at each end of the planned row, garden twine tied between the markers as a guide, a trowel or hoe, sharp sand, pelleted organic fertilizer, a watering can, and, if planting in grass, a bulb planter.*

2 *Using a trowel or hoe, dig a trench as wide, and three times as deep, as a bulb to one side of the garden twine line. Lay sharp sand to one bulb's depth in the bottom of the trench to maximize drainage and scatter pelleted slow-release organic fertilizer on top.*

3 *Place your bulbs slightly closer than usually recommended, to give you a good density of flowers for cutting without leaving the area looking too empty. Replace the soil and firm it gently with the flat of your hand. If the soil is dry, or dries out in the next few weeks, give it a good soaking.*

• The ground may be drier in fall so, to make the root ball and soil stick together in one big clod, give the clump a good soaking before digging it up. With more soil sticking to the roots, you damage the tiny, delicate rootlets less and so give the transplanted offspring a better start.

Collecting and planting seeds and seedlings

• Seed collecting starts in summer, but most is done in fall. To save the expense of buying annuals every year, it is well worth collecting seeds from all but F_1 (first-generation) hybrids, which do not come true from seed.

• Catch the seed cases when they are turning brown and drying out. Pick the seed case whole and store it in a labeled paper envelope. By the time you sort through these in the winter, they will be thoroughly dried and you can easily separate out the valuable seeds and discard the rest. Return them to the envelope and record what you have and in what quantities. Store them in a cool, dry place until you are ready to plant them in seed flats or in the open garden (see pages 33 and 35).

• Dig up any self-sown seedlings of hardy annuals and plant them in blocks or lines. Self-sown seedlings from perennials such as alchemilla, lupines, euphorbias, astrantia, giant sea holly, anchusas, and violets can be replanted in the same way or left to grow where they are.

• Put some of your hardy annual seeds, especially cornflowers and love-in-a-mist, straight into the ground. Some may not germinate, but enough will to make it worthwhile. These plants mature earlier and will extend your season of flowering.

Layering shrubs

• Propagate plants such as witch-hazel and mock orange that have low-lying branches by layering. Simply bend down a healthy, vigorous lower branch so that it can touch the ground. Dig out a 2in (5cm) trench about 10in (25cm) from the tip of the branch. Strip the leaves and side shoots except at the tip and pin the branch into the trench with a hairpin-shaped piece of wire. Cover it with soil and wait for roots to form. The following spring, sever the branch from the parent and you will have an independent offspring. After a month, dig it up, and replant it.

Taking cuttings

• As you dig up tender perennials for overwintering, take cuttings, too. Treat them as any semi-ripe cuttings (see page 39). You will then have strong plants for planting at the end of spring.

• Take heeled cuttings from perennial pinks by gently tearing off a side shoot, taking a small piece (a "heel") of the central stem with it. Dip this in rooting hormone powder, then insert it into a pot of sandy cutting starter mix. Store the cuttings over winter in a light, frost-proof cold frame and pot them in spring before planting in the garden.

Preparing the garden for winter

• Clear up dead foliage, prune, and mulch, wrap or even dig up to bring inside frost-tender plants.

• As some plants brown and die, cut them back to the ground so they can emerge green and fresh without having to push through their decaying leaves the following spring. Plants such as lamb's-ear and most of the euphorbias will become a soggy mess as soon as a hard frost hits them. These are the ones to cut right down to the ground. There is something beautiful about a garden reduced to its skeletal bones in this way.

• Leave some plants whose dead foliage and flower or seed heads are an asset to the winter garden. Thistles, acanthus, and alliums look good through the winter.

• Trim back bush roses to prevent wind rock, following the instructions for pruning on page 36.

• Provide protection from the hardest frosts. Semi-tender shrubs, herbaceous perennials, bulbs, and tubers need to be covered with a carpet of leaves, straw, or even a good layer of garden compost to protect their crowns. This applies mostly to plants of Mediterranean or Californian climates, such as artichokes, agapanthus, young *Arum italicum,* and *Helleborus argutifolius*, and shrubs such as evergreen ceanothus, abutilons, and young magnolias; these are safest if protected by netting or a light material designed to reduce frost damage. Aim to have them snugly wrapped by mid-fall.

• Dig up your tender tubers such as *Cosmos atrosanguineus*, dahlias, and the tender agapanthus, and overwinter in a cool, dry place, not touching one another. Dig up tender perennial penstemons and salvias, and cut them back before overwintering in a light, cool, frost-free place.

• Spread a layer of manure or garden compost over the whole garden and dig it in. If your soil is heavy, leave any large clods – they will be broken up better by the winter weather than by your struggling with them now. Lighten your soil by spreading some horticultural grit or sharp sand. Never walk over newly dug ground or you will undo all the good soil structuring you have done. Lay a plank down and stand on this if you need to go over the ground again.

Winter

In winter there is less to do in the garden, greenhouse, and potting shed. One of the main delights of winter is selecting what you want from the seed catalogs. Try to order early so your choices are available. The thing to be careful about, when you are seduced by the excitement of having all these lovely plants in your garden, is not to order too many. Remember the time you have to spend on them, as well as the space they require in the greenhouse, or on your windowsills.

Taking hardwood cuttings

• You can propagate from many trees and shrubs by taking hardwood cuttings. Start with ivies and willows that reward you every time by forming roots on each cutting you prepare. Then move onto the more difficult dogwoods and camellias, which are likely to have a lower success rate. Remove a woody branch, which in the case of willow can be up to 4–5 ft (1.2–1.5m) tall, and insert it in soil lightened with sand in a prepared bed. For ivies, cut one trailing branch into sections with three or four leaves each. Insert these cuttings into a sandy cutting starter mix and put them in a cold frame or cool greenhouse for the winter. If roots have not formed by spring, place them on a heated propagator bench to give them a boost – do this, too, for any trickier plants.

Taking root cuttings

• Take root cuttings when plants are dormant in winter so that parent and offspring both have time to recover and flourish by the next growing season. This is the best way to propagate the fall-flowering anemones (*A.* × *hybrida* and *A. hupehensis*), the pasque flower, most of the sea hollies, acanthus, and Oriental poppies. Mark the position of the parent plant in fall, because the leaves will have disappeared by winter and, unless it is marked, you will have no idea where it is. Dig up the whole plant carefully, and, using a sharp knife, slice some of the root into 3in (8cm) sections. Angle the thin end at 45 degrees to tell you it is the bottom. The top end should have a 90-degree cut.

• Have your pots of cutting starter mix waiting. The cut sections of root must not be left to dry out. Tie a bundle together with gardener's twine and put them into the mix, making sure you have kept each root facing the right way up. Cover them with 1in (2.5cm) of soil and place them in a cold frame or another light, frost-free place. Replant the parent plant.

• By spring, shoots will have appeared on the cuttings. Check that they have good roots and then plant them individually in pots. Leave them where they are until fall, when you can plant them in the garden.

Sowing seed

• Sow seeds that are slow to germinate. The superb deep purple lisianthus, for example, should be sown from fresh seed in mid-winter if it is to put on adequate growth to flower that year.

• If you forgot to sow your seeds of sweet Williams, lupines, and hollyhocks, sow them now. You will not have such strong plants as those planted in late summer or fall, but they will flower in the same year.

• If you did not sow your sweet peas during fall for storing in a cold frame over winter, sow them now so they are ready for planting in spring. Pinch out their growing tips so you will have strong, bushy plants.

Pruning

• Now is the time to prune, trim, and tidy deciduous shrubs and climbing and large shrub roses, while the framework of the plant is most apparent. Most of the big shrubs, *Elaeagnus angustifolia*, mock orange, and the statuesque *Rosa moyesii* will benefit from pruning in winter, as will any large rampant climbers.

• Start by removing dead, diseased, or damaged wood right from the base, then concentrate on weak and spindly branches. Also, remove any suckers from the main stem or at the base, since these divert energy from the main plant.

• Always stand back and assess the overall shape of the plant. In general, aim for a balanced, even silhouette. Be careful to preserve the graceful, arching habit of shrubs such as the species roses by removing more than a third of their stems, although some vigorous shrubs, such as lilac, can be safely cut back hard.

Flower Arranging

This school of flower arranging is accessible to everyone. There is no need for any expensive equipment or complicated techniques such as intricate wiring. All you need is a love of color and a sense of drama. Keep in mind a few basic ideas on structure, scale, and color, follow the advice for cutting and conditioning, and you will be well on your way.

You should aim to create a heightened version of what is in the garden, with a similar feeling of natural ease and beauty: avoid strict symmetry and dominating vertical or horizontal lines. Remember that a flower arrangement can be in an unconventional container. Conjure romantic globes with billowing flowers and branches of foliage; or construct enormous swags and medallions to hang inside or out. Keep the image of growing plants in mind, and have fun.

As well as creating average-sized bunches of flowers, think of making arrangements for both giants and pygmies. A huge vase of pussy willow, foxgloves, or cow parsley is an impressive sight. At the other extreme, one velvety auricula, with a face like a mime artist, is almost guaranteed to lift the spirits. Anything is possible.

Blues, greens, whites, and yellows make beautiful and peaceful combinations, but think, too, of mixing rich and powerful colors – oranges, purples, and near-blacks, or crimsons, golds, and royal blues. Balance their strength with calming acid-green or silver. Why not be even more adventurous? Raise eyebrows by using colorful containers to make zinging combinations such as fluorescent pink and turquoise or orange and lime-green. Be brave and let rip.

When you restrict the varieties of flowers, you can run riot with color. Be bold: mix red, yellow, carmine, purple, blue, and green to create a show-stopping display.

Cutting

The best part of having a cutting garden is harvesting your own produce from your own garden. I fill my pails with endless possibilities for combinations, gathering a bounty of all shapes, sizes, and colors. You can wander around surrounded by luscious scents, textures, and colors all of your own making, and any of which can be brought into the house – the choice is yours. And, as you pick, all the anxiety and diligence that have gone into making your cutting garden will, I am sure, be metamorphosed into pride and pleasure.

If you obey a few rules based on commonsense when you are picking, everything you cut from the garden will benefit and will have a longer vase life.

Cut when it is cool
You should always try to cut in the early morning or in the evening. These are the most beautiful times of the day, before the dew has fully evaporated, or when the last of the sun enriches the colors of the garden as a whole. During the day, particularly in the summer months with the increased heat, plants will transpire more. They will therefore probably be moisture-deficient and so more likely to droop as soon as they have been cut. Plants that have had the opportunity to restore their moisture balance overnight will be more able to withstand the trauma of cutting. To some extent the same applies when the plants have had some time to recover in the cool of the evening.

Invest in the right equipment
Good-quality pruners and scissors will repay their price in years of service. They must be really sharp. If they are blunt, you will crush the stem end and block it, and could damage the host plant. If you are picking lots of flowers, invest in a wheelbarrow so you can push your pails around the garden with you.

Care for your plants
Treat your garden with care. If you cut sensibly, it is easy to pick enormous amounts from a garden without its being apparent that you have taken much, or even anything at all. Always try to pick from the back of shrubs and large perennials, avoiding obvious gaping holes near the front. Think of the overall shape of the plant as you pick from it and try to improve, not destroy, it. With smaller plants take one or two stems from several plants, rather than all the flowers from one and none from the rest.

Cut flowers in loose bud
Most flowers are best cut in loose bud. Ideally they should be showing some color, yet still be somewhat closed. Find the stems on the plant with the most flowers at this stage. There will often be a flower or two which is more advanced, but these can be removed during conditioning if they have passed their best.

There are a few exceptions to this rule, including dahlias, zinnias, and marigolds, where the flower will not develop from a bud. These must be picked when already fully out (see notes given for each plant on pages 96–163). At the other extreme, some flowers – camellias, for instance – will come out from even very tight buds.

Cut your stems long
On the whole, the longer the stems, the easier the flowers will be to arrange. Cut each stem right down to the ground, or back to a main stem, so that you can make the most of the natural height of the plant. For a more three-dimensional arrangement, choose some twisting and turning stems as well as some of the more obvious straight ones.

Leave some bulb foliage
Bulbs are the exception to the rule about cutting stems as long as possible, since they need to have some leaves left for photosynthesis in order to store energy in their bulbs to carry them through the dormant season. If you cut lilies and crown imperials to the ground, you will cut off almost all the leaves. So try to cut the stems leaving about a third of the main bulk of the foliage. Only once the leaves have browned can you cut them off and clear them up.

Quickly place cut flowers in water
Once a plant has been picked, put it in water as soon as possible. This is most important in the heat of summer. Some plants, like peonies, will never fully recover if they are left out of water, and their heads will droop. Others may appear more resilient, but their cut life will be much curtailed. Keep one or more pails one-third filled with water near you.

Keep your sizes separate
If you are picking both short and tall plants, keep them in separate pails, or the taller, heavier plants will crush the flowers of the shorter, delicate ones. If the flowers of the shorter stems end up in the water, they may be harmed.

Strip the bottom leaves as you go

Strip the bottom leaves and side branches of each stem into an empty container as you go. If you remove them now, you will decrease the surface area that is transpiring and hence decrease the demands and stress on the newly cut flower. These leaves would need to be removed before conditioning anyway.

Think of arrangements as you go

As you pick in the garden, try to bunch plants loosely together, creating a balance of flowers and foliage, colors, and textures. Particularly if you have a lot of arrangements to do, this could save enormous amounts of time, and it will avoid repetition.

Choose the unusual

Use your imagination in what you pick. There will of course be flowers and foliage for picking that are obviously pretty to arrange. But look around for the less obvious, too. Check hedges, or any scrubby wild parts of your garden that you hardly ever go into. Keep an eye out for interesting buds, seed cases, twisting or unusual colored stems, berries, and hips, as well as flowers and foliage for your bunches. Experiment with your picking. If a plant flops the first time you use it, try searing the stem the next (see page 48). Make your own discoveries and you will have much more fun, and your boundaries will expand in an ever more satisfying way.

Equipment

Deep pail, filled to one-third with water, for long stems.
Shallow pail, filled to one-third with water, for short stems.
Empty pail for stripped leaves and side stems.
Basket to carry flowers from the middle of a border
to the pails.
Thorn-proof gloves for picking roses and blackberries.
Rubber gloves for picking euphorbias and rue.
Pruners for cutting woody stems.
Scissors for cutting fleshy stems.
Folding knife for slitting stems and removing thorns.

Stripping stems

Strip the bottom third of your cut stems, taking off all leaves, side branches, or thorns. Put the waste into a pail and then on the compost heap. Divide your flowers into tall and short and keep them in separate pails, so the larger and more robust ones do not crush the smaller, more delicate ones.

Dealing with rose stems

Strip the thorns from the bottom third of your rose stems so you do not prick yourself when conditioning and arranging. Cut the stem end again at a sharp angle and then make a 1in (2.5cm) slit up the middle of the stem to increase the surface area for water absorption and prevent a seal from forming on the newly cut end. This is ideally done under water so air locks cannot form.

Conditioning

Once you have gathered in your harvest, you need to put the flowers in a cool place out of direct sunlight, near a sink and a flat surface so that you can condition them. After conditioning, leave everything standing overnight or through the day in deep water, so the newly cut flowers have time for a good drink. Tepid water is absorbed better than water that is ice-cold, and it is a good idea to add some brand name cut-flower food containing nutrients and antibacterial agents. This sets up the flowers to withstand excess heat and bright sunlight much better. If you cut, arrange, and put the vases straight into the house, the life of your flowers will be shortened by several days.

For all plants there are some basic rules of conditioning.

Remove any leaves below the water line

The water line is just below the top of the vase and leaves that are below this should be removed from the stem. If you have not removed enough while outside in the garden, you should do this first. Any leaf that touches the water will quickly decay and produce a bacterial soup, which will stink and clog up the stems and shorten the life of the other flowers. Too much leaf also puts great demands on the flower stem of the cut plant, so aim for the minimum that looks nice. Don't overdo it, though, and leave a collection of bald, top-heavy beauties.

All stems should be recut

Before you give your flowers their long drink, you must recut the stems with really sharp pruners, scissors, or a knife. This is best done under water to avoid the risk of air locks forming in the capillary network of the stem. Cut them at an appropriate angle: flat for soft stems, which can absorb some water along the length of stem, and at a 45-degree angle for woody stems, so that you maximize the surface area for water uptake. Plunge them immediately into a deep vase of tepid water because newly cut ends begin to seal over at once.

Sear sappy and soft stems

If you find that a plant you particularly like always seems to droop, even if you put it straight into water in the garden, try searing the stem ends in boiling water. This technique is the savior of many a wilting cut flower. It is particularly useful for sappy, soft-stemmed plants (for example, euphorbias, smyrnium, acanthus, artemesia, poppies, hellebores, viper's bugloss, holly-

Searing sappy or soft stems
The vase life of flowers with soft stems or stems that "bleed" can be prolonged by searing them in boiling water. Keeping their heads clear of the steam, dip the newly cut stems in 1in (2.5cm) of boiling water for 20 seconds before plunging them into tepid water.

hocks). In the case of euphorbias, it also stops the leaking of the very allergenic white milk from the stem end (see euphorbia, page 96). Make sure that the flower heads are well away from the heat, either by angling the flowers away from the steam, or by wrapping the flowers in stiff brown paper. Dip the stems into 1in (2.5cm) of boiling water for about 20 seconds. During this time you will often see bubbles emerging as the stem seals off. Then place the flowers immediately in tepid water.

Even flowers with tough but nonwoody stems, such as roses, seem to benefit from this treatment. First cut their stems, preferably with a sharp knife, at a 45-degree angle. If the head has already flopped, which happens so often with bought roses, try searing the stems as soon as possible and they almost always miraculously pick up again over the next hour or so.

Hammer woody stems

The ends of woody stems of trees and shrubs (for example, lilac, viburnum, cotinus, philadelphus) should be crushed. Hammering the bottom 1–2in (2.5–5cm) of each stem increases the surface area for water absorption and prevents a skin or seal from forming over the stem end, blocking the plant's water uptake. Once the stems have been crushed, they should be plunged immediately into a deep vase of tepid water.

Hammering woody stems

To prevent a seal from forming and to increase surface area for water absorption, crush the bottom 1–2in (2.5–5cm) of each stem with a hammer or mallet on a hard surface. Then plunge the stems into tepid water.

Binding long, thin stems such as tulips

If you want straight tulips, they must be supported during the conditioning process. Wind string or florist's tape around the complete length of their stems and wrap them in stiff paper before leaving them in water overnight.

Bind long, thin stems

Heavy-headed flowers with long, thin stems (such as tulips) and bought greenhouse plants (such as gerberas) tend to bend after picking. If you leave them untreated as they suck up water in the conditioning process, the stems will become set in this bent position. Prevent this by binding the stems to hold them straight.

Support hollow stems

Hollow-stemmed plants with heavy heads (for example, amaryllis, lupines, or delphiniums) may break under the weight of the flower head even before you arrange them. To avoid this, gently insert a thin stick right up the hollow stem. Fill the stem with water, then plug the end with cotton secured with a tight rubber band.

Aftercare

Once you have gone to the trouble to pick, condition, and arrange your flowers, it is worth doing all you can to prolong their vase life. Just as cut flowers need a cool place for conditioning, so they will survive longer away from heat or direct sunlight. Research has shown that carnations kept at 50°F (10°C) will age eight times faster than those kept at 34°F (1°C). So avoid placing arrangements near a radiator in winter or in direct sunlight in summer.

Add nutrients and preservatives to the water

Cut flowers need sugars that can be utilized for metabolism, a substance to raise the acidity of the water, and an antibacterial agent. Brand name sachets of cut-flower food contain agents for all three. I find that it is worth going to a wholesale market and buying them in quantity. If you don't want to buy special food, add a few drops of bleach and a teaspoon of sugar to the vase and stir.

Make sure the flowers have clean water

Cut flowers last longer in clean water. Make sure you start with a pristine vase. Otherwise bacteria will build up in the dirty water, as we all know from the stench you get when throwing away flowers that have stayed in water unchanged for a week. The bacteria, acting on the cut stem ends, create a slime that blocks the capillaries through which water is drawn up to the leaves and the flowers. This blockage causes the plant to wilt. Check the water level every other day, since flowers will die quickly with only a tiny bit of water in the bottom of the vase. In hot weather you should try to change the water every other day. To do this, you do not have to destroy your arrangement: just leave the vase under running water for a couple of minutes and then replenish the cut-flower food. At the same time, you can remove any dead or dying flowers with your scissors to give the arrangement a face lift.

Choosing a Vase

If you marry your flowers to a vase that is sympathetic in shape and color, you are halfway to creating a beautiful arrangement. So it is important that when you begin to grow flowers for cutting, you should also invest in at least a basic variety of vases and containers (see opposite). I recommend the following: a simple, clear glass vase, full-bellied with a neck, about 8–12in (20–30cm) high (see page 72); a similar-shaped vase or a pitcher, about 18in (45cm) high, for generous, larger arrangements (see page 71); a tall straight or slightly shaped vase between 8in (20cm) and 12in (30cm) high (see page 53); a tall, narrow vase for a single rose or flowering tobacco (see page 82); at least one or two shallow ceramic or glass bowls for table centerpieces (see page 62); a few colored glasses for smaller posies and single flower heads for putting beside a bed or on your desk, and one or two 1–2in (2.5–5cm) vases for a single crocus or auricula (see pages 56–57 and 79). As you grow more and varied flowers, and become more adventurous in your arrangements, you will find that you want to add to your vase collection. Try tag sales and junk and antique stores as well as more unusual china and glass stores.

Height of vase

For any arrangement to be in harmonious proportion, choose a vase one-third to one-half the height of the tallest flowers and foliage you have picked. If the vase is more than this, it will make the flowers appear as if they are straining to peep out of the top. If it is less, then the whole arrangement will look as if it is about to topple over.

Color and style of vase

I love brilliant, contrasting colors, and so my favorite arrangements are often those with bright, zingy flowers in strong-colored ceramic or glass containers. A few stems of the crimson hyacinth 'Jan Bos', for example, will combine with a container of a contrasting color to produce a powerful attention-seeker. A subtle mixture of more delicate flowers, such as love-in-a-mist with cornflowers, delphiniums, and lady's mantle, needs a lighter, less dominant vase.

Similarly, great bosomy peonies and roses can look good in an elaborate vase, while simple, wild-style flowers on the whole look better in unpatterned, unfussy containers. It is important that the vase never overwhelms the flowers.

Acquire a good collection of vases *Choose plain glass or a neutral-colored material like pewter to get the most use out of your vases to begin with, but don't neglect other colors. You will soon learn which sizes, shapes, and colors suit your favorite flowers and arrangements.*

Stems too long *These cosmos stems look as if they could topple the vase over at any minute. This lack of balance is visually uncomfortable.*

Stems too short *Some of these stems look as if they are craning their necks to reach out of the vase. This disproportion is best avoided.*

Stems in good proportion *These stems are two to three times the height of the vase, creating an arrangement that looks stable and open.*

Equipment for arrangements

1   cone or funnel for extending stems
To lengthen stems in especially large arrangements. Push each stem into a cone, secure it with florist's tape, and fill the cone with water before pushing the cone spike into florist's oasis. To lengthen stems even further, tape each cone to a stick and then push the stick into oasis.

2   9 x 4¼ x 3¼ in (23 x 11 x 8cm) block of florist's oasis
Foam used by florists to hold stems in place. Easily cut to size and water-retaining once it has been soaked, it is especially useful for arrangements in shallow bowls.

3   water vial
To hold stem ends in swags, medallions, wreaths, and globes. Once they are placed, the water-filled vials can be hidden by the foliage. Most plants will survive for one to two days with this amount of water.

4   heavyweight pin-holders in 3 sizes
To hold average-sized stems, such as roses and euphorbias, in place. (Use marbles for finer stems and florist's oasis wrapped in chicken wire for very large or robust stems.) Stick the pin-holder to the bottom of the vase with florist's clay or double-sided tape.

5   glass marbles
To hold delicate stems in place, especially in glass vases. You need enough to fill about one-third of a vase.

6   glass stem-holder
To hold firm stems in place in a large, shallow bowl. Secure to the bottom of the vase with florist's clay or double-sided tape.

7   florist's clay (strong water-proof glue-tack)
To attach florist's oasis, pin-holders, anchor pins, and so on, to bowls and vases.

8   candle holder (shown inverted)
To insert into a block of florist's oasis to hold a candle upright.

9   anchor pin or oasis pin
To hold blocks of florist's oasis in place. Attach to the bottom of a bowl or vase with florist's clay or double-sided tape and push the oasis firmly down onto the four plastic teeth.

10   gardener's twine
To make wreaths and tie bunches.

11   roll of fine-gauge florist's wire
To tie and bind in swags, wreaths, globes, and medallions.

12   scissors
To trim leaves, stem ends, etc.

13   plastic sheeting
To protect the floor where you are working. If lifted by the four corners, it can be emptied into a trash can when you finish.

14   chicken wire, 12 in (30cm) wide
To wrap around florist's oasis in the construction of swags and globes. Also use for huge arrangements – bunch inside vases to hold stems in place.

15   watering can
To fill vases, water vials, etc.

16   18in (20cm) globe of florist's oasis
To create large globes for special occasions.

17   moss
To line a hanging basket, especially to pad the areas around florist's oasis. Also to hide oasis in large arrangements.

18   a pair of hanging baskets
To construct large globes. Fill with soaked florist's oasis and wire together.

19   heavy twine
To tie larger bunches and wreaths; hop-bine (Humulus lupulus) can be used instead.

20   circle of heavy-gauge wire
To secure large, heavy swags, and globes.

21   strong carry-all
To carry all your equipment.

Creating Arrangements

Making beautiful and impressive flower arrangements is easy since there are no hard and fast rules to slavishly obey. However, there are a few basic guidelines that work for me, even though I sometimes disregard them deliberately when the occasion or the plant demands it. Even though it is worth keeping the following advice in mind, it is important to use your imagination and follow your own inclinations.

Avoid strict symmetry at all costs
Neat domes of flowers usually look boringly restrained and predictable. Create a livelier arrangement by allowing branches to burst out in different directions, balancing an upward spike here with a downward bough of berries there. To emphasize this, use odd numbers of the dominating flowers and spikes of foliage. Work in threes, fives, and sevens, rather than fours, sixes, and eights. Use, for example, three of your most glamorous flowers, five of your middle-sized flowers, and nine or eleven of more abundant "padding" flowers.

Create a broken silhouette and a billowy effect
Cut stems in a variety of lengths. As you place your flowers, push some right into the heart of the arrangement, leaving others standing out.

It is painful to see beautiful plants poked into a vase without room for their natural lines, twists, and turns. In general, try to allow each stem to stand or hang as it would on the parent plant in the garden. Avoid creating any vertical and horizontal lines with the dominant flower, because this will segment the vase into zones and destroy the overall effect.

Arrange in three dimensions
Even if you are making an arrangement that is to sit against a wall or window, always aim to construct it "in the round." Don't fall into the "short-at-the-front-and-tall-in-the-back" trap. It is tempting to put all your best flowers where they will be most obviously seen. But doing this will give your arrangement an unnatural, two-dimensional look as well as make it unbalanced in weight, making it all too easy to topple over. If you arrange a vase that could be viewed at any angle, it will immediately look much livelier. And you will be surprised to find that you will be able to see all your flowers. Glimpsing them from varying viewpoints will make the arrangement far more dynamic.

Emphasizing the effect of strong flowers
When yellow and brick-red sunflowers are mixed with substantial, bursting artichoke buds, the arrangement becomes even more commanding, the focal point of a room.

Diffusing the effect of strong flowers
The impact of the same flowers as those seen above is softened by the feathery heads of dill, making a less powerful arrangement, one that is better able to blend into the background.

Teaming flowers and foliage
It is usually best to team strong foliage with strong flowers and light, fluffy foliage with more delicate flowers. Each enhances the other. Robust, architectural foliage, such as acanthus, green artichokes, or horse chestnut buds, will reinforce the flamboyant effect of flowers like Parrot tulips, sunflowers, and dahlias. If you want to soften the effect of flowers with strongly defined shapes, use feathery foliage such as dill.

Choosing foliage

Your selection of foliage is as important as your choice of flowers. I tend to avoid the heavy, dark, evergreen forms of privet, laurel, and boxwood. I think their glossy texture and dark tone weigh down an arrangement and swamp the color and light of the flowers. I choose enlivening acid-green at any opportunity and rarely make an arrangement without euphorbia or smyrnium in spring, and lady's mantle, bupleurum, or dill, in summer and fall.

Don't stop with just flowers and foliage

Often the addition of some branches, seed heads, or even fruit is the making of a bunch of flowers. Try and forage for something – pussy willow, filbert catkins, emerging spring leaves, ears of wheat, cattails, clematis seed heads, sprays of blackberries, or crab apples – from the wilder parts of the garden. What you choose to add can dictate the final effect of an arrangement, making it either more attention-seeking, or more muted.

Color contrast

It is always more interesting to use contrasting colors in an arrangement. Think of this when choosing foliage as well as flowers.

If you cut some sumptuous carmine snapdragons and cosmos, they could look somber on their own, since they are so closely matched in color, especially when teamed with one type of foliage. Adding a few deep blue salvias and gentians would immediately make the arrangement come alive. Adding acid-green and deep crimson foliage such as dill, bupleureum, and smokebush brings richer colors and greater interest. Don't be tempted to overdo the mixture. If you go on and add two or three more shapes and colors, the style and grace of the arrangement may collapse.

I feel that you can successfully have either limitless color or infinite flower variety, but not both at once. When a color jamboree is what's wanted, it is probably better to restrict the number of types of flowers. When the flower types are limited, anything goes (see page 45).

Subdued color *The color match between the cosmos and the snapdragons is almost too perfect and, with only privet foliage, there is not enough going on to arrest the eye.*

Balanced color *With blue (salvia and gentian), acid-green (bupleurum and dill), and deep purple foliage (smokebush), the arrangement is immediately livelier.*

Chaotic color *With even more colors and types of flowers (here, yellow coneflowers, purple lisianthus, and white cosmos), an arrangement can become so busy that it loses its presence.*

Creating a mixed arrangement

Start with the background foliage

Use your leafiest, bulkiest foliage to create the overall basic structure.

Failure *(left) These branches of oak are not thinned out. The stems are cut to equal lengths and placed neatly and too symmetrically, making the arrangement look dense and boring.*

Success *(right) Lots of leaves have been removed to emphasize the acorns and lighten the overall effect of the dark foliage. The stems are arranged so that one leans over the vase on one side and another curves into the air on the other. The result is asymmetrical and more natural.*

Add more background greenery

Choose something that will contrast with the fairly dark, solid shapes of the oak leaves. Fill out the arrangement to the point where you feel that it could almost be left without adding the flowers.

Failure *(left) The usually pretty bupleurum is lost in the dense green sea of leaves. The silhouette remains too solid, adding little interest to the arrangement.*

Success *(right) Strong foliage with boughs of crabapples and green love-lies-bleeding with its long, lime-green, dangly tassels contribute subtle color contrast and different shapes and textures.*

Add the most dominant flowers

Place flowers at very different levels, some cut quite short for the heart of the arrangement, and others standing tall, left long to break up the silhouette. Avoid overpacking so the plants can follow their natural lines and are not held too upright and alert.

Failure *(left) An even number of flowers has been placed symmetrically in the vase. Each one is forced too deeply into the foliage. The result looks cramped and suffocated.*

Success *(right) An odd number of sunflowers has been added, all at different levels in the arrangement. The effect is open and relaxed.*

Spring Arrangements

A Spring Tapestry

Illustrated on pages 56–57.

This array of mid-spring flowers and elegant glassware is inspired by the Pointilliste idea that dashes of color create overall richness and depth.

Equipment

a selection of glass bowls, plates, drinking glasses, vases, mini-decanters
8–10 glass marbles
1–3in (2.5–8cm) pin-holder
florist's clay or double-sided tape
2 pliable twigs, such as willow, about 12in (30cm) long

Plants

25 sweet violets (*Viola odorata*)
15 wood anemones (*A. nemorosa*)
9 flame-colored wallflowers (*Erysimum cheiri* 'Fire King')
5 stems of euphorbia (*E. amygdaloides* var. *robbiae*)
3 heads of daphne (*D. odora* 'Aureomarginata')
9 auricula primroses (*Primula auricula*)
1 plum snakeshead fritillary (*Fritillaria meleagris*)
3 heads of magnolia (*M. denudata*)
7 young cardoon leaves (*Cynara cardunculus*)
15 Lenten rose flowers and seed heads (*Helleborus orientalis*)

Method

Pick a selection of delicate flowers that look good up close. Some are so perfect that one stem is best on its own. Others look balanced when several flowers are combined. Add one or two vases of more robust flowers, like the wallflowers and the Lenten roses, to enhance the delicacy of the rest. Here, I have kept the flower heads quite short and all at a similar level to intensify the image.

Mix the violet stems with a few leaves in your hand and place them all together in a drinking glass.

Bend the pliable twigs into a zig-zag, so that they form a web in the shallow bowl to hold the fine anemone stems upright.

Place the wallflowers in a taller vase. Their strong stems will provide a structure; distribute the euphorbias among them.

Cut the daphne sprigs short and place them in a saucer of water.

Fill another drinking glass to about a third with 8–10 marbles and poke in the primrose stems, one by one.

Place the fritillary and magnolias in the narrow-necked decanters.

Use the florist's clay or tape to secure the pin-holder in a bowl. Distribute the cardoon leaves in the holder, then add the Lenten roses.

From a Spring Hedge

The splendor of the silver bowl provides a good contrast to the simplicity of these wild flowers.

Equipment

raised shallow bowl, 12in (30cm) wide
2 blocks of soaked florist's oasis, cut to fit 2in (5cm) above the bowl's rim
anchor pin
florist's clay or double-sided tape

Plants

7–11 stems each of the following:
Solomon's seal (*Polygonatum × hybridum*)
arum leaves (*A. italicum* 'Marmoratum')
sweet cicely (*Myrrhis odorata*)
15–20 cuckoo flowers (*Cardamine*)
22 blue and white bluebells (*Hyacinthoides hispanica*)
15–20 cowslips (*Primula veris*)

Method

Use the florist's clay or tape to secure the anchor pin in the bowl. Position the oasis on the anchor pin. Distribute the Solomon's seal and arum over the oasis in an irregular shape 1½ times the bowl's height. Let the sweet cicely curve to one side. Distribute the cuckoo flowers and bluebells evenly, but place the cowslips to accentuate the asymmetry of the arrangement.

Woodland with Parrots

These huge-headed, flamboyant Parrot tulips are best mixed with equally stylish and strong foliage. The horse parsley is perfect for this. To give height and lift to this robust arrangement, add some branches of maple 'Crimson King', with its newly emerged claret foliage and acid-yellow flowers echoing the color in the tulips.

Equipment
waisted glass vase, 12in (30cm) tall

Plants
9 branches of maple *Acer platanoides* 'Crimson King', 24–30in (60–75cm) long

7 stems of horse parsley (*Smyrnium olusatrum*), 18–24in (45–60cm) long

15 tulips (*Tulipa* 'Flaming Parrot'), 18in (45cm) long

Method
Arranging these plants could not be easier. The waisted vase holds the first few maple branches in place. The maples then provide both support and structure to hold the floppier stems and flowers of the horse parsley and tulips.

So simply create a good overall structure and height for the arrangement with the maples, leaving the tallest branches standing about 1½ times the height of the vase. Do not make it too symmetrical, but it should look balanced at this stage. Next, poke in the horse parsley stems placing them fairly evenly throughout the arrangement. Finally, add the tulips, making sure there are no blank holes. Since the tulips are the only flowers used – and powerful ones at that – you need to give them a fairly uniform distribution.

A Vivid Globe of Venetian Colors

This is a combination of many of my favorite colors and plants. These fiery oranges, resonant black-purples, and pale and acid-greens reflect the vivid and dramatic color schemes used in Titian's paintings. Imagine a line of these globes hanging above your head at a party overlooking the Grand Canal in Venice. Used en masse, or singly, they will enhance any party, inside or, as here, in a romantic garden setting.

Equipment
1 globe of florist's oasis, diameter
   8in (20cm), soaked
3ft (90cm) length of 2in (5cm)
   chicken wire
fine-gauge florist's wire
⅛in (3mm) heavy-gauge wire
wire cutters and scissors
length of chain or rope for
   hanging globe

Plants
Stems, 12–14in (30–35cm) long,
   of each of the following:
20 smyrnium (*S. perfoliatum*)
   or *Euphorbia cyparissias*
20 *Euphorbia cornigera* or *E. palustris*
20 yellow-green *Euphorbia
   polychroma*
20 European guelder rose (*Viburnum
   opulus* 'Roseum')
20 orange euphorbia (*E. griffithii*
   'Fireglow')
40 black tulips (*Tulipa* 'Queen of
   Night' and *T.* 'Black Parrot')
20 dark purple columbines
   (*Aquilegia vulgaris*)
5 trails of white anemone clematis
   (*C. montana*), left as long as possible

Method
Follow **Steps 1–6**.

1 Cut a piece of chicken wire long enough to encircle the florist's oasis globe, with a generous overlap. Cut a piece of the heavy-gauge wire so it is long enough to fully encircle the globe, and add on an extra 12in (30cm) length for hanging. The length of chain or rope will be attached to this.

2 Wrap the chicken wire around the globe, securing it carefully with fine-gauge florist's wire. Weave the piece of heavy-gauge wire through the chicken wire, completely around the globe, and twist it several times at the top where the two ends meet.

3 Attach the chain or rope securely to the wire. Hang the globe at easy working height, so you can poke in the flowers without having to reach up. Gradually cover the globe lightly with smyrnium or *Euphorbia cyparissias*, spacing the stems evenly.

4 In the same way add the *Euphorbia cornigera* and *E. polychroma* and the European guelder rose stems.
   Remember to check that the green oasis is well hidden at the bottom of the globe, too, as the view from underneath is most important.

5 Add the orange *Euphorbia griffithii* 'Fireglow', the black tulips, and the columbines, distributing them evenly.

6 (*right*) Add a few twists and turns of anemone clematis, breaking any symmetry. Move the globe into position.

The Painter's Palette

*This bold, brassy arrangement abandons all
rules of color association. Oranges, yellows,
pinks, purples, blues, and greens all clash in
glorious disharmony.*

Equipment
shallow glass bowl, 14in (35cm) across
    and 3in (8cm) deep
2 blocks of florist's oasis, cut to sit
    2in (5cm) above the bowl rim
anchor pin
florist's clay or double-sided tape

Plants
10–15 stems each of *Euphorbia palustris*
    and *E. amygdaloides* var. *robbiae*,
    8–10in (20–25cm) long
10 stems of California lilac
    (*Ceanothus arboreus*), 8–10in
    (20–25cm) long
10–15 each of Persian ranunculus
    (*R. asiaticus*) in red, picotee yellow,
    and plain yellow
10–15 each of poppy anemones
    (*A. cornaria* De Caen Group)
    in purple and magenta-pink
10–15 orange, yellow, or bicolored
    tulips (e.g. 'Apricot Parrot',
    'Mickey Mouse', 'Orange
    Favourite', 'Texas Gold'),
    10in (25cm) long
10–15 bright-colored Lily-flowered
    tulips (e.g. 'Aladdin'), 12–16in
    (30–40cm) long

Method
Use the florist's clay or tape to secure
the anchor pin in the bowl. Position
the oasis on the anchor pin. Seal the
euphorbia stems in boiling water.
Distribute the euphorbia and California
lilac evenly over the oasis, making
sure that some stems reach out over
the edge. Add the ranunculus, the
anemones, and the yellow, orange,
and bicolored tulips. Distribute each
type of flower to give an almost even
color pattern. Finally, position the
Lily-flowered tulips to stand above
and slightly to one side.

The Height of Spring

A lush arrangement of spring cherry blossoms looks unfussy, simple, and stylish. Spikes of acid-green euphorbia and sticky chestnut buds make the arrangement more substantial. If you prefer a lighter, silhouetted effect, you can leave them out.

For maximum impact, position the arrangement in the middle of a large table. Choose a site that has back or side light, so the sun can flood through the petals and highlight their simple beauty.

Equipment

glass vase, 18in (45cm) tall, with a
  wide mouth and narrow waist,
  which will hold the stems securely
  but allow the blossoms to splay out
75–100 glass marbles

Plants

Stems or branches, 3–4ft (90–120cm)
  long, of each of the following:
15 euphorbia (*E. characias*)
15 branches of white cherry blossom
  (*Prunus* 'Taihaku')
15 Mazzard cherry blossom
  (*Prunus avium*)
10–15 European horse chestnut
  (*Aesculus hippocastanum*) with newly
  emerging leaves

Method

Gently place the marbles in the vase.
Position the euphorbia spikes evenly,
in a not-too-tidy dome, poking the
stems right into the marbles. This
mesh of stems will hold the other
branches where you position them.

Add the heads of white cherry and
then the Mazzard cherry blossom,
allowing some to flop out over the
sides of the vase, with the blossom
hanging as it might on the tree.

Finally, add the chestnut buds,
some cut taller, some shorter, to
break up any symmetry that remains.

A Midsummer Feast

Illustrated on pages 64–65.

Vibrant flowers and breezy seed-laden foliage from wheat field and garden combine beautifully to make swags and sheaves. They are used here to decorate a tent and a long table for a great outdoor summer feast.

The Swag

It's much more interesting and colorful to create swags of brilliant flowers to dress up a plain white tent rather than hire an elaborate one with a fancy ruched blue or pink lining.

Equipment

surveyor's tape
blocks of oasis
kitchen knife and wire cutters
1–2in (2.5–5cm) gauge chicken wire
¹⁄₈in (3mm) heavy-gauge wire
fine-gauge florist's wire

Plants

approximate plant quantities for each
    3ft (90cm) of swag, all stems
    4–6in (10–15cm) long:
30–40 stems of hornbeam (*Carpinus
    betulus*), with seed cases
30–40 stems of lady's mantle
    (*Alchemilla mollis*)
15–20 bunches each of 3–5 sprigs of
    cornflowers (*Centaurea cyanus*)
15–20 bunches each of 3 sprigs of
    lavender (*Lavandula stoechas* subsp.
    pedunculata)
15–20 mixed poppies and poppy
    seed heads

Method

Measure the front of the tent, or where you want to hang your swags, and divide the distance into manageable sections, not more than 6ft (1.8m) long. Loop the tape by as much as you want the swags to curve. Follow **Steps 1–5**.

1 Using a sharp knife, cut the oasis into square blocks; the swag needs to be as light as possible, and it will then hold its shape better. Soak the blocks thoroughly.

Cut the chicken wire to the length of each swag, adding 4–6in (10–15cm) at each end to bind and secure the blocks of oasis.

Cut a length of heavy-gauge wire twice the length of the swag, plus 4ft (1.2m) for securing the swag ends to the tent. Bend the wire in two.

2 Thread the double length of heavy-gauge wire through the chicken wire from one end to the other, securing it with fine-gauge florist's wire at 18in (45cm) intervals. Place the soaked blocks of oasis on the double wire, along the length of the chicken wire.

3 Wrap the chicken wire around the oasis, overlap the two edges, and use the fine-gauge florist's wire to join them securely. Bend the chicken wire ends in and secure them, leaving a 12in (30cm) loop of heavy-gauge wire at one end and two wire ends 12in (30cm) long at the other.

4 Hang the structure in place, twisting the heavy-gauge wire loop and ends around the tent poles or the eyelets in the canvas. Ensure that the double run of heavy-gauge wire is on the bottom, taking the weight of the swag.

Begin adding the plants. Distribute the hornbeam seed cases evenly, putting in as many above and below as at the sides.

5 (*right*) Add the lady's mantle until the oasis is almost covered. Insert the bunches of cornflower and lavender sprigs, then distribute the poppies, concentrating them on the most conspicuous areas.

Finally, give the whole swag a good spray with a water atomizer.

The Wheat Sheaf

*A colorful sheaf of bright poppies, grasses,
oats, and wheat tied simply with hop-bine
makes a lovely, simple, and fresh table
decoration.*

Equipment
hop-bine (*Humulus lupulus*) or twine

Plants
mixed wild grasses, wheat, and wild
    oats, 18–24in (45–60cm) long
10–15 lady's mantle (*Alchemilla mollis*),
    12–18in (30–45cm) long
20 cornflowers (*Centaurea cyanus*),
    18in (45cm) long
10–15 love-in-a-mist (*Nigella damascena*),
    12–18in (30–45cm) long
30–40 corn poppies (*Papaver rhoeas*)
    and Iceland poppies (*P. nudicaule*),
    cut slightly shorter and to different
    lengths

Method
The sheaf is too big to hold in your
hand all at once, so I make up four
bunches and tie them together.

Sear the stem ends of the poppies
and do not recut them. For each
bunch, take a handful of the mixed
grasses, hold them halfway along
their stems and tie together loosely
with twine. Holding the bunch in one
hand, poke in the flowers, all facing
more or less the same way: the lady's
mantle, cornflowers, and love-in-a-
mist, and then the poppies. Place
some poppies high and some low –
but their stems should not reach to
the bottom of the sheaf. Tie the
bunches together securely with the
hop-bine or twine. Trim the stem
ends (except for the poppies) so that
they are even.

Stand the sheaf on the table with
the stems splayed slightly so it stays
upright. You can keep the flowers
fresh by standing the sheaf in a little
water; take it out and dry the stem
ends when the table is laid. Scatter a
few poppy petals among the plates.

Honeysuckle and Rose Globe

Create your own sweet-smelling mixture of flowers and foliage at the height of summer. Twine scented roses and honeysuckle around a globe, allowing the stems to bend and twist, just as they would if they were growing in the wild. For maximum enjoyment, raise the globe to head height. Resist any urge to overtidy the beautiful natural chaos of the plants.

Equipment

wire globe, about 32in (80cm) diameter
stainless steel pail
a few half-bricks or rocks, to weight the pail
florist's clay, to stick on the rim of the pail to hold the globe in place
pedestal or small decorative stand or table
30–40 florist's water vials in two sizes, 3in (8cm) and 5in (13cm)
fine-gauge florist's wire
scissors and wire cutters
rope to hang globe as you work

Plants

the following stems, cut as long as possible:
30–40 lady's mantle (*Alchemilla mollis*)
30–40 mixed oats, grasses, and wheat
the following stems, 2–3ft (60–90cm) long:
10–15 honeysuckle (*Lonicera*)
10–15 briar rose, or a single Rambler rose, such as *Rosa mulliganii*

Method

Follow **Steps 1–6**.

1 Before you arrange the plants, check the position of the pedestal with the pail and globe in place. When you are happy, remove the globe, weight the pail, and fill it with water.

2 All stems, except the wheat, need to be in water. Place those that won't reach the pail in florist's vials. Create sprays of lady's mantle, oats, and grasses, and put each in a shorter vial.

3 Hang the globe at a height where you can work on it comfortably. Start at the top, winding the honeysuckle stems in and out, and allowing the stem ends to hang down to sit in the water.

4 Tie in the honeysuckle stems with the florist's wire at roughly regular intervals. Weave in the rose stems and tie them in.

5 Place any stem that will not reach the water in one of the larger vials. Tuck the vials inside the globe.

6 (*right*) Fill holes with the lady's mantle sprays and wheat. Lower the globe and place it on the pail, securing it on the florist's clay. Make sure all the hanging stems stay in the water. (You can also hang the globe; all stems must then be in vials.)

Posy in Crimson, Carmine, and Gold

This posy is the most luscious combination of the richest color, scent, and texture. Mix deep crimson-black sweet Williams, sweet peas, and Rosa 'Souvenir du Docteur Jamain' with carmine stocks, cosmos, and Rosa 'Nuits de Young', and add gold marigolds with crimson centers. For a real treat, place the vase beside your bed so you can wake up to this exotic mixture of highly scented flowers.

Equipment

silver or pewter cup, 5in (13cm) tall

Plants

5–7 each of the following stems,
  8–10in (20–25cm) long:
roses (*Rosa* 'Nuits de Young' and
  R. 'Souvenir du Docteur Jamain')
carmine stocks (*Matthiola incana*)
cosmos (*C. bipinnatus* 'Versailles
  Carmine')
sweet Williams (*Dianthus barbatus*
  Nigrescens Group)
sweet peas (*Lathyrus odoratus*
  'Matucana' and *L.o.* 'Pageantry')
cypress spurge (*Euphorbia cyparissias*)
perennial bupleurum (*B. falcatum*)
yellow marigolds (*Calendula* Art
  Shades Group)
lamb's-ear (*Stachys byzantina*)

Method

This arrangement starts with flowers rather than foliage because it is the flowers that are dominant here. Make a structure 1½ times the height of the vase, using all the crimson and carmine flowers and letting them spread out from the cup. Start with the roses, and add the stocks, cosmos, sweet Williams, and sweet peas. Then place the acid-green spurge and bupleurum, distributing them evenly. Add the marigolds and finally the stems of lamb's-ear, letting them curve out from under the flowers as if to contain and support them in their luxurious, velvety folds.

Summer Abundance

This sumptuous celebration of summer is worthy of a still-life painting. Here for the picking are flowers of unsurpassed stature and opulence. Go over the top in creating this one, with huge alliums and agapanthus, great wands of eremurus and delphiniums, and heavy-headed, heady-scented lilies.

Equipment

china urn, 18–24in (45–60cm) tall

Plants

5–9 each of the following stems, using
  as much height as possible:
eremurus (*E. stenophyllus*)
delphiniums (*D.* Giant Pacific
  hybrids)
Alpine sea holly (*Eryngium alpinum*
  'Amethyst')
dill (*Anethum graveolens*)
bells of Ireland (*Moluccella laevis*)
alliums (*A. giganteum*)
lupines (*Lupinus* 'The Governor')
lilies (*Lilium* 'Casa Blanca')
orange marigolds (*Calendula* Art
  Shades Group)
agapanthus (*A. campanulatus*
  var. *albidus*)

Method

First position the dominant structural flowers – the eremurus and the delphiniums – to give the arrangement its height and architecture. Make sure they are asymmetrically placed.

Add the sea holly, green dill, and bells of Ireland. Put in the alliums, lupines, and lilies next, placing some high and some lower, and giving emphasis to the center rather than the silhouette. Use the bright, contrasting marigolds to punctuate the center.

Finally, position the towering stems of agapanthus, using them to break up any neat lines and symmetry that may creep in.

Vase of Pure White, Cream, and Green

In the heat of summer, it is refreshing to have an arrangement of light, pure white and green flowers and foliage. Mix great bunches of scented roses, acanthus, and teasel with glowing white foxgloves and white fireweed. Combine them with lady's mantle, bishop's flower, masterwort, and caper spurge to make a stylish yet unpretentious arrangement.

Equipment
waisted glass vase, 12in (30cm) tall

Plants
the following stems, 18–36in
   (45–90cm) long:
10 teasels (*Dipsacus fullonum*)
10 bishop's flower (*Ammi majus*)
10–15 lady's mantle (*Alchemilla mollis*)
7 masterwort (*Astrantia major*)
5 caper spurge (*Euphorbia lathyris*)
5 white foxgloves (*Digitalis purpurea*
   f. *albiflora*)
5 white fireweed (*Epilobium*
   angustifolium f. *album*)
7 spiny bear's breeches (*Acanthus*
   spinosus)
7 *Rosa* 'Iceberg'

Method
Use the teasels and bishop's flower to make a structure 2½ to 3 times the height of the vase. Place a few teasel heads high to mark the height and cut the rest shorter to put at the heart of the arrangement.

Next add the bright, fluffy lady's mantle, masterwort, and spurge, distributing them evenly. Position the foxgloves and the white fireweed, placing some to catch the light and create a radiant outline.

Then add the bear's breeches and roses, making sure they are balanced yet asymmetrical within the display. Let the bear's breeches create height to one side. Put the roses at the heart and slightly to the other side, curving out from the neck of the vase.

A Colorful Collection

The velvety textures and rich colors of the scarlet lychnis, green flowering tobacco, and purple-blue anchusas and alliums contrast well with the clear simplicity of the blue- and gray-striped pitcher. The single zinnia in its blue glass continues the theme. Flowers often look more beautiful grouped in a collection of vases, decanters, and pitchers than they would if simply standing on their own.

Equipment
blue glassware
pitcher, 12in (30cm) tall

Plants
5–7 each of the following stems,
    18–24in (45–60cm) long:
anchusas (*A. azurea*)
salvias (*S. patens* and *S. × superba*)
flowering tobacco (*Nicotiana* 'Lime
    Green')
alliums (*A. cernuum, A. neapolitanum*
    Cowanii Group, *A. sphaerocephalon*)
triteleia (*T. laxa* 'Koningin Fabiola')
lychnis (*L. chalcedonica* and
    L. × arkwrightii 'Vesuvius')
orange alstroemerias (*A. ligtu* hybrid)
globe artichokes (*Cynara cardunculus*
    Scolymus Group)
plus: a single zinnia (*Z.* 'Envy')

Method
For this arrangement, place the flowers first and the artichoke foliage last. Using the robust anchusas and salvias, make a structure about 1½ times the height of the pitcher. These stems make a network into which you can insert the flowering tobacco, alliums, and triteleia, creating an up-and-down rhythm in the bunch.

Add the contrasting bright lychnis and alstroemerias before placing some artichoke foliage at the heart of the arrangement and some right on the edge.

Place the single green zinnia in the blue glass to highlight the acid-green color scattered among the flowers.

Party Pompon

This vivid and dashing bauble is spectacular for a summer party. If you are eating outside, hang it from a tree or close to the table. It looks equally striking hanging from a beam in an outdoor arbor or tent or above the table in your dining room. Don't aim for a tight, neat look, but make an extravagant statement: a dramatic globe some 3ft (90cm) across of richly colored late-summer flowers and foliage.

Equipment

2 wire hanging baskets with chains, 12in (30cm) diameter
moss, to line the baskets
4 blocks of soaked oasis
⅛in (3mm) heavy-gauge wire
wire cutters and kitchen knife
rope or twine
tent peg (optional)

Plants

15–20 each of the following foliage stems, 16in (40cm) long:
golden privet (*Ligustrum ovalifolium* 'Aureum')
smokebush (*Cotinus coggygria* 'Royal Purple')
silver-leaved elaeagnus (*E. angustifolia*)
the following stems of background flowers, 20in (50cm) long:
10 bear's breeches (*Acanthus mollis*)
15 bells of Ireland (*Moluccella laevis*)
20 bupleurum (*B. griffithii*)
15 dill (*Anethum graveolens*)
10 sea hollies (*Eryngium giganteum*)
5 Scotch thistles (*Onopordum acanthium*)
15 each of the following richly colored flowers, 18in (45cm) long:
claret-red gladioli (*G.* 'Black Lash')
claret-red dahlias (*D.* 'Black Fire')
sunflowers (*Helianthus annuus* 'Henry Wilde' or 'Valentine')

Method

Strip the bottom 3–4in (8–10cm) of leaves and cut the stems at an angle so they are easy to poke through the moss and into the oasis blocks. Follow **Steps 1–5**.

1 Remove the chain of one basket, leaving the chain from the other basket free to hang the arrangement. Line the baskets with moss.

2 Cut one block of florist's oasis into quarters. Place another whole block into one of the baskets, wedging it in with a quarter block at each side. Put two blocks on top of each other in the center of the other basket, securing them with a quarter block on each side.

3 Set the two baskets rim to rim and bind them together securely with the heavy-gauge wire.

4 Hang the globe at a height so it is easy to work on. If necessary, attach rope to the bottom of the globe and pin it to the ground with a tent post to prevent it from swinging. Start with the golden privet, pushing the stems into the oasis, covering the globe evenly.

5 (*right*) Add the smokebush and elaeagnus so the gray and purple leaves are evenly distributed. Insert the background flowers, one type at a time, all around the globe. Push in the gladioli and dahlias. Finally, add the sunflowers, placing them randomly.

Fall Arrangements

A Fall Gift

Illustrated on pages 76–77.

This rich, bright, multicolored bunch of flowers and leaves in clear plastic wrap will impress and cheer any friend or relation. With carmine-pink, claret-red, clear turquoise, and deep orange blossoms, all set against the silver and green of cyperus, artemisia, and elaeagnus, it would be hard to beat this mixture for rich color.

The plastic wrap looks attractive and protects the flowers for a journey. Never transport cut flowers in a hot car without water – they will wilt in a few minutes. Wrap the stem ends in soaked paper towel, place them in a plastic bag, and secure it with a rubber band.

Equipment
twine
clear plastic wrap
scissors

Plants
5–7 each of the following,
    18in (45cm) long:
elaeagnus (*E. angustifolia* or
    E. 'Quicksilver')
artemisia (*A. arborescens* 'Faith Raven'
    or *A. pontica*)
bupleurum (*B. fruticosum*)
iris seed heads (*I. foetidissima*)
salvias (*S. uliginosa*)
feather-top (*Pennisetum villosum*)
5–7 each of the following,
    12in (30cm) long:
dahlias (a mixture of bright and dark
    colors, e.g., *D.* 'Glow' or 'Queen
    Fabiola' with 'Natal' or 'Arabian
    Night')
Michaelmas daisies (*Aster novi-belgii*)
cyperus (*C. albostriatus*)

Method
Strip all the bottom leaves of the flowers that you would expect to be below the water line in the vase.
Follow **Steps 1–4**.

1 In your hand, make a structure from the elaeagnus and add the artemisia and bupleurum, leaving some elaeagnus stems standing out. The foliage should be balanced yet not too symmetrical, with some stems curving down at the front.

3 Now add the final touches of the contrasting sky-blue salvias, the bright green cyperus, and feathery grasses, putting some at the heart and some at the edges of the bunch, so the arrangement is balanced and yet not neat. It will now be difficult to hold so many stems together.

2 Still holding the bunch in your hand, add the dahlias and Michaelmas daisies, distributing them evenly, and then poke in the iris seed heads.

4 Either get someone to help you by tying the stems as you hold them, or lay the bunch carefully on a table, hold it with one hand, and tie it with the other. Trim the stems all to the same length. If you cut any woody stems, slit them again about 1in (2.5cm) so they will readily absorb water.

A Fall Collection

By fall the summer abundance is past, so collect a few stems of different things – whatever is still around – and arrange them by color. None of the vases here would make an impact on its own but, combined, each one becomes part of a handsome group. The hop wall medallion and a scattering of hop seeds on the table serve to link the different elements of the display.

Equipment
glasses and vases of varying heights,
    including a thin-necked vase
15–20 marbles for the small vases,
    to hold fragile stems in place
⅛ in (3mm) heavy-gauge wire, for
    the base of the hop medallion

Plants
hop-bine (*Humulus lupulus*)
the following flowers and foliage, cut
    to 1½ to 2 times vase heights:
5–7 ampelopsis (*A. glandulosa* var.
    brevipedunculata)
3–5 euonymus (*E. europaeus*)
3–5 red abutilons (*A.* 'Clementine')
7–9 cosmos (*C. atrosanguineus*)
3–5 deep red violets (*Viola* variety)
7–9 dahlias (*D.* 'Bishop of Llandaff')
3–5 purple violets (*Viola* variety)
3–5 large-flowered nicandras
    (*N. physalodes*)
3 anchusas (*A. azurea* 'Royal Blue')
7–9 gentian heads (*Gentiana triflora*
    var. *japonica*)

Method
Make the hop-bine medallion first (see page 88). Entwine one end of hop-bine into the other to secure it. Arrange the ampelopsis, euonymus, and abutilons in separate vases. Place the cosmos and red violets in the thin-necked vase and the dahlias in a vase on their own. Put marbles in each of the small vases. Push the purple violets, nicandras, and anchusas gently into the marbles in one small vase and the gentian flowers into the other.

Fall Table Centerpiece

The freshness of yellows and greens is a surprise at this time of year. In this dramatic table centerpiece, they provide a startling contrast to deep crimson, burnt-orange-brown, vibrant orange, and sultry purple.

Equipment
shallow fruit bowl, about 12in (30cm) wide and 4in (10cm) deep
soaked oasis block
anchor pin
florist's clay or double-sided tape

Plants
7–10 each of the following, 12–18in (30–45cm) long:
blackthorn stems (*Prunus spinosa*)
viburnum stems (*V. opulus*)
Chinese lanterns (*Physalis alkekengi*)
gloriosa daisies (*Rudbeckia*)
tithonias (*T. rotundifolia* 'Torch')
zinnias (*Z.* Scabious-flowered Group)
penstemons (*P.* 'Blackbird' or 'Sour Grapes')
15 yellow red-hot pokers (*Kniphofia* 'Yellow Hammer' or *K. citrina*)

Method
Secure the anchor pin to the bowl with the florist's clay or tape. Place the oasis on the anchor pin, so that the block stands 1–2in (2.5–5cm) above the rim. Make a balanced but not too symmetrical structure from the blackthorn and viburnum stems, spreading out over the table but with the emphasis to one side. Let the Chinese lanterns curve over the edge of the bowl, where they will be highlighted. Add the gloriosa daisies, tithonias, and zinnias, mainly at the heart of the arrangement. Finally, place the penstemons and the yellow red-hot pokers, twisting and turning all around the outside, giving height to one side to counterbalance the downward curve of blackthorn and Chinese lanterns on the other.

Venetian Glass

*This is proof that it takes no more than one stem of a dramatic and beautiful flower to make an arrangement. In the right vase, a solitary stem can have more impact than an elaborate vase of ten or twenty different types of flowers and foliage. In spring try this with a single, frilly, flamboyant Parrot tulip. In summer choose one perfect sunflower, or a stem of a huge-headed Oriental poppy. In fall the giant flowering tobacco brings the bonus of heady, exotic evening scent, and in winter you might try witch hazel (*Hamamelis*) or a towering stem of dogwood (*Cornus mas*).*

The choice of vase is equally important. For the elegant tobacco flower, choose a narrow silhouette. Larger-headed flowers like Parrot tulips and sunflowers need a vase with a more rounded shape, so that the proportions are balanced.

Equipment
Venetian glass jar, 20in
(50cm) tall

Plant
single 4–5ft (1.2–1.5m) stem
of giant flowering tobacco
(*Nicotiana sylvestris*)

Method
Remove enough of the bottom leaves to allow the stem of the giant flowering tobacco to be safely anchored in the base of the tall vase. Place the tobacco so that it does not stand bolt upright, but continues a graceful line from the vase, curving gently upward to its full and magnificent height.

Red-Hot Leaves

To decorate your entrance hall or living room, gather a billowing harvest of different leaves, berries, hips turning color, and cat-tails, with just a few dahlia, delphinium, salvia, and leonotis flowers set among them. Aim at creating the effect of a pile of dazzling red leaves with splashes of flower color and contrasting white snowberries – a condensed version of fall in the garden borders.

Equipment
pewter pitcher, 12in (30cm) tall

Plants
5 each of the following stems,
    24–36in (60–90cm) long:
American smoke tree (*Cotinus obovatus*)
red oak (*Quercus rubra*)
cattails (*Typha*)
7–11 each of the following stems,
    18–30in (45–75cm) long:
euphorbia (*E. griffithii* 'Fireglow')
rose hips (*Rosa moyesii* 'Geranium')
snowberry berries (*Symphoricarpos albus*)
5–7 each of the following flowers,
    24–36in (60–90cm) long:
delphinium (*D.* Black Knight Group)
leonotis (*L. ocymifolia*)
dahlias (*D.* 'Edinburgh')
blue salvias (*S. guaranitica* or *S. farinacea*
    'Victoria')
red salvias (*S. elegans* or *S. fulgens*)

Method
Using the smoke tree and oak stems, make a balanced but asymmetrical framework about twice the height of the pitcher. Add the euphorbias to fill in any gaping holes. Place the vertical emphasis next, using the cattails, delphiniums, and leonotis. Then arrange the hips and berries fairly symmetrically. Use the heavy hips to curve over the lip of the pitcher, to bring the arrangement down toward the table. Finally, add the dahlias and salvias at the center.

A Winter Feast

Illustrated on pages 84–85.

A relaxed three-part table arrangement is centered on large, festive candles. Bright bursts of informal flowers are mixed with waving spikes of old man's beard, clematis, and filbert catkins.

The center raised classical vase is complemented by two smaller glazed terracotta side bowls. The center vase arrangement differs slightly from those in the two side bowls. The combination appears simple, yet grand.

For a country look, aim to combine plants that associate well in nature – many of these delicate flowers might be found growing wild on a sheltered bank at the edge of a wood.

Equipment

1 raised classical or formal vase, preferably on a plinth, about 15in (38cm) high

2 side bowls, preferably raised and matching the color of the formal vase

3 ivory candles, 16in (40cm) long, for the raised vase

2 ivory candles, 12in (30cm) long, for the side bowls

3 anchor pins

florist's clay or double-sided tape

2 blocks of florist's oasis

scissors

Plants for each side bowl

10 stems of filbert catkins (*Corylus avellana*), 12in (30cm) long

5 arum leaves (*A. italicum* 'Marmoratum'), with stems 6–8in (15–20cm) long

5–10 *Cyclamen hederifolium* leaves, with stems 4–6in (10–15cm) long

3 *Clematis cirrhosa* stems, 18in (45cm) long

5 honeysuckle stems (*Lonicera fragrantissima*), 12in (30cm) long

5–10 hellebore stems (*Helleborus orientalis*, green and white forms), 8–10in (20–25cm) long

10–15 *Narcissus* 'Cheerfulness', 8–10in (20–25cm) long

3–5 white hyacinths (*Hyacinthus orientalis* 'Sneeuwwitje' or *H.o.* 'L'Innocence')

Method for side bowls

Secure the anchor pins in the bowls using either florist's clay or double-sided tape. Cut one block of oasis in half and then trim both halves so that they fit the bowls and rise 1in (2.5cm) above their rims. Position the pieces of oasis on the anchor pins. Follow **Steps 1–3**.

Plants for the center vase

5–10 stems, 2–3ft (60–90cm) long, of each of the following:

violet willow (*Salix daphnoides*)

filbert catkins (*Corylus avellana*)

old man's beard (*Clematis vitalba*)

bird's foot ivy (*Hedera helix* 'Pedata')

clematis (*C. cirrhosa*)

15–20 cyclamen leaves (*C. hederifolium*), with stems 6–8in (15–20cm) long

10–15 stems, 8–12in (20–30cm) long, of each of the following:

arum leaves

hellebores (*Helleborus orientalis* and *H. foetidus*)

daphne (*D. laureola*)

narcissi (*Narcissus* 'Cheerfulness')

15–20 snowdrops

5–7 white hyacinths (*Hyacinthus orientalis* 'Sneeuwwitje' or *H.o.* 'L'Innocence')

Method for the center vase

Secure the anchor pin in the vase using either florist's clay or double-sided tape. Cut the second block of oasis to fill the vase so that it sits at least 1in (2.5cm) above the rim. Position the oasis on the anchor pin. Push the 3 long candles into the oasis. Make the arrangement in a similar way to that shown in **Steps 1–3** for the side bowls. Start with the willow and filbert stems, making a relaxed but even arrangement around the candles. Insert the old man's beard, ivy, clematis, cyclamen, and arum leaves, and then add the flowers, keeping the arrangement open and light. When you place the finished vase and bowls on the table, scatter a few ivy leaves between them. If you like, add some small candles.

1 Push the candle firmly down into the center of the oasis, and place the filbert stems around it, spacing them evenly but asymmetrically.

2 Insert the cyclamen and arum leaves. Let the clematis stems trail out to one side and balance these with the honeysuckle, keeping the stems long so the arrangement is light, flowing, and relaxed.

3 Fill in with the flowers, distributing them evenly but avoiding any rigid symmetry. The final effect should be quite open. Light the candles just before the guests are seated.

Winter Branches

This arrangement of winter branches looks beautiful in a well-lit corner of a room or on a table in an entrance hall. Use violet willow and filbert as the base, as I have here, or a mixture of yellow and red dogwoods and any of the brightly colored willows. The large amaryllis flowers add a touch of glamor and warmth and, like the branches, last two to three weeks in water in a room that is not overheated.

Equipment

12in (30cm) tall glass vase with a neck
9–12 thin sticks
cotton balls
9–12 rubber bands

Plants

10–12 stems of violet willow (*Salix daphnoides*), 2½–3ft (75–90cm) long
6 stems of filbert catkins (*Corylus avellana*), 2½–3ft (75–90cm) long
9–12 stems of mixed red and white amaryllis (*Hippeastrum*), some 1½ft (45cm) and some 2–2½ft (60–75cm) long

Method

Cut the sticks to the correct length for inserting in the hollow amaryllis stems, right up to the flower head. This prevents their huge, heavy heads from breaking the stems. Secure the sticks with balls of cotton. Rubber bands secured around the stem ends will prevent them from splitting in the water.

Arrange the violet willow into a balanced and yet not too symmetrical structure, at about 1½ times the height of the vase. Let the filbert stand naturally, with the catkins hanging as they would on the tree.

Place the amaryllis, using the shorter stems to form a heart to the arrangement, and placing the longer ones to highlight their bright and sumptuous silhouettes.

A Winter Medallion

This dramatic yet simple wall hanging is easy to make. You can leave it hanging for many months, renewing it with freshly blooming flowers. I have chosen hellebores, but Narcissus *'Paper White' or* Iris unguicularis *will look equally lovely.*

Before you construct the medallion, decide where you are going to hang it and put a hook in the wall. Work out how large you want the finished medallion to be, according to the expanse of wall.

Equipment

⅛in (3mm) heavy-gauge wire
fine-gauge florist's wire
scissors
wire cutters
odorless hair spray (optional)
10–15 florist's small plastic water vials (optional)
a picture hook or tack for hanging

Plants

10–15 freshly cut stems, 3ft (90cm) long, of each of the following:
pliable willow, e.g. weeping willow (*Salix babylonica*), or red or yellow dogwood (*Cornus*)
violet willow (*Salix daphnoides*), or a pussy willow
10–15 stems, 1½–2ft (45–60cm) long, of each of the following:
filbert (*Corylus*) or other catkins, such as alder (*Alnus*)
old man's beard seed heads (*Clematis vitalba*), or any other fluffy clematis seed heads, such as *C. tangutica* or *C.* 'Bill Mackenzie' (a light mist of hairspray, applied as soon as possible after picking, will help hold the seed heads in place)
10–15 stems of hellebores (*Helleborus orientalis*), 1ft (30cm) long

Method

Follow **Steps 1–7**.

1 Form a wire circle from the heavy-gauge wire and fasten the ends with the fine-gauge wire. Bend three pliable willow or dogwood stems around the wire hoop, weaving them in and out. These stems will hold themselves in place once you have wired their thick ends onto the circle; you can then tuck in their thinner ends.

2 Starting at a different spot, add more stems, poking the cut ends into the willow framework. Always weave the willow around the wire in the same direction to create a regular shape. Add further branches until you construct a substantial base. Bind the branches together firmly with the fine-gauge florist's wire.

3 Add all the violet or pussy willow stems, one at a time, winding them around the base and poking in the ends. Make sure you weave them in the same direction as the first willow or dogwood stems. With the fine-gauge florist's wire, secure the main stems of willow.

4 Add the catkins, poking them in randomly and at different angles, so that the medallion doesn't look too stiff and formal.

5 Hang the medallion on the wall. If the circle looks at all asymmetrical or out of shape, carefully bend it back into a circle.

6 Insert branches of old man's beard at random intervals, taking care not to knock off its fragile seed heads.

7 (*right*) If you want to extend the bloom longer than a few hours, before adding your flowers insert their stems into florist's plastic water vials. Hide the vials among the willow branches.

A Winter Desk

Many of the small late-winter flowers are particularly lovely when seen up close. Only then can you really enjoy the delicate veining of their petals, their subtle scents, and intricate structures. The little winter irises and daffodils, witch hazel, sweet box, and species crocus are all best appreciated at close quarters.

Equipment

4in (10cm) diameter glass bowl
2 metal goblets 3–4in (8–10cm) high
drinking glass about 3in (8cm) high
tiny colored scent bottle
8–10 glass marbles
1in (2.5cm) pin-holder
florist's clay or double-sided tape

Plants

7–9 *Iris reticulata*
1 stem of sweet box (*Sarcococca humilis*)
3 stems of witch hazel (*Hamamelis mollis*)
1 *Narcissus* 'Topolino'
5 *Narcissus* 'Tête-à-Tête'
3–5 *Iris danfordiae*
10–15 winter aconites (*Eranthis hyemalis*)
10–15 dried copper beech leaves
1 *Crocus tommasinianus*

Method

The bowl of aconites and beech leaves displays these buttercup-yellow flowers as they might appear surrounded by the leaves in the garden. Fill the bowl with water, float the dried leaves on top and push the short aconite stems in between them. Fill one of the metal goblets about a third full with glass marbles. Top with water and push the stems of the *Iris danfordiae* and the *Narcissus* 'Tête-à-Tête' between the marbles. Use the florist's clay or the double-sided tape to secure the pin-holder in the bottom of the other metal goblet. Push the witch hazel stems into the anchor pin and add the *Narcissus* 'Topolino'. Put the little crocus in the scent bottle. Place the *Iris reticulata* in a small glass about half their height and add the sprig of sweet box.

Flower Curtain for a Winter Party

This light cheesecloth curtain embroidered with fresh flowers and foliage makes an elegant and romantic party decoration. The cool green hellebore petals take on a glowing luminosity as sunlight streams through them; at night, by candlelight, their angular flowers and seed heads are thrown into sculptural relief. For best effect, arrange a double row of flowers down one edge; massed, the flowers create shadows that hide the wires.

Begin by hanging lengths of cheesecloth at the windows. Simply turn over the tops and, making gentle gathers, pin them at regular intervals along the top of the curtain pole with thumbtacks.

For a swagged effect, loosely tie back the floral border side of the curtain using a curtain tie of the same material.

Equipment
2 lengths of cotton cheesecloth
curtain pole and thumbtacks
fine-gauge florist's wire
scissors and craft glue

Plants
Quantities depend on the size of the curtain and the flowers available in the winter cutting garden.
Stems, 3–4in (8–10cm) long, chosen from the following plants:
green hellebore heads (*Helleborus argutifolius, H. foetidus, H. orientalis*)
snowdrops (*Galanthus nivalis, G.n.* 'Flore Pleno')
cyclamen leaves (*C. hederifolium*)
hyacinths (*Hyacinthus orientalis* 'Sneeuwwitje' or *H.o.* 'L'Innocence')

Method
Follow **Steps 1–5**.

1 Cut the wire into as many 1½in (4cm) lengths as you have flowers, bending each to form a U-shaped staple, as shown.

2 Gently push one end of the staple and then the other just through the stem. Then push both staple ends completely through together.

3 Attach the flowers to the curtain by pushing the staples gently through the fabric.

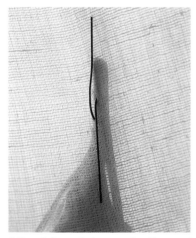

4 Bend the ends in opposite directions so they lie flat behind the stem and flower head, holding them securely in place.

5 Arrange the wired flowers in a double border down one or both vertical edges of the curtain. Dab glue on the back of the ivy and cyclamen leaves, and stick them randomly across the cheesecloth.

Harbinger of Spring

This little vase of miniature flowers, one of my favorite types of flower arrangement, is very easy to assemble. Each flower is seen individually and, viewed up close, you can fully appreciate the different textures, colors, structures, and scents.

Toward the end of winter the earliest bulbs, such as grape hyacinths, squills, and miniature daffodils, begin to bloom in the more sheltered, sunny spots of the garden. Mix these with late winter flowers, such as pulmonarias, cyclamen, crocus, and polyanthus to create a brilliant, gemlike collection for your bedside table.

Equipment

colored-glass container 3–4in
   (8–10cm) high

Plants

5–10 stems, cut as long as possible,
   of each of the following:
yellow and purple crocuses
pulmonarias (*P.* 'Sissinghurst White'
   and 'Blue Ensign')
polyanthus varieties
squills (*Scilla* or *Chionodoxa*)
narcissi (*Narcissus cyclamineus* or
   N. 'Canaliculatus')
cyclamen (*C. coum*)
grape hyacinths (*Muscari*)
snowdrops (*Galanthus nivalis* varieties)

Method

Start with the stronger and more fully formed of your flowers, such as the crocuses, pulmonarias, and polyanthus, to create your structure. Poke the finer ones, like the squills, narcissi, cyclamen, and grape hyacinths, in between these stems, making sure each type of flower is not clumped together. Last, add the snowdrops.

Flowers and Foliage through the Seasons

The flower and foliage plants included here are all personal favorites. They may exist in particularly rich and exotic colors, they may have an irresistible scent, or they may have especially long and productive flowering seasons. Almost all are easy to grow, without too many special requirements. With so many annuals you are guaranteed to have a good number of quick-growing plants that are harvestable in a matter of months.

So for one reason or another, each and every plant in this catalog is a bonus to the cutting garden. When you make your choice, try to include varieties of plants that look good at more than one time of year. Look for plants that have beautiful flowers as well as ornamental leaves or fruits. With agapanthus the umbels of blue and white flowers on their long stalks are invaluable in summer, but their green seed heads are equally good for autumn appeal. With peonies the same is true. Their spring emerging leaves, their spring and summer flowers, and then their seed cases in fall are all excellent for cutting.

Large quantities of flowers in the house are a treat at any time of the year, but don't forget to make choices for the colder, harsher months of the year, when the weather brings you inside and there is less to divert you in the garden. In making your choice from my selection, you will have a beautiful and productive all-season cutting garden.

A riot of spring color from a giant globe containing acid-green and bright red euphorbias
(E. cornigera, E. polychroma, and E. griffithii 'Fireglow'), purple aquilegias
(A. vulgaris) and the deep purple tulip 'Black Parrot', and white Clematis montana.

Spring

In the wild, spring is the flowering of the year, the first great burst of life. To the gardener, spring brings untold riches in the filling out of increasingly colorful and frothy borders. For the small arrangement there are species tulips, primulas, miniature daffodils, and fritillaries. For bigger, more dramatic displays there are armfuls of fruit blossoms, basketfuls of punchy Parrot tulips, and boughs of newly emerging, chartreuse-green leaves.

Green and Silver

Cardoon, globe artichoke
CYNARA
Main entry: Summer Purple, page 132.
The soft gray-green leaves of the cardoons (1) cut young are a dramatic foil to hellebores or velvet polyanthus (see page 58).

Spurge, milkweed
EUPHORBIA
Evergreen and deciduous subshrub, perennial, biennial, and annual
Zones: E. characias *7–10;*
E. amygdaloides *var.* robbiae,
E. lathyris, E. marginata,
E. seguieriana *8–9;* E. amygdaloides
7–9; E. cornigera *6–9;* E. cyparissias,
E. dulcis, E. griffithii *varieties,*
E. polychroma *4–9;* E. palustris
E. schillingii *5–8*
Height: E. cyparissias, E. dulcis *12in (30cm);* E. amygdaloides *'Variegata',*
E. polychroma, E. seguieriana *18in (45cm);* E. amygdaloides *var.* robbiae,
E. marginata *2ft (60cm);* E. palustris,
E. cornigera, E. griffithii *varieties,*
E. schillingii *3ft (90cm);* E. lathyris,
E. characias *varieties 4ft (1.2m)*
Good varieties for cutting *I use euphorbias with any and everything. Their upright habit and vivid, acid-green flower bracts provide the perfect contrast in the flower bed and flower arrangement to all colors from pastels to richest ecclesiastical*

tones. For a succession lasting throughout the year, start with the large evergreen variety, E. characias (5). Two of the best cultivars are E.c. subsp. wulfenii *'John Tomlinson' and 'Lambrook Gold'. Both combine successfully with large bunches of blossoms (see page 63). Two other early spring euphorbias are E. amygdaloides (3) and E.a. var. robbiae (4). These mix well with bright tulips or a colorful bunch of anemones (see page 62). They are followed by the flat-topped E. polychroma, E. cornigera, and the taller E. palustris (page 109). A mixture of these and orange E. griffithii with black aquilegias and the black tulip 'Queen of Night' looks glamorous (see page 61). In late spring I also use cypress spurge, E. cyparissias (2), with its delicate acid-green flowers and bracts, in smaller bunches.*

During summer and on into fall, euphorbias continue to be a mainstay of my cutting garden (see pages 116 and 137). For acid-green in winter E. cornigera often goes on flowering in a sheltered spot – I have picked some to mix with anemones (Anemone × hybrida) on Christmas Day.

I used to scoff when I read that you should never cut euphorbia without gloves on because it has a highly allergenic milky sap. But this is a plant to which you can gradually develop a sensitivity and I certainly have. If I fail to put on gloves or rigorously wash my hands after picking, my face now swells up like a basket ball. The reaction seems most violent on a hot day.

Conditioning *The stems should last about 10 days. Seal their ends with boiling water, to stop the sticky sap from leaking out (see page 48). If you don't, it will cover your hands as you work with them and turn the water cloudy. Leaking sap also blocks the capillary action of the stems, and so prevents them from drinking.*
Cultivation *When buying euphorbias from a nursery, I recommend choosing*

smaller plants and paying less. They are all quick-growing, and you will have a good-sized plant in one growing season. I have different varieties on each side of the center path in my cutting garden, so there are always one or two within easy reach to pick through most of the year. Depending on the space available, and how many varieties you decide to have, I would suggest planting most euphorbias in clumps of three. However, E. characias, the largest euphorbia, makes a good single specimen.

Most euphorbias prefer full sun but tolerate partial shade and like reasonably drained, fertile soil. They will benefit from a mulch of garden compost or manure in spring. Wood spurge, E. amygdaloides, and its variants, which are woodland-edge perennials, will tolerate a poor dry soil and even spread beneath a shady wall or hedge. Grow from seed, cuttings, or by division. The annual E. marginata should be sown early in the greenhouse, and then planted out in full sun. E. palustris, if sown early

❶ *Cynara cardunculus* (leaf)
❷ *Euphorbia cyparissias*
❸ *Euphorbia amygdaloides*
❹ *Euphorbia amygdaloides* var. *robbiae*
❺ *Euphorbia characias*
❻ *Helleborus argutifolius* (seed heads)
❼ *Smyrnium olusatrum*
❽ *Smyrnium perfoliatum*

SCALE
2in (5cm)

SCALE
2in (5cm)

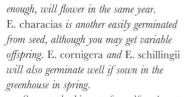

enough, will flower in the same year.
E. characias *is another easily germinated from seed, although you may get variable offspring.* E. cornigera *and* E. schillingii *will also germinate well if sown in the greenhouse in spring.*

Some euphorbias are free self-seeders, too. E. characias, E. lathyris, E. dulcis, *and* E. amygdaloides *will produce volunteers, which should be collected from beneath the parent plant and potted when young.* E. characias *produces biennial stems of leaves one year and flower spikes the next. You should cut these back as they brown to allow room for new growth, perhaps leaving one or*

two spikes for self-seeding.

E. amygdaloides *var.* robbiae *and* E.a. *cultivars,* E. cyparissias, E. dulcis, E. schillingii, *and* E. griffithii *cultivars all have rapidly spreading roots. Allow new plants to become established and then divide. They will take off readily from even the smallest clump.* E. seguieriana, E. polychroma, E. cornigera, *and* E. palustris *form large root balls, which can also be readily divided. You need to be careful when choosing a planting site for* E. cyparissias, *because it tends to take over. Deciduous perennials, like* E. polychroma, *should be cut to the ground in fall.*

Many of the euphorbias can be propagated successfully from cuttings.

Hellebores
HELLEBORUS
Main entry: Winter Green, page 149.
The chiseled, sculptural seed heads of the Corsican hellebore, H. argutifolius (**6**), *are best combined with the black Tulipa 'Queen of Night' or, for a 'Cruella de Vil' look,* Fritillaria persica.

Alexanders, horse parsley
SMYRNIUM
Biennial Zones: 7–9
Height: 2–3ft (60–90cm)
Good varieties for cutting *The elegant* S. perfoliatum (**8**) *has lime-green bracts arranged like tutus up the stem, surrounding chandeliers of tiny yellowish-green flowers. I like it best of all on a brightly lit windowsill mixed with* Dicentra *'Bacchanal' and the plum snakeshead fritillary. The larger horse parsley,* S. olusatrum (**7**), *is also good value cut. With a chunkier, more robust feel, it combines well with the flamboyant Parrot tulips and crown imperials. Its one drawback is its unpleasant smell; I use only a few stems at a time and would not put it in an enclosed room.*
Conditioning *Strip the bottom leaves and then give the stem a good soak overnight. It will otherwise have a tendency to droop.*
Cultivation *Horse parsley prefers a sunny open site with a fertile, well-drained soil.* S. perfoliatum *likes some shade and in the garden mixes well with other deciduous*

woodland plants, such as hellebores and Solomon's seal. Horse parsley is rarely found in nurseries, but S. olusatrum *can be grown from seed and treated as a biennial.*

S. perfoliatum *can be a tricky plant to establish from seed, but once established it will freely self-seed. If you know someone with a good-sized patch, the best thing is to dig up some of this. In mid-summer it goes dormant so dig it up when the leaves reappear in late fall. Though widely described as a biennial, it often does not flower, seed, and die until the third year.*

Tulip
TULIPA
Main entry: Spring Orange and Red, page 108. *Of these three Viridiflora tulips, the cream and green* T. *'Spring Green'* (**11**) *is excellent mixed with white cherry blossom, lilac peonies, and white dicentras, and looks dramatic when combined with the black Parrot tulip and the attractive berried ivy.* T. *'Hummingbird'* (**9**) *is elegant, its pale green contrasted to grapefruit-yellow, while the smaller* T. *'Pimpernel'* (**10**)*, with its gray-green-edged white flowers and foliage, is a drama queen. It is best arranged on its own in a brightly colored glass. As its flowers age they turn deep red, but keep their green edges.*

9 *Tulipa* 'Hummingbird'
10 *Tulipa* 'Pimpernel'
11 *Tulipa* 'Spring Green'

White

Juneberry, serviceberry, snowy mespilus
AMELANCHIER

Deciduous shrub and tree Zones: 5–9
Height: to 20ft (6m)

Good varieties for cutting *There is widespread confusion between the commonly available amelanchiers, A. canadensis (**4**), A. laevis, and A. lamarckii, which are very similar – even botanists argue about which is which. So never mind its label in the nursery, just look out for the shrub or small tree that has fine oval leaves and an overall delicate structure and form. In mid-spring I love its combination of newly emerging, copper-colored foliage with white blossoms: its chalky white clouds of fine flowers charm until the wind blows them away. I use it as the main structure in a huge all-white spring mixture containing white lilac, Viridiflora tulips, white pompon peonies, and the white dicentra D. spectabilis 'Alba'. It proves its worth again in fall with its small leaves turning an iridescent mix of reds, oranges, and ochers.*

Conditioning *It is worth hammering the cut stem ends and giving them a cool, deep overnight drink before arranging.*

Cultivation *This is a good tree for a small garden, because it never gets too big. Plant just one, unless you have enormous amounts of room, and then you could have three to five in a shrub garden.*

In keeping with other trees, amelanchier is best planted in late fall when the leaves have been shed but it is not too frosty and cold for the tender roots to settle. Choose a site in sun or semi-shade, with soil that is well drained but not too dry. Mulch with manure or well-rotted garden compost in early spring. Amelanchiers thrive in neutral to acidic soils (most of them cannot tolerate lime) and as with many acid-loving plants, the lower the pH, the stronger their fall color.

It's unlikely that you will want to propagate amelanchiers since buying a good-sized specimen is best, but if you do want to increase your stock, do so from division or seed or, if you have a shrubby specimen, by layering (see page 42).

Anemone, windflower
ANEMONE

Perennial
Zones: 4–8 (A. × hybrida 6–9)
Height: A. blanda and A. nemorosa cultivars 4in (10cm); A. coronaria 8–10in (20–25cm); A. hupehensis 24–30in (60–75cm); A. × hybrida 5ft (1.5m)

Good varieties for cutting *Anemones are excellent for cutting year-round. The European wood anemone, A. nemorosa (**3**), with its simple star-shaped flowers, is lovely on its own. Beautiful cultivars include the wisteria-blue form, with buttercup-yellow anthers, A.n. 'Robinsoniana', and the double white, green-streaked A.n. 'Bracteata Pleniflora'. A well-illustrated bulb catalog will help you to choose your own favorites.*

*Grecian windflower, A. blanda (**1**), has a greater number of finer petals and flowers*

1 Anemone blanda
2 Anemone coronaria
   (De Caen Group)
   'The Bride'
3 Anemone nemorosa

*from late winter until mid-spring. Among many color variants is the sky-blue A.b. 'Atrocaerulea' (see pages 112 and 113). The poppy anemone, A. coronaria, cultivars are another spring mainstay for cutting. I like these best as single colors: the rich velvety deep blue-purple, the zany carmine-pink, or the pure white 'The Bride' (**2**) are all good, but they are difficult to find unmixed. You may want to plant them in a trial area for the first year, and transplant them into color blocks in the cutting garden for the next year. I always choose the single De Caen Group, not the double St. Brigid.*

From late summer, and sometimes until early winter, you will find flowers of the A. × hybrida and A. hupehensis types (see page 139), which with their tall, straight stems are invaluable for cutting. They all last well for up to two weeks in water.

SCALE
2in (5cm)

Cultivation *The A. nemorosa and A. blanda types thrive in dappled shade, with a humus-rich, well-drained soil. They are particularly good for naturalizing in grass or in woodland, where they will spread to form a spectacular carpet before the leaf canopy obscures them A. coronaria needs full sun and well-drained soil to flower well. Given these conditions, it will flower for months on end. A. hupehensis and A. × hybrida like an open position but will grow in shade. Their colonizing roots can be invasive, especially in light soil. Despite their height, they do not need staking.*

The corms of A. blanda, A. nemorosa, and A. coronaria are cheap to buy, so get them in quantity. They grow better if soaked for 24 hours before planting. They form leafy clumps that can be divided in two or three years, once the colony has become established. Divide them as the leaves die down in early summer.

With the larger perennial anemones, A. × hybrida and A. hupehensis, buy three to five of your chosen forms. Buy decent-sized plants if you want tall flowers the first year. In two to three years you will start getting a good harvest of large saucers on tall stems.

Propagate by division or root cuttings in the winter – even the smallest section of root is likely to grow a plant, as you will discover if you try to move them. They almost invariably reappear in their old position. Although it is some trouble (and so worth it only for the rarities), anemones can also be grown from seed sown in late summer, but the seed has to be fresh. Collect this when the seed heads still look green and unripe.

A. coronaria St. Brigid Group is the one propagated commercially, from seed sown in spring to flower from late summer to the following spring. However, the plants have to be kept at a minimum temperature of 45°F (8°C) throughout the winter.

Cow parsley
ANTHRISCUS SYLVESTRIS

Biennial Zones: 4–8
Height: 3ft (90cm)

Good varieties for cutting *In the wild, the delicate, fluffy white cloud of cow parsley (**5**) makes an eye-catching spectacle* in late spring, and its finely cut foliage is also a real asset in any garden. Cut tall, the flowers look simple and dramatic on their own displayed in a plain glass vase. Picked shorter, they add a light rural feel to a mixed arrangement. I also use cow parsley to make cheap yet strong hanging pompons for late spring parties.

Cultivation Cow parsley grows in any soil but prefers a well-drained, sunny spot. It does not like being transplanted, so sow the seed where you want the plants to flower and then when the first, atypical (cotyledon) leaves appear thin to about 12in (30cm) apart. Don't wait for the recognizable feathery leaves, because the plants will resent disturbance at that stage.

CLEMATIS

Evergreen and deciduous climber and perennial
Zones: C. cirrhosa 7–9; C. × durandii, C. montana, C. tangutica 6–9; C. vitalba, C. viticella 5–9
Height: C. × durandii 6ft (1.8m); C. 'Rouge Cardinal', C. cirrhosa, C. viticella 6–10ft (2–3m); C. tangutica 10ft–12ft (3–4m); C. montana 20ft (6m); C. vitalba 30ft (9m)

Good varieties for cutting *There isn't really a clematis that is not good for picking, but the problem is their short flower stems. You can get around this if you're feeling brutal and brave, by cutting a whole bough of flowers, or even several. In spring, the cultivars of the anemone clematis, C. montana* (**6**), *are ideal for this. With their strong woody stems covered from top to bottom with open, fresh-faced flowers, and extremely vigorous and quick growth, they can take this treatment two or three years after planting. I use them as the main feature in late spring and early summer bridal bunches. You can cut them long and trailing, and then bind them together to give you any length of train you want. They will not last all day without water, but if you make up the bunch just before it is needed, they look fine for many hours. You can make an incredible bouquet, both pretty and dramatic, by mixing the anemone clematis with boughs of guelder rose and adding tall, curving*

Solomon's seal to form the crown. Clouds of white clematis flowers can be bound one stem to another, and then another, to trail halfway down the church behind the bride.

When making up a bridal bunch, do it in front of a full-length mirror, holding it as the bride will be, and putting in the flowers to be viewed from that angle. Leave the stem ends bare in water until just before the bunch is needed, then dry them as much as you can, before covering in plastic wrap, followed (and hidden) by the ribbon or tape.

In summer there are lovely rich velvety red and purple clematis such as 'Royal Velours' (see page 126), to choose from, while in fall the yellows (C. tangutica and 'Bill Mackenzie') and in winter the fluffy seed heads of old man's beard are mainstays (see pages 88–89 and 137).

Cultivation *Clematis are best planted in spring. Like most climbers, they thrive with their roots cool, in the shade, and their stems climbing up a wall or tree, or over trellis in full sun. The montanas take shade and can even be grown to cover a shady wall. C. × durandii and others that do not cling are best grown in the herbaceous border or tied into a hazel or bamboo wigwam.*

All clematis like a soil that is retentive of moisture without getting waterlogged. For maximum flowers, fertilize regularly. Cut dead wood from winter, spring, and early-summer flowerers (C. cirrhosa, C. montana, C. tangutica) after flowering, also shaping them then. C. × durandii and the herbaceous clematis should be cut down close to the ground in the fall. Those that flower later, like the Viticella cultivars, should be cut down to within 12in (30cm) of the ground, in late winter or early spring, even if they have started sprouting.

You are not likely to want more than one of each of these large plants. If you do want to propagate, take softwood or semi-ripe cuttings from the cultivars in early summer. For the species, sow seed in the fall. C. viticella self-seeds successfully.

4 *Amelanchier canadensis*
5 *Anthriscus sylvestris (dark-leaved)*
6 *Clematis montana*

SCALE
2in (5cm)

Lily-of-the-valley
CONVALLARIA MAJALIS

Deciduous perennial Zones: 4–9
Height: 8–9in (20–23cm)

Good varieties for cutting *The species lily-of-the-valley*, C. majalis (1), *not only produces the most sweetly scented, white, bell-shaped flowers in late spring but also does so from the dark, uncompromising corners of your garden where little else thrives. I cannot resist picking bunches of them to put by my bed.*

C.m. 'Fortin's Giant' is an excellent cultivar that has larger flowers and broader foliage than most. It flowers two weeks later than the species, so if you plant both you will prolong the picking season. For lovers of pink, there is a flushed-pink variety, C.m. var. rosea, which looks like a mini-bluebell. There is also a good variegated form that requires a sunny site or it reverts to the usual green-leaved type.

Cut flower and leaf together for a fresh-looking and fresh-smelling arrangement. The strong green foliage balances the delicate, pretty flowers. You will find that the scent fades and the flowers brown after four to five days, or sooner in a warm room.

Cultivation *This is a plant that will grow where it wants, and not necessarily where you want it, so the best course is to plant clumps of 10 to 15 crowns in early fall in several spots, preferably in semi-shade*

(although full sun and deep shade will also do) and see where they thrive. Planting lily-of-the-valley in different sites in varying degrees of light and sun will also prolong your picking season, with those in full sun flowering up to a month earlier.

If bought dry, lily-of-the-valley's long, thonglike roots should be laid out about 1in (2.5cm) deep, horizontally, and made as firm as possible. Almost any soil will do, except wringing wet bog or clay. Give your colonies a topdressing of manure or garden compost in the fall once the leaves have died down. If lily-of-the-valley is happy it can become invasive, and you may find yourself digging it out to control its spread.

Propagate by division in early spring, every three or four years, but not more often. In dividing the clumps, dig up and then plant them as square sods, with earth and creeping rhizome together. They can also be grown from seed sown in fall.

Bleeding heart, Dutchman's breeches
DICENTRA

Perennial Zones: 3–8
Height: D. 'Bacchanal' 18in (45cm); D. spectabilis 24in (60cm)

Good varieties for cutting *The fine lime-green leaves, light structure, and dangly heart-shaped flowers of the white dicentra, D. spectabilis 'Alba' (3), combine beautifully with the Viridiflora tulip 'Spring Green', Solomon's seal, and the loveliest white cherry blossom, Prunus 'Taihaku'.*

Another favorite is D. 'Bacchanal'. It has delicate velvet-crimson flowers over elegant grayish finely cut foliage. I like this in a small arrangement with Euphorbia cyparissias and the dog's-tooth violet. Its long flowering season compensates for the lack of flower profusion at any one time, and it will form a good ground-covering clump, the foliage lasting into fall.

Conditioning *Give all dicentras a good drink before arranging.*

Cultivation *Buy three to five plants of each variety you like, and they will quickly become established and merge into a good-sized clump. They thrive in part-shade in a humus-rich, moist but well-drained soil, and*

❶ *Convallaria majalis*
❷ *Iris 'Natascha'*
❸ *Dicentra spectabilis 'Alba'*
❹ *Hesperis matronalis var. albiflora*

like a cool position. Shelter the plant from wind and late frosts, which will damage any new shoots. They will also put up with full sun, provided that the soil does not dry out.

The foliage of D. spectabilis yellows and dies back soon after flowering. You can tidy this up as it collapses, but otherwise you should avoid cutting the foliage in its full green, because it weakens the plant. Plant in fall or early spring.

Propagate by division when dormant in late winter; these are, however, plants that hate disturbance, so division should be kept to a minimum. D. spectabilis 'Alba' can also be grown from seed, germinating more easily after cooling for a time in the refrigerator. D. formosa is more difficult to propagate from seed.

Snakeshead fritillary
FRITILLARIA MELEAGRIS

Main entry: Spring Yellow, page 109.
The white fritillary, F.m. subvar. alba (5), is best alone or with the plum-colored form.

Dame's rocket, sweet rocket
HESPERIS MATRONALIS

Main entry: Spring Pink, page 104.
White sweet rocket, H.m. var. albiflora (4), is ideal for mixed arrangements or in a heady bunch with its pink cousin.

Bluebell
HYACINTHOIDES

Main entry: Spring Blue and Purple, page 112. *A white form of the bluebell H. non-scripta (6) is lovely arranged with* the tulip 'Spring Green' and white anemones (A. coronaria De Caen Group 'The Bride'); or simply combine it with blue and white bluebells (see page 58).

Hyacinth
HYACINTHUS
Bulb Zones: 4–9
Height: 7–8in (17–20cm)
Good varieties for cutting *The best of the hyacinths for cutting are the slender old-fashioned Fairy or Roman hyacinths (see page 152). I find the usual forced forms rather chunky as cut flowers, with their short, thick stems and heavy heads, although I do enjoy the lurid, almost fluorescent pink H. orientalis 'Jan Bos' (see page 154). A few stems of these on their own, even if not exactly beautiful, should certainly make you smile. Another freak form that I am very keen on is H. 'Distinction' in an intense, velvety carmine-purple-pink. The white-tinged-green H.o. 'L' Innocence' (7) and the*

deep blue H.o. 'King of the Blues' are both worth growing for their scent. Place a single stem beside a bed or in the bathroom.
Cultivation *Hyacinths like a sunny, open site. They thrive in any well-drained soil, preferably enriched with manure. Bulbs are cheap to buy. Plant 3–4in (8–10cm) deep, and about 8in (20cm) apart, in fall. For bumper flowers, apply liquid fertilizer after the flower spikes have appeared. I also force hyacinths both for cutting and for pots to cheer up the house in winter.*

You can propagate them by removing the bulb offsets if you lift them in late summer. These will flower when about three years old, but will not be full size until they are seven years old. I am too impatient for this and so buy more bulbs every fall.

IRIS
Main entry: Winter Blue and Purple, page 158. *The delicate, ghostly white, miniature Reticulata iris 'Natascha' (2) is best when three to five stems are arranged on their own in a small glass. Put them beneath a table light, so the orange flash and violet veins of the petals are individually lit.*

MAGNOLIA
Deciduous and evergreen shrub and tree
Zones: M. grandiflora 7–9; M. stellata 5–9; M. denudata 6–8
Height and spread: M. stellata 8–10ft × 10–20ft (2.5–3m × 3–6m); M. denudata both 30ft (9m); M. grandiflora both usually 30–40ft (9–12m), rarely up to 100ft (30m)
Good varieties for cutting *I always feel magnolias are particularly suited to urban gardens, which are on the whole more sheltered and less prone to ruinous late frosts. The luxurious, waxen flowers are all spectacular for cutting. The star magnolia, M. stellata (9), is an especially good one to grow because, although like many magnolias it is slow-growing, it is unusual in starting to flower when still young. It is free-flowering and perfectly combines texture and form, with its soft, velvet buds and calyx surrounding whorls of curving cream petals with darkened centers. The flowers are often damaged by frost, but with so many buds on each branch, there are always more to come.*

The Yulan magnolia, M. denudata (8), is another beauty. Once established it will be densely covered in the fragrant, pure white,

shapely saucerlike flowers, which feature in so many Japanese and Chinese paintings. Pick a sprig of this to enjoy at close quarters.

Those who garden on a grander scale, and who have an expanse of sunny wall, should consider the huge, evergreen, summer-flowering southern magnolia M. grandiflora (see page 121), although it takes several years to flower.
Conditioning *The loose stamens of M. grandiflora will fall and cover the table they are standing on, so remove these before arranging in a vase.*
Cultivation *Magnolias thrive best in rich, deep soil that retains moisture but is not boggy. They need sun or part-shade, and shelter from strong winds. Most species prefer neutral to acidic soil. When planting, dig a large hole that will allow plenty of room for the root ball plus lots of organic material. The fleshy roots are easily damaged, so plant in late spring when the risk of hard ground frost has passed. Where the climate is more severe, you may need to protect the evergreen species with netting in winter. Mulch annually with rich garden compost until the plant is well established.*

SCALE
2in (5cm)

⑤ *Fritillaria meleagris subvar. alba*
⑥ *Hyacinthoides non-scripta*
⑦ *Hyacinthus orientalis 'L'Innocence'*
⑧ *Magnolia denudata*
⑨ *Magnolia stellata*

① *Myrrhis odorata*
② *Rosa banksiae var. banksiae*
③ *Viburnum x burkwoodii*

SCALE
2in (5cm)

Sweet cicely
MYRRHIS ODORATA

Perennial Zones: 4–8
Height: 2–3ft (60–90cm)

Good varieties for cutting *Sweet cicely, M. odorata* (1), *is an old-fashioned herb, now often naturalized as a garden fugitive. Its finely cut, fernlike foliage is a real asset in the garden, where it will grow in shade under a tree, or beside a hedge. It looks lovely growing with the strong, heart-shaped leaves of Siberian bugloss. I grow it for its light, feathery flowers, which start about a month before cow parsley or bishop's flower, particularly if it is growing in sun. From the middle of spring, I use it, and the foliage, too, to lighten up any wild flower bunch (see page 58).*

Conditioning *Give the leaves and flowers a good soak at least overnight before arranging, or they may droop.*

Cultivation *It thrives in shade or sun, in well-drained soil. If you keep cutting the flowers, the plants will preserve energy, and will soon form good established clumps. Plant three to five plants in the fall, or early spring. It will then self-seed freely.*

This is an easy plant to grow from seed in spring. Sow in a seed bed, thinning to 12in (30cm) as needed, or propagate by division and transplanting roots, in summer or fall.

Daffodil, jonquil
NARCISSUS

Main entry: Spring Yellow, page 109.

Favorite narcissi of mine are the delicate and highly scented N. poeticus var. recurvus (6) *and the pure white, multiheaded Triandrus, such as N. 'Ice Wings' and N. 'Thalia', with their smaller heads and long, thin flower shape and reflexed petals.*

Peony
PAEONIA

Main entry: Spring Pink, page 105.

The double white peony P. lactiflora 'Shirley Temple' (4) *has a delicious scent and outside petals of pinkish white with the middle pompon brushed with cream.*

Solomon's seal
POLYGONATUM

Rhizomatous perennial Zones: 4–9
Height: P. odoratum 2ft (60cm);
P. falcatum 20–36in (50–90cm);
P. multiflorum 40in (1m); P. × hybridum 4ft (1.2m); P. biflorum (syn. P. commutatum) 5ft (1.5m)

Good varieties for cutting

Solomon's seal is invaluable as a background flower for spring. If an arrangement is not inspiring me or just does not seem to jell, I often find that Solomon's seal saves the day. With its tall arching stems, silver-green foliage, and dangly white bellflowers, it makes an interesting asymmetrical silhouette that can be used to advantage in all sizes of arrangement, standing tall in a huge vase, or cut down to mix with more delicate plants. I also find it useful as a structural plant for late spring globes. Try mixing it with fluffy-headed lilac and peonies.

As well as the stately P. × hybridum (5), *a cross between P. multiflorum and P. odoratum, there are other more exotic varieties, such as the variegated form P. falcatum, with its reddish stems and white-edged leaves. P. odoratum is a good dwarf and its scent is strong. If you have room for a giant, grow P. biflorum to mix with white lilac, peonies, and cow parsley in a huge spring bunch.*

Cultivation *Solomon's seal thrives in a cool, shady situation, with a humus-laden, retentive soil. It will, in fact, grow almost anywhere that is not hot and dry. Plant a good clump of five to seven and let them*

spread. Top-dress annually with well-decayed manure, and otherwise leave well alone – this plant also resents disturbance.

Propagate by division of the near-surface rhizomes in spring or fall. Plant them again immediately, or store them, but only for a short time, in moist potting mix.

Banksian rose
ROSA BANKSIAE var. BANKSIAE

Main entry: Summer Pink, page 124.

The early-flowering, powder-puff Banksian rose, R. banksiae var. banksiae (2) *is one of the most delicate roses. It needs a sunny, sheltered wall to climb over. It is ideally suited to arranging: try just three sprigs on their own, perhaps on a dressing table.*

Lilac
SYRINGA

Deciduous shrub and tree Zones:
S. vulgaris 4–8; S. microphylla 5–8
Height and spread: S. vulgaris cultivars 15ft × 8ft (5m × 2.5m); S. microphylla 6ft × 6ft (1.8m × 1.8m)

Good varieties for cutting *Many people refuse to have lilac in the house since it once meant bad luck. It would be a real pity to miss out on that delicious wafting scent, so rid yourself of superstition and pick vast bunches of it. The straightforward S. vulgaris varieties are the most robust for cutting. I am not keen on the mauve forms, which look tinged with gray. I also tend to choose the single-flowered forms rather than the double ones, which can remind me of curly poodles. I like the pure white S.v. var. alba* (7) *and S.v. 'Maud Notcutt', which has larger individual flowers than the vulgaris form. The small-flowered, cream S.v. 'Primrose' is pretty mixed with early yellow roses such as 'Canary Bird'. I would also grow the most floriferous 'Andenken an Ludwig Späth' (see page 113) and the double S.v. 'Charles Joly' for strength of color in the purples.*

Other pretty species varieties tend to have no scent. S. microphylla 'Superba' is an exception, with its deep pink buds and smaller, paler, fragrant flowers in early summer. To produce a second crop of flowers in the fall, thin the spent flower twigs.

Conditioning *Hammer the woody stem ends. The flowers will last longer if you strip the leaves, but if I am arranging lilac on its own, I keep some of the leaves for a more natural look.*

Cultivation *Lilacs are unfussy plants that will grow in most fertile, well-drained soil in sun, although they will not tolerate very acidic conditions. They thrive on limestone. Plant in late fall. They do not like being transplanted and will take a couple of years to settle down before flowering well, so don't despair before that. No regular pruning is needed, but you should take your plant back to an attractive shape and structure*

after flowering, and remove any weak shoots. Also, rid the plant of any suckers, which divert energy and flowering potential from the main stems. Young plants benefit from deadheading or regular picking.

If you want more than one of each variety, you can propagate from softwood cuttings or layering (see page 42) in late summer.

Tulip
TULIPA
Main entry: Spring Orange and Red, page 108. *I love the Lily-flowered tulip 'White Triumphator' (11) for its look of purity and haughtiness. Arrange several on*

their own in a tall narrow vase to keep the heads held high. The sumptuous, blowzy, peony-flowered, white tulips are ideal for sentimental bunches, for weddings, or for when friends have a baby. Combine them with deep purple anemones (A. coronaria), and some emerging hornbeam, oak, or beech leaves, with the twigs just rising above a tightly tied bunch of these flowers.

More my type are the showy, raspberry-ripple T. 'Carnaval de Nice' (8) and the ripple-edged Parrot T. 'Estella Rijnveld' (9), which may be a bit too flamboyant for most gardens, but are perfect for picking. Arrange them on their own or mixed with the pure

white, double T. 'Mount Tacoma' (10), tumbling out of a simple white pitcher in the middle of your dining room. As the flowers open completely and before their petals begin to drop, they look more and more like spectacular tropical birds.

VIBURNUM x BURKWOODII
Main entry: Winter Pink, page 154.
The wonderfully fragrant, spring-flowering viburnum V. × burkwoodii (3) has white flowers with buds flushed with pink and lasts for up to a week in water. Unlike many of the leggy members of this family, it is a handsome bush even when not in flower.

SCALE
2in (5cm)

❹ *Paeonia lactiflora*
　 'Shirley Temple'
❺ *Polygonatum x hybridum*
❻ *Narcissus poeticus* var. *recurvus*
❼ *Syringa vulgaris* var. *alba*
❽ *Tulipa* 'Carnaval de Nice'
❾ *Tulipa* 'Estella Rijnveld'
❿ *Tulipa* 'Mount Tacoma'
⓫ *Tulipa* 'White Triumphator'

Pink

Poppy anemone, windflower
ANEMONE CORONARIA

Main entry: Spring White, page 98. *The radiant carmine-pink De Caen Group poppy anemone (1) has an almost unrivaled intensity of color. I use these pink anemones in zingy, multicolored arrangements, mixed with tulips and euphorbias (see page 62). They also look good on their own in a bright green vase for a bedroom or bathroom.*

Cuckoo flower, lady's smock
CARDAMINE

Annual and perennial Zones: 3–9
Height: 18in (45cm)

Good varieties for picking *From the very beginning of spring the lilac-pink cuckoo flower, C. pratensis (4), covers the banks of our road, and creeps in around the damp edges of the garden. Its delicate color and form mix beautifully with the bluebells and wood anemones that also grow wild on the banks. For the garden there is an improved form, with slightly bigger flowers, C.p. 'Flore Pleno'.*

Arrange them simply in a blue glass vase on their own or mix them with other spring wood and meadow wild flowers – cowslips,

bluebells, and Solomon's seal (see page 58). *I may sound sanctimonious, but I think it is always better to grow your own wild flowers in the garden, and leave the ones along the road-sides to lift someone else's spirits.*

Flowering earlier than C. pratensis is its big brother, C. quinquefolia (see page 153). You can often pick this from late winter to early spring, for informal bunches.
Cultivation *Cardamines thrive in sun or semi-shade, and moist or wet soil. Plant five to seven in a damp corner of your garden in fall or spring. They will gradually spread. Propagate from seed sown in pots in a cold frame in the spring or by division in fall (see pages 32–34 and 41).*

Anemone clematis
CLEMATIS MONTANA

Main entry: Spring White, page 99. *C.m. 'Elizabeth' (5) is a vigorous, pale pink climbing clematis that is ideal for bridal bouquets or for table decorations, where it can weave its way across the tabletop. To create a fresh pretty look, try combining anemone clematis with white lilac and green guelder rose pompons.*

DAPHNE x BURKWOODII

Main entry: Winter Pink, page 153. *D. × b. 'Somerset' (6), one of the latest daphnes to flower in late spring or early summer, has, like all its family, a sensational scent. I put three to five stems in a green glass decanter for a bathroom or bedroom.*

Dog's-tooth violet, trout lily
ERYTHRONIUM

Tuberous perennial Zones: 2–7
Height: E. dens-canis 5in (13cm); E. 'Pagoda', E. californicum 12in (30cm)
Good varieties for picking *European dog's-tooth violet, E. dens-canis (2), is a wild woodland flower in Italy, and you often*

come across clumps of its beautiful dappled leaves standing out against the coppery tones of the wood floor. You would never find this delicate intense plant in a florist's shop and yet it is a beauty. Just put three to five stems with their leaves in a shallow glass, and have them on your desk or by your bed for close inspection. With their bending and twisting reflexed petals, they also form an elegant silhouette against the light on any windowsill. There are now many color varieties available: I am keen on the rich purple E. dens-canis 'Frans Hals'.

The more robust trout lilies E. 'Pagoda' (see page 109) and E. californicum do not have the striking leaf markings, but their larger flowers last better in water. Arrange these on their own, too, or mix them with the species tulip T. tarda.
Cultivation *These tubers are expensive. Invest in just a few and let them spread. You must not allow the tubers to dry out, so plant them immediately on arrival or store them in moist bark or potting mix until you are ready. Plant them 3–4in (8–10cm) deep*

and about 2–3in (5–8cm) apart in humus-rich, well-drained soil in a shady position. They hate disturbance.

It is possible to propagate these plants from bulb offsets in summer, but the flowers will not be produced until the bulb is at least three to four years old.

Dame's rocket, sweet rocket
HESPERIS MATRONALIS

Perennial Zones: 4–9
Height: 3–6½ft (90cm–2m)
Good varieties for cutting *The tall, pale lilac sweet rocket, H. matronalis (7), is excellent for cutting. It has a slight, sweet scent, particularly at night, and a densely flowery habit. It will flower continuously from the end of spring through to mid-summer, and the more you pick the longer it will go on producing flower spikes. Grow both the pink-purple and the white forms, mix them together in a bunch, and arrange them in a huge pitcher for the kitchen table; or mix them with boughs of the Mazzard cherry, Prunus avium.*

1 *Anemone coronaria* De Caen Group
2 *Erythronium dens-canis*
3 *Tulipa saxatilis*
4 *Cardamine pratensis*
5 *Clematis montana* 'Elizabeth'
6 *Daphne* × *burkwoodii* 'Somerset'

SCALE
2in (5cm)

SCALE
2in (5cm)

❼ *Hesperis matronalis*
❽ *Paeonia officinalis*
❾ *Tulipa* 'China Pink'
❿ *Paeonia lactiflora*
   'Sarah Bernhardt'

SCALE
2in (5cm)

SCALE
2in (5cm)

Cultivation *Sweet rocket will do well in shade as well as full sun, and the white variety can form a lovely luminous haze at dusk beneath trees in a garden with the scent wafting over you as you walk. Plant five to seven plants and you will have plenty for cutting. This biennial could not be easier to grow from seed. Sow it in rows in a seed bed at the beginning of summer, and thin to 8–12in (20–30cm). Either leave it where it was sown and pick it from there, or transplant it to its flowering position in the fall. Mulch with manure in late spring.*

Peony
PAEONIA
Shrubby and herbaceous deciduous perennial Zones: 3–7
Height: P. lactiflora *and* P. officinalis *cultivars 2–2½ft (60–75cm)*
Good varieties for cutting *Peonies (8), like lilies, swags of roses, and tall iris, always seem luxurious and extravagant flowers to pick. As you chop them off with the pruners, they make you feel slightly*

wicked and, at the same time, excitingly indulgent. I almost find myself looking over my shoulder, waiting to be warned, like a child stealing candy. My favorites are the deep crimson and carmine double forms, such as P. officinalis *'Rubra Plena',* P. lactiflora *'Inspecteur Lavergne', and, the darkest of all,* P.l. *'Monsieur Martin Cahuzac'. I also like the scented double white* P.l. *'Shirley Temple' (see page 103), which has a beautiful creamy-yellow center.*

The blowzy pink peonies you see at late spring and early summer weddings are not my style. The color and form remind me of cotton candy or ballroom dance dresses, with their layer upon layer of pink material. If you favor such a peony, however, P.l. *'Sarah Bernhardt' (10) is one of the best, because it does also have a faint scent.*

The single peonies with their purer appearance and great cup faces look similar to waxen magnolias, and are also good cut. Sadly, the flowers of the shrubby tree peonies do not last more than a day or two, so I tend to leave them on the bush.

The young, reddish-tinged leaves of P. lactiflora *are also lovely for spring picking (see page 107). Take them sparingly since they may be flowering stems. I also pick the three-headed, sculptural seed heads in late summer and fall (see page 117).*
Conditioning *Peonies can be temperamental. Do not leave them out of water after picking, because once they have drooped it will be difficult to perk them up again. Pick them in bud or full flower, and if the water is kept clean and fresh, they may last for up to two weeks.*
Cultivation *Peonies thrive in rich, well-drained soil that does not dry out in summer. Plant them in full sun. You may need to stake them, because the flower heads, particularly in the double forms, are often heavy enough to bend over and possibly break the stem. Give them a dressing of bonemeal every fall and a compost mulch in spring.*

When you cut them, it is important to take only one or two stems from each plant, since the leaves grow on the same stems as the flower. This will leave enough foliage for photosynthesis, and hence food storage for root development.

You need to plant clumps of three to five of each variety to give you enough for cutting. The crowns should be planted just below the surface, with the resting buds not more than 1½in (4cm) below the soil. If you plant them too deep, they will not flower so freely.

Propagate by division in the fall.

Tulip
TULIPA
Main entry: Spring Orange and Red, page 108. *After a long journey and several days of searching, I found cliff tulip, Tulipa saxatilis (3), on a rocky hillside at the western end of Crete. This, by far the most brazen species tulip with its bright pink petals and deep egg-yolk-yellow base and center, should not be mixed with anything else, but valued and presented as a real empress in its own right.*

The strong pink tulips, such as Lily-flowered T. 'China Pink' (9), I mix only with bright green smyrniums and euphorbias, which both contrast with their color and also cool them down.

Orange and Red

Columbine
AQUILEGIA

Perennial Zones: 5–9
Height: 20–30in (50–75cm)

Good varieties for cutting *The beautiful and elaborate columbines remind me of a nun's headdress. Although they last only three to four days in water, they make elegant cut flowers that are well worth growing.*

Grow a mix of fine long-spurred varieties, such as the McKana Hybrids in red, pink, white, blue, single, and bicolored forms, and display them in a jumble of color for informal table centerpieces. Or grow generous blocks of the bicolored, long-spurred A. olympica in red-and-gold (1) or blue-and-white varieties and single-colored varieties like the short-spurred, almost black A. atrata (see page 112). Arrange these in a glass on their own or combine them with other flowers that highlight their coloring.

Conditioning *Stand them in deep water for several hours before arranging.*

Cultivation *The McKana Hybrids like sun and moist, well-drained soil. Other columbines thrive in light shade – they can even be planted against a sunless wall.*

Columbines are short-lived perennials and you need to restock regularly. They are grown easily from seed in spring. Sow under cover and line them out into a fertile seed bed for the summer. Move to their flowering positions in fall. Or sow fresh seed in late summer, thin, and pot on in the fall, storing the young plants in a cold frame through the winter. They will self-seed, hybridizing madly, so to keep your colors true, separate them well when planting in the garden.

English wallflower
ERYSIMUM CHEIRI

Perennial and biennial Zones: 3–9
Height: 12–20in (30–50cm)

Good varieties for cutting *The sweet, old-fashioned smell of wallflowers mixed with snapdragons and forget-me-nots always reminds me of cottage-type gardens. Wallflowers come in all the best colors, from deep rich black-crimson 'Blood Red' (3), burnt marmalade-orange 'Fire King' (2), and bright vibrant yellow 'Cloth of Gold' to white and cream 'White Dame'.*

Planted, they are best in color blocks in the garden rather than in multicolored mixtures. I use them as a broad scalloped edging to my annual cutting patches, underplanted with forget-me-nots, and backed by clumps of horse parsley (Smyrnium olusatrum). The unmixed rule does not apply when they are cut: there is nothing nicer than a wonderfully scented pitcher of mixed wallflowers for the center of your kitchen table or in a large container for the family room. They last well even in a hot room, which brings out their scent more intensely. They also look good arranged with Euphorbia amygdaloides var. robbiae, cut short for a small vase (see page 56). Being all-round, robust plants, wallflowers will last up to 10 days in clean water.

Cultivation *Wallflowers are available in the fall as bare roots in garden centers, but take care not to buy assorted colors or dwarf varieties, which are not as good for cutting. They like a sunny position in fertile, well-drained soil and, treated as biennials, are easy to grow from seed. Sow in color lines 8–12in (20–30cm) apart, directly in a seed bed in early summer. Thin the plants to 12in (30cm) apart (save and transplant the thinnings if you wish) and then in mid-fall transplant to their flowering positions. Try to keep a good clump of earth around the root when you transplant, for the tiny spider's web of rootlets gives the plant a good start before the depths of winter.*

1 *Aquilegia olympica*
2 *Erysimum cheiri 'Fire King'*
3 *Erysimum cheiri 'Blood Red'*
4 *Euphorbia griffithii*
5 *Euphorbia griffithii (spring leaves)*
6 *Fritillaria meleagris*

SCALE
2in (5cm)

SCALE
2in (5cm)

opulent colors – the rich violet-purples of poppy anemones and the warm burnt oranges and reds of the wallflowers. Cool this mixture with the contrasting acid-green of new hornbeam leaves or the ever-useful smyrniums and euphorbias. Or you can display them with flamboyant flowers like tulip 'Carnaval de Nice' and the Parrot tulips, using the handsome peony leaves as your main foliage. The reddish-stained new leaves of P. lactiflora and P. mloko-sewitschii (**12**) are also lovely cut, mixed with hellebores and young artichoke leaves.

Auricula, polyanthus
PRIMULA
Main entry: Spring Yellow, page 110.
The red polyanthus are great favorites of mine because they look so warm and inviting (**8**–**10**). Arrange them on their own from late winter through to the end of spring in an array of colored glasses. They also look lovely mixed with other small spring flowers, such as squills and violets.

Auriculas (**7**), with their thick, velvety petals, are the flowers that the Victorians and Edwardians were so fond of for their still-life paintings. They should be cut a few stems at a time and arranged simply on their own to be admired in the light from a window or under a table lamp.

Persian ranunculus
RANUNCULUS ASIATICUS
Main entry: Spring Yellow, page 111.
Looking like an elegant anemone, this bulb is showing off its richest Burgundy-red tones (**13**). Mix it with pink, yellow, and orange ranunculus, or the red poppy anemone and bupleurum.

Spurge, milkweed
EUPHORBIA
Main entry: Spring Green and Silver, page 96
The vibrant orange-brick-red of E. griffithii varieties (**4**) is a must in any cutting garden. They last well when cut and mix beautifully with other lime-green-flowered euphorbias and almost any of the tulips (see page 61). I also pick them in the fall, when the foliage has turned a tomato-soup red, to mix with bright and browning cotinus, oak, and amelanchier leaves (see page 143). The young, emerging leaves (**5**), with their vibrant red veining, are also intense and bright mixed with ranunculus and tulips in the spring.

Snakeshead fritillary
FRITILLARIA MELEAGRIS
Main entry: Spring Yellow, page 109.
One of the most delicate wild flowers, the fritillary (**6**) grows freely in meadows. Show off its plum-colored, snakeskinned bells on their own or with the white form (page 101).

Peony
PAEONIA
Main entry: Spring Pink, page 105.
The rich crimson of the pompon peony Paeonia officinalis 'Rubra Plena' (**11**) is irresistible when mixed with other deep,

7 *Primula auricula*
8 *Primula Cowichan Garnet Group*
9 *Primula Cowichan Garnet Group*
10 *Primula variety*
11 *Paeonia officinalis* 'Rubra Plena'
12 *Paeonia mlokosewitschii* (spring leaves)
13 *Ranunculus asiaticus*

SCALE
2in (5cm)

Tulip
TULIPA

Bulb   Zones: 3–9
Height: Greigii 6–12in (15–30cm);
Fosteriana, Single, and Double Early
12–16in (30–40cm); Darwin, Lily-
flowered, Parrot, Viridiflora, Single, and
Double Late 18–24in (45–60cm)

Good varieties for cutting   *Tulips
make supreme cut flowers. So much so that
there is not a month in the year when they
are unavailable in the cut-flower markets.
In the garden, you can plan to have one tulip
or another to cut at least through the whole
of spring. I have no great favorites among
the early Fosteriana or Greigii varieties, but
I love the Single Early 'Prinses Irene' (6),
with its strong, vibrant orange base color,
and violet purple marking at the bottom of
each petal, and the bicolored red and yellow
'Mickey Mouse' (see pages 110 and 111).
Coming after these in spring are the Darwin
Hybrids, the Single Lates, the Viridifloras,
and the Lily-flowered forms. An excellent
Darwin Hybrid is T. 'Gudoshnik' (4) with
its red-on-yellow marbling, and you must
grow the dramatically beautiful, deep purple-
black Single Late T. 'Queen of Night' (see
pages 112 and 113). Of the Viridifloras,
cream-and-green T. 'Spring Green' (see page
97) and green-and-orange T. 'Artist' (2) are
both unusual and stylish. The Lily-flowered
varieties, with their curving stems and pointed
silhouettes, are supremely elegant. Nearly all
this group are worth growing: the single
colors are lovely and there are some good
bicolors, too. Grow 'Queen of Sheba' or
'Aladdin', both red with yellow margins,
or the vibrant orange T. 'Ballerina' (3)
with its bonus of a freesialike scent.*

*Next come the Double Late forms. T.
'Uncle Tom' (7) is a rich deep claret, but it
is hard to beat the theatrical raspberry-ripple*

① *Tulipa acuminata*
② *Tulipa 'Artist'*
③ *Tulipa 'Ballerina'*
④ *Tulipa 'Gudoshnik'*
⑤ *Tulipa 'Orange Favourite'*
⑥ *Tulipa 'Prinses Irene'*
⑦ *Tulipa 'Uncle Tom'*

*T. 'Carnaval de Nice' for style and panache
(see page 103). The weird spidery T.
acuminata (1) is in a class of its own.
I often pick a stem to have on my desk in
a tall narrow glass.*

*The climax comes with the astonishing
Parrot tulips, which look like a Latin
American festival procession: orange mixed
with green, as in 'Orange Favourite' (5),
yellow veined with red ('Flaming Parrot',
page 111), white dappled with red and
green ('Estella Rijnveld'), and deep purple-
black upon black (Black Parrot', pages 112*

*and 113). Nothing in the garden can beat
these in the glamor stakes.*

Conditioning   *Tulips last well in water.
Strip the bottom leaves and soak the stems
for about eight hours, tightly wrapped with
two or three sheets of newspaper, to keep
their stems upright: if floppy stems absorb
water, they will stay bent, hiding their faces.*

Cultivation   *Tulip bulbs are cheap to buy
from bulb wholesalers. Buy 25, or, if you
have room, 50 to 100. For easy picking,
plant them in rows or blocks. Like most
bulbs, tulips enjoy a good baking in the sun*

*in summer and a well-drained soil. Position
them about 4in (10cm) deep, and 4–6in
(10–15cm) apart, in mid-fall. Left in the
ground, they will form bulb offsets that will
eventually flower; however, if you are too
impatient to wait, buy more each year. If you
cut heavily, you may find you exhaust all the
bulbs and few will flower the following year.
It is always worth putting in more than you
will want to cut, so there are still some
flower heads to look at and more of a chance
for a decent show next year.*

*You can lift the bulbs to store until
planting time once the leaves have died down
by mid-summer, when photosynthesis will
have provided energy to carry them through
the dormant season. For ease I usually leave
the bulbs in the ground, only lifting and
dividing them every three to five years.*

SCALE
2in (5cm)

Yellow

Trout lily
ERYTHRONIUM
Main entry: Spring Pink, page 104.
The beauty of the trout lilies is in their minutely detailed flowers and the elegant outline of their swept-back petals. Arrange the yellow-flowered E. 'Pagoda' (1) on its own or mixed with the species tulip Tulipa turkestanica or the perfect T. clusiana 'Cynthia' (see pages 110 and 111).

Spurge, milkweed
EUPHORBIA
Main entry: Spring Green and Silver, page 96. *The yellow-green euphorbias provide some of the best spring foliage. Mix E. polychroma (3) and the taller plant E. palustris (4) with each and every color.*

Fritillary, crown imperial
FRITILLARIA
Bulb Zones: 4–9
Height: F. meleagris 10–12in (25–30cm); F. persica, F. imperialis to 5ft (1.5m)
Good varieties for cutting *A prima-donna among spring flowers, the statuesque crown imperial, F. imperialis 'Lutea' (5), has tall curving stems below a circle of huge,*

yellow, hanging bells. It is spectacular on its own or even better mixed with the 'Flaming Parrot' tulip and boughs of the horse chestnut's sticky buds. I also love the burnt toffee orange form F.i. 'Rubra Maxima' in a fiercely exotic mix with the other queen of fritillaries, F. persica, Euphorbia characias subsp. wulfenii, and the shaggy 'Black Parrot' tulips. The only drawback to these fritillaries is their musky smell, but I hardly notice it. At the other end of the scale are the perfect checkerboard, white or plum-colored bells of the snakeshead fritillary (see pages 101 and 106).*
Cultivation *Fritillaries like a deep rich soil and prefer full sun, although the crown imperial tolerates some shade. Grow F. persica in a well-drained site with the protection of a sunny wall. Avoid disturbing these plants once they are established, since they may stop flowering. Top-dress annually with well-decayed manure.*

The snakeshead fritillaries, cheap to buy from wholesalers, can be planted by the 100 in an area of unmown grass. Or plant them in a large clump by a path, but put in a conspicuous label so you don't dig them up later on. Put them in 4in (10cm) deep and about 6in (15cm) apart.

The larger, more expensive fritillaries do not flower until they are four to six years old so buy them from a good wholesaler, who supplies mature bulbs. If you buy cheaply you are likely to be buying a younger bulb. Plant several bulbs 6in (15cm) deep and 8–12in (20–30cm) apart. Although you can propagate fritillaries from seed or offsets, you will have to wait for them to flower.

Daffodil, jonquil
NARCISSUS
Bulb Zones: 3–9
Height: miniatures 6in (15cm); full-size 12–18in (30–45cm)
Good varieties for cutting *I used to have reservations about the huge, yellow or orange-and-yellow, trumpeted varieties of daffodils. I now love them. A good robust one is 'Mrs. R.O Backhouse', whose color fades out to a gentle apricot and which looks lovely in a tall white pitcher. 'Professor Einstein' has bright orange centers that look*

fantastic contrasted in large bunches with tall grape hyacinths. I much prefer these unsophisticated flowers to the split-corona and double forms.*

Of the daffodils I pick for their scent, the tiny Tazetta N. 'Canaliculatus' (2) is hard to beat. It is lovely mixed with other small-flowered bulbs like scillas, muscari, and polyanthus. Another good Tazetta is the lightly scented pale cream N. 'Geranium' (6).

Easy to force indoors for winter are the especially fragrant N. 'Paper White' (see page 152) and N. 'Soleil d'Or'. The elegant and delicate pheasant's-eye narcissi also have a swoony scent, particularly in the evening.
Cultivation *Daffodils can be grown in any well-drained soil in sun or even in quite shady borders. They are inexpensive bulbs if*

1 *Erythronium 'Pagoda'*
2 *Narcissus 'Canaliculatus'*
3 *Euphorbia polychroma*
4 *Euphorbia palustris*
5 *Fritillaria imperialis 'Lutea'*
6 *Narcissus 'Geranium'*

SCALE
2in (5cm)

SCALE
2in (5cm)

SCALE
2in (5cm)

you buy 50 or 100 at a time from a good wholesaler. You will get bigger and better flowers if you plant them by the end of summer, because unlike tulips they benefit from being longer in the ground. However, planted later they will do well enough and even better the following year. They benefit from picking and deadheading, so the bulb does not deplete its food store trying to produce seed. After flowering, don't cut the leaves, or mow over them if they are in grass, until they have turned yellow. This allows the leaves time to feed the bulb to sustain it until the next season.

Plant the large forms 3–4in (8–10cm) deep, and 4–6in (10–15cm) apart; the miniature varieties should be about 2–3in (5–8cm) deep and the same apart. If you are planting in grass, make a hole in the turf 2–3in (5–8cm) deep and about 3in (8cm) wide with a trowel or tubular bulb planter. Place a bulb in each hole and replace the clump of soil or sod. If you are planting them indoors for forcing, use a potting mix combined 2:1 with sharp sand or grit for drainage (see pages 40–41).

You can propagate by division no sooner than six weeks after flowering. The clumps should be divided and replanted every three to five years.

❶ Primula auricula 'Blairside Yellow'
❷ Primula Gold-laced Group
❸ Primula vulgaris
❹ Primula veris
❺ Viola variety

Auricula, cowslip, polyanthus, primrose
PRIMULA
Perennial Zones: 4–9 (auriculas 3–8)
Height: 6–12in (15–30cm)

Good varieties for cutting *By the end of winter the primulas and polyanthus start to flower, beginning with the luscious, rich Venetian colors of the Cowichan polyanthus (see page 107). Arranged in separate colored glasses they look as rich as a church procession. The Gold-laced polyanthus (**2**), cowslips, and primroses come after them. The English primrose, P. vulgaris (**3**), looks lovely in a shallow glass on its own, while the cowslip, P. veris (**4**), with its longer stems, also looks good as the central attraction in a wild flower display (see page 58).*

*In mid-spring the auriculas (**1**) come into flower. Their texture is so rich and plush that they seem almost made up. A creamy fluff called farina covers the stem and buds, and sometimes the petals even maximize their looks with eyeliner (see page 107).*

One of the main problems with growing polyanthus of any kind is that birds often get to the flower buds before you do. Avoid this by constructing a simple web of black thread tied on short twigs pushed into the ground to stand about 3in (8cm) above the flowers.

Cultivation *Gold-laced polyanthus, the English primrose, and the cowslip all require moist but well-drained soil in sun or partial shade. Originating from woodland plants, most will grow in full shade, too. Auriculas need a grittier, alkaline soil in sun.*

All primulas and polyanthus can be grown from seed, sown at the start of the year; you may even have flowers the same year. Alternatively, visit a good nursery and pick those that are in flower to be sure of obtaining the best color forms. Buy at least five of any one type, so you can make up a decent clump, which will provide you with more flowers the more you pick them. Plant them 12in (30cm) apart, and the gap between them will quickly close. They will then self-seed, and you can build up a good stock by dividing the clumps the first fall.

❻ Ranunculus asiaticus
❼ Ranunculus asiaticus
❽ Tulipa 'Mickey Mouse'
❾ Tulipa tarda
❿ Tulipa turkestanica

SCALE
2in (5cm)

Persian ranunculus
RANUNCULUS ASIATICUS

Bulb Zones: 9–10
Height: 18–22in (45–55cm)

Varieties good for cutting *These semi-tender bulbs come in glowing colors: Burgundy red, warm marmalade-orange, bright sunflower-yellow (6), and royal carmine-pink. There are forms with red veined on yellow (7), and yellow edged with claret, and many variations on this theme.*

The double forms are like mini-peonies when they first appear, and as they open up come to look more like big anemones with their dark bulbous centers and buttercup petals. The singles look like a much bigger and more glamorous older sister of the European field buttercup. Use them in your spring multicolored arrangements (see page 62), mixed with tulips, anemones, ceanothus, and euphorbias. Or simply arrange them in a tightly tied posy, the rich colors mixed together with pussy willow and new maple leaves and flowers.

Conditioning *Carefully strip all but the top leaves of these plants because they become slimy on contact with water. The flowers will last up to two weeks in clean water.*

Cultivation *These are plants that like a position in full sun with a very well-drained potting mix. In frost-prone areas, grow them in the greenhouse. Plant out in large pots or better still in a greenhouse bed, 3in (8cm) deep and 4–6in (10–15cm) apart. They are difficult to propagate so I buy the bulbs, which are cheap and widely available.*

Pussy willow
SALIX CAPREA

Main entry: Winter Green and Silver, page 150. *Although pussy willow, S. caprea (13), often appears early in winter, these silver-green buds rarely plump up with all their soft yellow fluff until the beginning of spring. I cut it all the time and mix it, tall or short, with almost anything for the first few weeks of the spring. It also looks good on its own, cut long, the tall branches arranged in a tall vase on a windowsill where the sun will catch the yellow haze of anthers and pollen that surround each flower.*

Tulip
TULIPA

Main entry: Spring Orange and Red, page 108. *In spring, tulips dominate the center stage of cut flowers. The yellow ones illustrated here, all stars in my book, range from delicate T. tarda (9), T. turkestanica (10) and T. clusiana 'Cynthia' (12), by way of the elegant 'West Point' (11) and 'Golden Melody' (16) to bicolored 'Mickey Mouse' (8), frilly 'Texas Gold' (15), and spectacular 'Flaming Parrot' (14).*

Pansy, violet
VIOLA

Main entry: Spring Blue and Purple, page 113. *From early spring through to the fall frost, I pick little yellow violets (5) to arrange on their own in a shallow glass. These violets are rarely seen in florist's shops, and it is so easy to grow your own.*

11 *Tulipa* 'West Point'
12 *Tulipa clusiana* 'Cynthia'
13 *Salix caprea*
14 *Tulipa* 'Flaming Parrot'
15 *Tulipa* 'Texas Gold'
16 *Tulipa* 'Golden Melody'

SCALE
2in (5cm)

Blue and Purple

Windflower
ANEMONE
Main entry: Spring White, page 98.
Enjoy clear blue A. blanda 'Atrocaerulea' (7) in a simple glass on its own by your desk or in a mixed early spring posy. The luxurious velvety blue A. coronaria De Caen Group (8) brings a plush richness to almost any color you mix it with (see page 62).

Columbine
AQUILEGIA
Main entry: Spring Orange and Red, page 106. *The purple-black columbine A. vulgaris (1) is lovely with black tulips and acid-green euphorbias (see page 61).*

California lilac
CEANOTHUS
*Evergreen and deciduous shrub and tree
Zones: C. arboreus, 9–10; C. 'Concha' 7–9; C. × delileanus 'Gloire de Versailles' 6–9
Height and spread: C. × delileanus 'Gloire de Versailles' 5ft × 5ft (1.5m × 1.5m); C. 'Concha' 5ft × 8ft (1.5m × 2.5m); C. arboreus 20ft × 25ft (6m × 7.5m)*
Good varieties for cutting *Ideally, grow the rich deep blue forms of ceanothus, such as the evergreen wall shrub C. 'Concha' (3). If you have sufficient space, pick one of the larger varieties, such as the evergreen C. arboreus (2). This will give you armfuls of flowers to arrange on their own, perhaps in a huge plain pewter pitcher, or to use as background foliage and flower for multicolored arrangements (see page 62). If you are restricted for space, choose a smaller shrub. Evergreen C. 'Frosty Blue' has mid-blue flowers in late spring. It is fast-growing and will tolerate lots of picking. The deciduous C. × delileanus 'Gloire de*

Versailles' is smaller still, and has the great advantage that it will flower over a long period: it will produce attractive flowers from mid-summer until fall.
Conditioning *Hammer or slit the stem ends for 1–2in (2–5cm) soon after picking, then stand in deep water for several hours.*

Cultivation *Plant at least one species for spring and one for fall picking. Plant in full sun and light, well-drained soil, preferably by a wall that will give protection from cold and drying winds. The evergreens can be short-lived, so take semi-ripe cuttings in summer. Remove dead wood only from evergreens. Deciduous ceanothus can have their laterals pruned in early spring to within 4in (10cm) of the previous year's growth.*

Bluebell
HYACINTHOIDES
*Bulb Zones: 5–8
Height: 24in (60cm)*
Good varieties for cutting *The rich blue carpet of a bluebell wood is a sight that lifts the spirits. The English bluebell, H. non-scripta (9), is best arranged on its own or mixed with cowslips and Solomon's seal in a wild flower arrangement (see page 58). There are white and blue cultivated forms with larger flowers, but the blues tend to be washed out. Best of all is the white form (see page 101).*
Conditioning *Pick bluebells when they first emerge or they will flop in 24 hours. It is better to use scissors when you pick them rather than just to pull them up, as children are inclined to do, and risk damaging the bulb. Cut above the white part of the stalk, which does not suck up water as effectively as the green part does.*
Cultivation *The best place to grow bluebells is in a woody area or among shrubs. Otherwise plant them in heavy soil against a damp shady wall or under a tree. Plant in the fall, 4–6in (10–15cm) deep. Propagate by division in late summer or by seed sown in the fall.*

1 *Aquilegia vulgaris*
2 *Ceanothus arboreus*
3 *Ceanothus 'Concha'*
4 *Syringa vulgaris 'Andenken an Ludwig Späth'*
5 *Tulipa 'Black Parrot'*
6 *Tulipa 'Queen of Night'*

SCALE
2in (5cm)

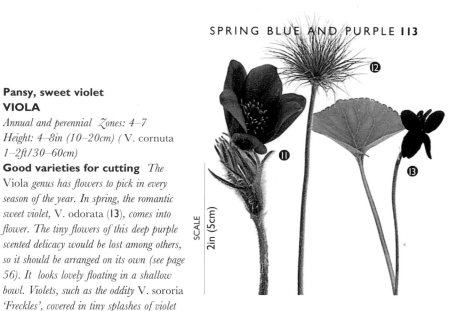

Spanish lavender
LAVANDULA STOECHAS
Main entry: Summer Blue and Purple, page 134. *This showy lavender (10) is one of the first to flower in mid-spring. With deep purple "rabbit's ear" tassels on purple and gray fragrant heads, it mixes well with almost anything. For a simple pretty bunch, combine it with bishop's flower, white and blue poppy anemone, and yellow Persian ranunculus. For a more glamorous look, arrange tall branches of lavender in a vase and simply poke tulip 'Flaming Parrot' into the lavender's woody structure. Use it, too, in early-summer party swags (see pages 64–67).*

Pasque flower
PULSATILLA
Perennial Zones: 5–9
Height: P. halleri 6–15in (15–38cm); P. vulgaris 6–9in (15–23cm)
Good varieties for cutting *Plant the exotic-looking, plush-purple Pasque flower, P. vulgaris (11), in large clumps, and you may coax it to spread as a rich velvet carpet, as it once did in its wild state. When you pick it, place just a few stems and leaves in one or two small glasses. Find a place where they will be back-lit, to catch the fine halo of tiny hairs that covers flowers, foliage, and stem. The seed heads (12) are lovely mixed with the deep-colored flowers of Viticella clematis, which are not unlike those of P. vulgaris itself. Among the various color forms are a deep crimson and a pure white. In addition, there is a larger-flowered, purple species, P. halleri, with huge, upward-facing flowers with a pointing purple proboscis in the deep yellow center. None of these, however, has quite the exquisite beauty of the wild species.*
Cultivation *Pulsatillas thrive in full sun in a well-drained, alkaline soil. They are worth propagating in quantity as they are plants that look best massed in a generous carpet which will really be noticed. The delicate flowers are easily swamped in the general border. Propagate by root cuttings during the winter or by seed sown when still fresh in the early summer. Trim off the seeds' wispy tails. They germinate quickly and should be thinned early on.*

Lilac
SYRINGA
Main entry: Spring White, page 102.
This deep purple lilac, S. vulgaris 'Andenken an Ludwig Späth' (4), is best in bud when the intensity of its color is greatest. Put it in a simple arrangement with Tulipa *'Spring Green'. Or mix it with* T. *'Queen of Night' (6),* T. *'Orange Favourite', and* Euphorbia griffithii, *and add the yellow-greens of* E. polychroma *and* E. palustris.

Tulip
TULIPA
Main entry: Spring Orange and Red, page 108. *The almost black* T. *'Black Parrot' (5) and* T. *'Queen of Night' (6) with their strong shape have great glamor and style. Contrast them in a tightly tied bunch with* T. *'Spring Green', peonies, and euphorbias, or with orange and acid-green euphorbias in a hanging globe (see page 61).*

Pansy, sweet violet
VIOLA
Annual and perennial Zones: 4–7
Height: 4–8in (10–20cm) (V. cornuta *1–2ft/30–60cm)*
Good varieties for cutting *The* Viola *genus has flowers to pick in every season of the year. In spring, the romantic sweet violet,* V. odorata (13), *comes into flower. The tiny flowers of this deep purple scented delicacy would be lost among others, so it should be arranged on its own (see page 56). It looks lovely floating in a shallow bowl. Violets, such as the oddity* V. sororia *'Freckles', covered in tiny splashes of violet on white, are good in small arrangements. Then there are the mini-violets, in many combinations of yellow and purple. The smaller species violets have less cheek and more chin than the violets usually grown as annuals, which have rounder faces with chubbier cheeks.*

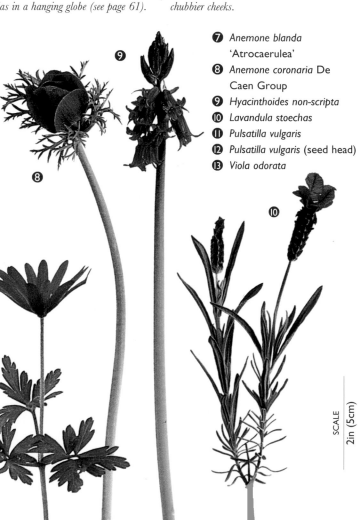

7 *Anemone blanda 'Atrocaerulea'*
8 *Anemone coronaria* De Caen Group
9 *Hyacinthoides non-scripta*
10 *Lavandula stoechas*
11 *Pulsatilla vulgaris*
12 *Pulsatilla vulgaris (seed head)*
13 *Viola odorata*

During summer the many color forms of the rhizomatous perennial V. cornuta *will continue to flower for months. These have longer stems than most and can be mixed with other flowers such as the small-flowered Icelandic poppy,* Papaver nudicaule. *The mauve-blue form combines beautifully with orange Icelandic poppies.*

Also grow the annuals V. *'Jolly Joker', a gaudy orange and purple, and the near-black* V. *'Penny Black', which lasts over 10 days in water. In cooler climates, if you keep picking or deadheading these violets, they will continue to flower all through the summer and well into fall.*

For the winter, choose any of those in the catalogs designed for cold-weather flowering. Plant up pots in the fall and put them by your back door for easy picking and dead-heading. Bring indoors before hard frosts.
Conditioning *Strip the bottom leaves.*
Cultivation *Some species violets prefer a cool shady site, but most of the cultivated forms do best in full sun. Group them in clumps of five to seven plants, planted 8–12in (20–30cm) apart.*

All the annuals and the species violets are easy plants to grow from seed. Many of them self-seed so freely you will have violets forever. If you sow them in early spring, they will flower later the same year. The species violets spread by runners, too, so can easily be propagated by division in mid-spring. The perennials, like V. cornuta, *are best from softwood cuttings. They all benefit from fertilizing and deadheading to keep them flowering longer.*

Summer

Summer is the time to have huge displays of flowers all over the house, giving a sense of luxury and abundance for everyone to enjoy. You can create statuesque and sumptuous vases of lilies, roses, iris, delphiniums, sunflowers, mock orange, eremurus, bear's breeches, and artichokes. Who could want more? Room by room, a different glorious display will greet you. For smaller arrangements, cut fragrant sweet peas, pinks, sweet Williams, phlox, roses, and honeysuckle. With all the color and vigor of annuals in full flood at this time of year, you will never lack for choice.

Green and Silver

Bear's breeches
ACANTHUS

Semi-evergreen, herbaceous perennial
Zones: A. mollis *8–10;* A. spinosus, A. hungaricus *6–10*
Height: 3–5ft (90cm–1.5m); A. spinosus *to 6ft (1.8m)*

Good varieties for cutting *The imposing, foxglovelike flower spikes of the acanthus are a mixture of green, purple, white, and pink. Each is clad in 20 or 30 flowers with dominant purple bracts that look like the dark, hooded eyes of one of Michelangelo's sibyls. Mix them with other strong and structural flowers such as sunflowers and artichokes, or arrange many stems on their own in a tall vase.*

For the greatest number of flower spikes, choose A. spinosus, *although* A. hungaricus *is also free-flowering.* A. mollis *(1) and* A. spinosus *Spinosissimus Group, whose elegant, finely divided foliage is an asset in any garden, produce fewer flowers.*

Conditioning *Beware of the long, sharp spikes in the flowers when cutting and arranging. Plunge the stem ends into boiling water for 20 seconds and they will last for up to two weeks in water.*

Cultivation *Plant acanthus in groups of three or five in spring, and protect the crowns with a mulch in the first winter. They may take a year or two to settle in and start flowering, so be patient. Acanthus will grow in shade, but for lots of flower spikes choose a site with deep, well-drained, fertile soil in full sun where its roots can bake. They can become invasive and, once established, their long, thonglike roots are difficult to eradicate.*

Propagate acanthus from root cuttings in winter (see page 43) or by division in fall or early spring (see pages 37 and 41).

Lady's mantle
ALCHEMILLA MOLLIS

Deciduous perennial Zones: 4–7
Height: 12–20in (30–50cm)

Good varieties for cutting
A. mollis *(2), with its acid-green, light and frothy flowers and downy foliage, is the bread and butter of the summer florist: it is a robust and long-lasting cut flower. The bright plateaux of green make perfect foreground foliage with any combination. This is the diplomat among flowers; you can mix it with any and everything.*

Use it in a pretty, country-style bunch with love-in-a-mist flowers and seed heads, blue and white cornflowers, white sweet peas, and snapdragons. Better still, use its vibrant color as a contrast to other bright and resonant tones. Mix it in a tightly tied posy with Viticella *clematis 'Royal Velours',* C. *'Rouge Cardinal', or* C. *'Jackmanii', Cosmos 'Versailles Carmine', and bright orange and yellow, tissue-paper Iceland poppies. The intensity of the green, rich crimson, deep carmine, yellow, and orange will make even those usually blind to the power of flowers stop in their tracks.*

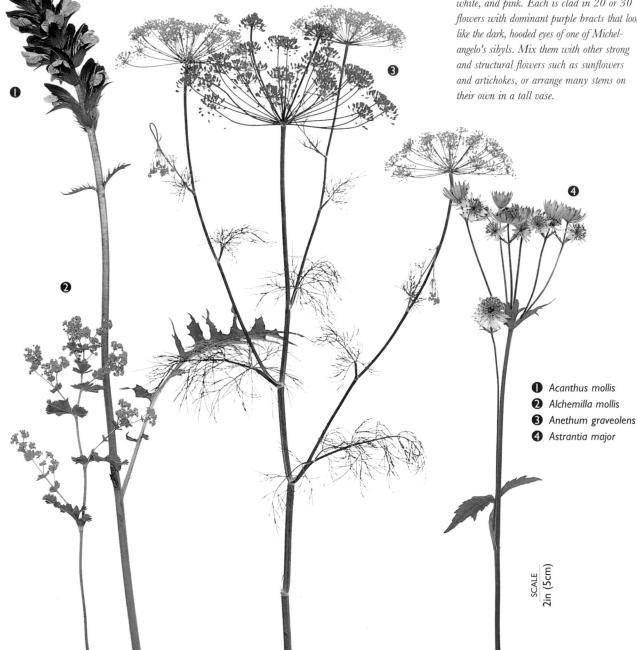

❶ *Acanthus mollis*
❷ *Alchemilla mollis*
❸ *Anethum graveolens*
❹ *Astrantia major*

SCALE
2in (5cm)

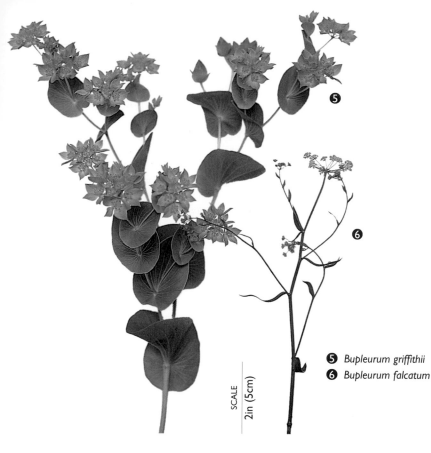

5 *Bupleurum griffithii*
6 *Bupleurum falcatum*

SCALE
2in (5cm)

Alchemilla is also ideally suited for using in oasis. The density of the flower heads will quickly cover up the ugly green blocks of foam. I use it and hornbeam seed cases as the foliage in a summer swag (see pages 64–67), where combined with blue cornflowers, lavender, and poppies they last for three or four days if kept out of the sun.

Conditioning *To prolong their cut life, give them a good drink before arranging.*

Cultivation *Alchemilla is easy to grow, and will thrive in all but boggy soils. It looks its best en masse, lining the sides of a path, rather than dotted throughout the garden. Plant in sun or partial shade. As the flowers lose their brightness in late summer, cut the plants to the ground. They will soon be covered in fresh, fluffy foliage and you may get a second flush of smaller blooms.*

Alchemilla will spread rapidly and readily, starting from only a few plants. It self-seeds promiscuously into any nook and cranny and these seedlings can be gathered up and replanted to flower the following year. What is more, a small plant will reach a good size by the end of one growing season, and can be divided into two or even three small plants in fall or early spring (see pages 37 and 41).

Dill
ANETHUM GRAVEOLENS
Hardy annual
Height: 2–5ft (60cm–1.5m)
Good varieties for cutting
Grow dill, A. graveolens (3), in as large a quantity as space allows. A native wheat-field plant of southern Europe and North and South America, it is an elegant and striking filler in the garden, and invaluable in any bunch of flowers. The tiny individual florets combine into light and fluffy yellow-green umbrellas, which give a lift to any arrangement. Mix it, as your primary foliage, with startling oranges and blues, with whites and greens, or best of all as a stark contrast to the rich Venetian colors of carmine, crimson, purple, and lapis-lazuli.

Conditioning *Strip all but the top leaves, and plunge the cut stem ends into boiling water for 20 seconds. It will then last for about 10 days in water.*

Cultivation *Plant small plants 8–10in (20–25cm) apart. Dill will thrive in any poor, well-drained soil in full sun as long as you water the plants well initially, and keep them moist and well weeded until they become established. Cutting makes for bushy, vigorous plants, and prevents them from*

going to seed, but will exhaust them in the end. Repeat sowings or plantings, every three to four weeks, are needed for a good supply.

Propagate from seed sown in situ in thick lines or blocks in the garden (see page 35). The seeds are large, so can be placed individually before being lightly covered with soil. Thin to 8–10in (20–25cm) apart in each direction, and provide some support using stakes (see page 37).

For early flowers, sow under cover in early spring, using pots or single-cell insets (see page 33). Do not sow in seed flats because dill does not like being transplanted. Space the seed evenly in your pot, or sow four per compartment, and then cover them with perlite. Germination takes two to four weeks. Wait until the risk of frost is minimal before planting outdoors.

Dill is another promiscuous self-seeder and may become a menace. If you fail to pick the flower heads for the house, you should cut them down before the seeds ripen and disperse. Keep dill and fennel separate, or they will cross-pollinate.

Masterwort
ASTRANTIA
Deciduous perennial Zones: 5–7
Height: 2ft (60cm)
Good varieties for cutting
This highly sculptural, dagger-petaled flower resembles those stylized plants often seen in illuminated medieval manuscripts. It has an elegance and presence that add character to any bunch of flowers. Each astrantia flower is in fact a collection of many, surrounded by a collar of jagged bracts. Mix the green and white A. major (4) simply with golden-yellow-centered Lilium regale. The over-powering scent of the lilies will drown the astrantia's slight musty smell, and the pointed petals of the two together make a beautiful filigree pattern. Alternatively, try it with lady's mantle and the heavy-headed scented pink roses R. gallica 'Versicolor' (Rosa Mundi) and R. 'Fritz Nobis'. There is also an excellent, large, white-flowered form, A.m. subsp. involucrata 'Shaggy' ('Margery Fish'), which is showier than the rest. This is useful for bridesmaids' bunches and bridal bouquets.

Conditioning *Give the stems a long drink in tepid water.*

Cultivation *Astrantias are extremely rewarding and easy to grow. Plant A. major in groups of three in part shade or full sun in a moist position.*

These vigorous plants spread by under-ground runners and are easily propagated by division after only one or two growing seasons (see pages 37 and 41). Buy a small number of the varieties you want and increase your stock from these, but keep them apart because they are self-seeding and will interbreed freely.

BUPLEURUM
Annual, perennial, and evergreen shrub
Zones: B. fruticosum 7–9;
B. falcatum 4–9
Height and spread: B. griffithii 20in × 12in (50cm × 30cm); B. falcatum 3ft × 2ft (90cm × 60cm); B. fruticosum 5ft × 5ft (1.5m × 1.5m)

Good varieties for cutting *The star of this genus and a superb plant for cutting is the hardy annual B. griffithii (5). Its domes of flat, bright green flowers, with 15 or 20 to every stem, provide some of the best foreground foliage you can grow. They last for up to two weeks in water, and give a perfect relaxed structure into which you can poke flowers of any color to make a beautiful and informal bunch. Combine B. griffithii with bishop's flower and bells of Ireland as your foliage and then add sweet peas, sweet Williams, poppies, and trumpet or martagon lilies. It is not strong enough to balance heavy-headed plants like sunflowers, artichokes, or dahlias, but is the perfect foil for almost anything else.*

The perennial bupleurum, B. falcatum (6), is less robust and showy but is also good when cut. Its smaller, yellow-green heads resemble a miniature version of dill and, like dill, it combines well with the deep clarets and carmines of Cosmos bipinnatus 'Versailles Carmine', the beautiful roses 'Nuits de Young' and 'Souvenir du Docteur Jamain', and richly colored stocks (see page 70).

Later in the year, the shrubby evergreen B. fruticosum also comes into its own. The flowers, which are coarser than those of

B. griffithii, *are very attractive to insects, so it is best to avoid using them when they are fully open. I cut the buds and the seed heads for late-summer and fall arrangements.*
Cultivation *These are sun-loving plants.* B. griffithii *should be grown in large quantities and will thrive in any good, well-drained soil in full sun.* B. falcatum *should be planted in a clump of three at the front of the border in mid-fall or mid-spring. It will thrive in any ordinary soil.*

I B. fruticosum *is large, and you will not pick it in great quantities, so plant only one.*

It is slightly tender and will benefit from a warm site, ideally with the shelter of a wall. Cut it back periodically after flowering so it does not get too woody.

B. griffithii *should be sown in situ in mid-spring (see pages 34 and 35). Keep it well watered, and once fully established keep picking to promote the growth of laterals to help the plant to bush out. It does not respond well to transplanting.*

B. falcatum *should be propagated from seed sown in a cold frame in mid-spring, and* B. fruticosum *either from seed or from*

① Cynara cardunculus Scolymus Group
② Eryngium alpinum 'Amethyst'
③ Eryngium giganteum
④ Euphorbia lathyris
⑤ Euphorbia schillingii
⑥ Euphorbia seguieriana

semi-ripe cuttings in late summer (see pages 38 and 39).

Cardoon, globe artichoke
CYNARA
Main entry: Summer Blue and Purple, page 132. *The edible buds of the globe artichoke,* C. cardunculus *Scolymus Group* (**1**)*, make perfect strong foreground foliage to complement intense colors like scarlets and oranges (see page 73) or heavy-headed sunflowers, 'Casa Blanca' lilies, and dahlias.*

Sea holly
ERYNGIUM
Biennial and perennial, some evergreen
Zones: Onopordum acanthium *6–10;* Eryngium planum *5–9;* E. alpinum, E. × tripartitum, E. × zabelii *5–8*
Height: E. × tripartitum *24–30in (60–75cm);* E. × zabelii, E. alpinum, E. planum *30–36in (75–90cm);* E. giganteum *4ft (1.2m);* Onopordum acanthium *8ft (2.5m)*

Good varieties for cutting
Eryngiums rank with spurges, poppies, sunflowers, and Parrot tulips as my favorite plants for cutting and for the garden. The sculpted heads in steely gray or rich royal blue are hard to beat. They are sympathetic mixers, combining well with a wide range of flowers, but can also be head-turning primadonnas, holding center stage. Grow them and grow lots of them.

Among the best are the biennial or, more accurately, short-lived perennial Miss Willmott's ghost (E. giganteum*) (**3**), and the new* E.g. *'Silver Ghost'. These may take some years to flower, and will then die, scattering their seed. Their statuesque silver flowers are the perfect foil to several stems of heavy-headed lilies, like* Lilium *'Casa Blanca'. Other fine sculptural beauties are the indigo-blue, spiky flowers of* E. × zabelii *'Violetta' (see page 133) and the similar-*

structured, largest-flowered eryngium, E. alpinum (**2**)*. Mix these with poppy seed heads, bupleurum, orange and yellow Peruvian lilies, and eremurus spikes, all contrasted to the sumptuous deep-purple of lisianthus. The smaller-headed* E. planum *and* E. × tripartitum *are also excellent.* E. × tripartitum *flowers right through the summer and into fall, and its dominant, fluffy, blue center and spiky ruff look good with almost any color.*

Another fabulous plant is the Scotch thistle, Onopordum acanthium. *It is invaluable for huge arrangements and lasts over two weeks in water.*

Conditioning *Give eryngiums a long drink in deep tepid water.*

Cultivation *Eryngiums thrive and color best in full sun. They are easy-going about soil type and will even grow with excessive lime and in poor stony soils. Most like some moisture but, being tap-rooted, they dislike becoming cold and waterlogged, so always introduce plenty of grit on planting.* E. alpinum *will tolerate some shade, but at the price of good deep blue coloring. Plant them in groups of three to five in spring or fall.*

The results from seed are unreliable, so if you have a good color form, propagation from root cuttings in winter (see page 43) is safest. If you propagate from seed, sow as soon as you have gathered the seeds in fall. Sow in shallow pans of light soil, and put them into a cold frame to let the frost get to them. The seed germination of eryngiums is slow: seedlings may take two years to appear. Plant them outdoors before the tap root develops significantly.

E. giganteum, *which dies after flowering, is a free self-seeder. It can often be successfully introduced into a garden by a random sprinkling of fresh seed gathered from a friend. Alternatively, beg a young seedling or two and wait for them to colonize your garden. Learn to recognize the seedlings to avoid weeding them out before they flower.*

Spurge, milkweed
EUPHORBIA
Main entry: Spring Green and Silver, page 96. *Euphorbias are the jewel in the crown for the flower arranger. In summer,*

E. sikkimensis *is the first to flower. This is followed by* E. schillingii (**5**), *which will carry on well into fall. Their spreading, acid-green flower heads are the perfect foil for any tall and stately bunch.* E. seguieriana (**6**), *a compact delicate plant, is invaluable for the smaller summer posy. Another must is the primeval-looking, biennial caper spurge,* E. lathyris (**4**), *with its deep hooded eyes arranged regularly up the stem.*

Bells of Ireland, shell flower
MOLUCCELLA
Half-hardy annual
Height: M. laevis *2–3ft (60–90cm);* M. laevis *'Long Spike' 3–4ft (90cm–1.2m)*
Good varieties for cutting
M. laevis (**9**), *another top ranked annual cutting plant, should be grown in as large a quantity as space allows. These towering, curling, and curving spikes of vivid green chalices, intricately veined with cream,* provide an invaluable tall and elegant final touch for almost any arrangement. Place five to seven spikes of them to break up symmetry and add vertical emphasis to any neat dome of flowers. The handsome 'Long Spike' form of *M. laevis is particularly good.*
Conditioning *Remove the lower leaves and any side branches – the brittle stems break easily at these junctions so take great care. Give them a long cool drink.*
Cultivation *This plant grows easily in full sun in rich, well-drained soil. Provide a network of twigs to support the stems. If they collapse, they will regrow upright toward the light, but you will have lost some height.*

Sow seed under cover while it is still cool (55–60°F/13–15°C) in mid-spring. Thin when large enough to handle, and gradually harden off for planting outdoors once there is minimal risk of frost. Or sow into a seed bed outside in late spring for late-summer and fall cutting.

7 *Nicotiana 'Lime Green'*
8 *Paeonia variety*
9 *Moluccella laevis*
10 *Stachys byzantina*

SCALE
2in (5cm)

SCALE
2in (5cm)

Flowering tobacco
NICOTIANA
Main entry: Fall White, page 139. *The pale chartreuse-green N. 'Lime Green' (**7**) is a long, elegant flower. In texture and tone it is the perfect complement to any of the rich ecclesiastical colors, or to vibrant scarlets and oranges (see page 73). It lasts for up to two weeks in water.*

Peony
PAEONIA
Main entry: Spring Pink, page 105. *Many of the peonies have interesting and dramatic seed heads, like the three-pointed jester's caps shown here (**8**). They combine well with any strong and sculptural summer and early-fall flowers.*

Lamb's ears, rabbit's ears
STACHYS
Perennial and subshrub, some evergreen
Zones: 4–9
Height: S. byzantina *12–15in (30–38cm) (flowering spikes may reach 3ft/90cm)*
Good varieties for cutting
S. byzantina *(syn.* S. lanata, S. olympica*) is an evergreen, furry, silver-leaved plant with spreading velvety rosettes (**10**). It throws up* tall spikes of tiny magenta flowers swaddled in the softest, woolliest of leaves throughout summer. These look just like floppy lamb's ears. In the garden, stachys makes an excellent traditional group with lady's mantle and alliums for carpeting the ground beneath old roses. Cut the flowering spikes and use them as your foliage in hand-tied posies, or in little bunches for the bedside (see page 70). Or make a silver velvet frame to encircle a bridesmaid's bouquet. The taller, more robust forms, are extremely useful in larger arrangements.
Conditioning *Strip the bottom leaves and give the spikes a good drink in shallow water, taking care not to overwet the foliage.*
Cultivation *These plants are easy to grow in any well-drained soil and are particularly tolerant of poor soils. Mass them along a path or beneath your roses, choosing an open site in full sun. They can look moth-eaten as the year progresses, so cut them back after flowering in early fall. Lots of fresh growth will soon appear.*

Propagate S. byzantina *by division (see pages 37 and 41). This is a vigorous plant that spreads rapidly by furry offshoots, and so it can be divided after only one growing season. It will also self-seed freely.*

White

AGAPANTHUS

Main entry: Summer Blue and Purple, page 130. *The white-tinged-pink pompon A. campanulatus var. albidus (1) looks lovely in a arrangement of long stems on their own, or with white lilies and peony seed heads.*

Bishop's flower
AMMI MAJUS

Hardy annual
Height: 2–4ft (60cm–1.2m)

Good varieties for cutting *Bishop's flower, A. majus (2), is the florist's cow parsley. Like Solomon's seal or guelder rose, its tall, lacy flowers transform any bunch into a light, airy arrangement. Cut short, it mixes with love-in-a-mist, cornflowers, sweet peas, poppies, and snapdragons. It is also a beauty arranged on its own, 10 to 15 stems cut to their full length in a waisted glass vase for the centerpiece on a large table. Use it, too, in stylish yet simple pompons for a summer party. Cut the stems to 12–18in (30–45cm) to cover oasis globes to hang from the ceiling.*

Conditioning *Strip all the bottom leaves and some of the higher ones, since they will yellow way before the flowers begin to age.*

Cultivation *This is an easy plant to grow in full sun. It needs plenty of water and will flower for many weeks if it is regularly picked and not allowed to run to seed. For 3–4ft (90cm–1.2m) plants, sow in fall directly into the flowering position. The plants overwinter well and you will have flowers to pick by late spring. For smaller plants, sow in the flowering site in mid-spring. Bishop's flower self-seeds freely so transplant the seedlings into beds or rows.*

Snapdragon
ANTIRRHINUM

Main entry: Summer Orange and Red, page 125. *The cottage-garden snapdragon A. majus 'White Wonder', (3) with its large, white, flaxlike flowers, is a great mixer for any simple pretty bunch.*

Monarch of the veldt, Namaqualand daisy
ARCTOTIS FASTUOSA

Main entry: Summer Orange and Red, page 125. *The chocolate and orange centers of the pale creamy white daisies A. fastuosa 'Zulu Prince' (4) look like patterns on a butterfly's wings. Their stems tend to be quite floppy, so they are best poked into an arrangement only at the end, when the other flowers and foliage can lend support to hold their heads up high.*

Bellflower
CAMPANULA

Main entry: Summer Blue and Purple, page 131. *The clear white, virginal bells of campanula C. persicifolia var. alba (5) are useful and long-lasting. Mix them with white foxgloves, yellow roses, deep purple lisianthus, and sprays of dill for wedding posies.*

COSMOS

Half-hardy annual and tuberous perennial
Zones: C. atrosanguineus 6–9
Height: C. atrosanguineus 2ft (60cm); C. bipinnatus 4ft (1.2m)

Good varieties for cutting *The annual cosmos is definitely among the plants that best earn their keep in the cutting garden. These tall bushy annuals flower and flower, providing cut flowers of sumptuous colors and fragile texture from late spring until the first hard frost. Grow C. bipinnatus 'Purity' (6), whose crinkled, saucer-shaped flowers mix with everything, and the deep carmine-pink C.b. 'Versailles Carmine' (see page 126). Put them on their own in a pitcher on a windowsill, where their thin petals will catch the light.*

1 *Agapanthus campanulatus* var. *albidus*
2 *Ammi majus*
3 *Antirrhinum* majus 'White Wonder'
4 *Arctotis fastuosa* 'Zulu Prince'
5 *Campanula persicifolia* var. *alba*

SCALE
2in (5cm)

From late summer through fall, the deep claret-crimson tender perennial C. atrosanguineus, *the chocolate-smelling cosmos, comes into flower (see page 142).*
Conditioning *Give these robust, long-lasting flowers a good cool drink.*
Cultivation *Cosmos like full sun and a moist but well-drained soil. The annuals thrive with regular top-dressing, watering, and picking. In mild areas, tubers of half-hardy* C. atrosanguineus *may be overwintered in the ground if protected with a deep mulch. In more severe climates, lift them and store them as for tender tubers (see page 42). Start them into growth in the greenhouse and plant in early summer.*

Propagate annuals from seed in early spring. Sow under cover in some heat. Thin them when they are large enough to handle and gradually reduce the heat. Transfer to cold frames and plant out once there is little risk of frost (see page 35). Propagate the chocolate cosmos from basal cuttings in spring or from semi-ripe cuttings in late summer (see pages 34, 36, and 39).

DELPHINIUM
Main entry: Summer Blue and Purple, page 132. *Any of the towering white delphiniums (7) are beautiful for cutting, and the more you pick, the more the laterals are encouraged to develop and flower. Use them in a stately white arrangement, or mix with royal and deep blue delphiniums.*

Foxglove
DIGITALIS
Biennial and perennial, some evergreen
Zones: 4–8
Height: D. grandiflora *2½ft (75cm);*
D. purpurea *varieties 3–5ft (90cm–1.5m)*
Good varieties for cutting *Much as I love* D. purpurea, *the biennial common foxglove, I find its plum-pink a harsh and difficult color to combine with other flowers, but there are many other stately foxglove species and cultivars that are perfect for cutting. Best of all is the pure white* D.p. f. albiflora *(9), with its great spikes of massed hanging bells, for an all-white, virginal piece. Cut it short and use its soft, velvety texture to complement deep crimson*

and claret snapdragons, stocks, and sweet Williams, with blue thistles, anchusas, and viper's bugloss. Or mix it with foxgloves from D. Excelsior Group *(8). The smaller and finer, yellow perennial* D. grandiflora *is also good as a cut flower.*
Conditioning *When you cut foxgloves, put them into a deep pail of tepid water and leave for several hours before arranging. They will then last for over a week. The bottom flowers will brown or drop before the top buds have developed and opened. Remove any flowers hanging on by the stigma.*
Cultivation *The biennials grow best in semi-shade and acidic, humus-rich, moist but well-drained soil; but they will tolerate most conditions, even pebble beaches, though there they will grow to only half the height. Plant clumps of 10 to 15 if you have room in your garden; otherwise, grow them in a row. The perennial forms like sun but will take some light summer shade. They dislike cold, wet weather. Prolong the picking season by cutting the center spike: this promotes the growth and flowering of the lateral branches.*

Sow the fine seed of biennials under glass in late spring or early summer (see pages 32-34). Do not cover with potting mix. Thin out at an early stage and plant in a seed bed for the rest of the summer. Transplant to the final flowering position in fall. They self-seed freely, but some will revert to the colored wild form. Pull out any seedlings with red stems if you want to grow white flowers.

Fireweed, willow herb
EPILOBIUM
Herbaceous perennial Zones: 3–7
Height: 5ft (1.5m)
Good varieties for cutting *The pink fireweed,* E. angustifolium, *which covers many a highway and railroad cut, is too leggy and invasive a plant for the cutting garden. But the white form,* E.a. 'Album' *(10), with its wandlike white flower spikes, has a haunting and ethereal air. It is very*

good for bulking white and green arrangements (see page 72).
Conditioning *Strip the lower leaves and sear the stem ends in boiling water for 20 seconds, before giving them a long cool drink.*
Cultivation *Plant in sun or shade, where it will quickly spread to brighten a corner. It prefers a moist but well-drained soil.*

Propagate by softwood cuttings of side shoots in spring (see page 39).

⑥ *Cosmos bipinnatus* 'Purity'
⑦ *Delphinium*
⑧ *Digitalis* Excelsior Group
⑨ *Digitalis purpurea* f. *albiflora*
⑩ *Epilobium angustifolium* 'Album'

SCALE
2in (5cm)

SCALE
2in (5cm)

Sweet pea, everlasting pea
LATHYRUS

Hardy annual and perennial climber
Zones: L. latifolius *5–9*
Height: L. chloranthus *5–8ft (1.5–2.5m);*
L. latifolius, L. odoratus *10ft (3m)*

Good varieties for cutting *Everyone is cheered by the scent of the sweet pea,* L. odoratus. *Grow monotone groups of your favorite colors over elegant hazel wigwams in a flower border, and a color razzmatazz in a sunny corner of the vegetable patch to fill a simple pitcher of clanging and clashing reds, mauves, pinks, blues, and whites. White sweet peas such as 'White Supreme'* (1) *mix well in any country-style bunch with lark-spur, lady's mantle, and cornflowers. I grow the deep claret-black 'Pageantry' mixed with the bicolored purple and carmine* L.o. *'Matucana' (see pages 70 and 134) and the handsome but unscented, lime-green* L. chloranthus *'Lemonade'.*

In fall, when your scented sweet peas are over, the long-flowering everlasting pea, L. latifolius, *is useful with silver foliage of wormwood and pale blue bog sage.*

Conditioning *Avoid direct sunlight and heat, which ages sweet peas rapidly.*

Cultivation *Sweet peas like a deep, humus-rich, well-drained soil in full sun. Soak seed for annuals overnight before sowing into tree pots (see page 33). Sow in early fall under cold glass if you want to have strong and*

sturdy plants for putting out in early spring. Or sow them in late winter in some heat, and plant them as soon as they begin to bulk up. They can also be sown in situ in spring. Always pinch back the leading shoot once you have one pair of true leaves. Remove climbing tendrils and tie the main stem into your framework as it grows. This will give you nice long strong stems for cutting. Do not let sweet peas set seed – pick any seed pods where you have missed cutting the flowers.

Grow perennials from seed sown in fall, or by division in spring. Cut them down to the ground in late fall.

Lily
LILIUM

Bulb Zones: 4–8
Height: L. *'Fire King',* L. longiflorum *3ft (90cm);* L. *'Casa Blanca',* L. *Pink Perfection Group,* L. regale *4–5ft (1.2–1.5m);* L. monadelphum *18in–6ft (45cm–1.8m)*

Good varieties for cutting *For a heady and luxurious treat, there is little to beat the pure white 'Casa Blanca' lily. Its huge open blooms, with crinkle-edged petals and burnt-brick-red pollen, exude a sump-tuous, room-filling scent – the stuff seduction scenes are made of. These are a treat in any bunch, but look best simply contrasted with stark, lichen-covered branches to highlight their beauty and drama. Any of the lilies with an Oriental ancestry, like 'Casa Blanca'* (3), *are well worth the expense of the bulb.*

The pure white Easter lily, L. longi-florum, *is used widely by florists for its delicious scent and long life in water, but it is also worth trying more unusual varieties of the elegant, trumpet-shaped lilies.* L. regale (4), *with its alternating deep pink and white outside petals and white with golden center, exudes a perfume to wake Sleeping Beauty. Even better is the dusky, romantic, deep plum hue of Pink Perfection Group – a silken thing of glamor and allure.*

The turkscap lilies, L. martagon *and the similar* L. monadelphum *(syn.* L. szovitsianum*), have intriguing curly, reflexed petals and flowers arranged up the stem like a baroque chandelier (see page 129).*

The coarser, unscented Asiatic lilies are also good cut, though they last less well.

Choose the deep ambers, bright oranges and near-clarets to mix with acid-green for a rich, hot bunch. The oranges, like 'Fire King' (see pages 126 and 127), are also good mixed with blue delphiniums in a hanging globe.

Don't forget the seed heads of lilies, which can look beautiful cut. Pick the seed pods of L. martagon in late summer to mix with delphiniums and dahlias.

1 *Lathyrus odoratus*
   'White Supreme'
2 *Magnolia grandiflora*
3 *Lilium* 'Casa Blanca'
4 *Lilium regale*
5 *Lupinus* Noble
   Maiden Group

Conditioning *When cutting lilies, leave enough stem and foliage to allow for photo-synthesis and food storage to sustain the bulb through winter and spring. Strip the anthers from the stamens before they cover your clothes with their sticky, staining pollen.*

Cultivation *Almost all lilies like a good, free-draining site in full sun, preferably with a cool root-run. Martagon lilies also do well in part shade. When planting, particularly on*

SCALE
2in (5cm)

heavy soils, envelop the bulb in mortar sand, or they will die in wet, cold weather.

Buy your lily bulbs from a reliable source. Experiment with the easiest to grow, like L. regale, and build up your repertoire from there. Choose bulbs that will give you flowers throughout summer. Plant them in good generous clumps, tightly packed, so that you can cut several flowering spikes without depriving your garden. Add humus and a fertilizer rich in potassium and phosphate, like bonemeal, to the soil. Do not use strong nitrogenous fertilizers and manure.

Plant in late summer, very early fall, or spring, 3–6in (8–15cm) deep according to the size of the bulb. Lilies can be left undisturbed for years, and only moved when they become overcrowded.

Lupine
LUPINUS
Main entry: Summer Blue and Purple, page 134. *The white Noble Maiden Group lupine (5), with its tall spikes of solid flowers in continuous whorls, makes a fresh strong addition to either a pure white arrangement or a multicolored array.*

MAGNOLIA
Main entry: Spring White, page 101. *The huge evergreen M. grandiflora (2), with its vast, waxen, frisbee-sized flowers, is slow to flower, but will eventually be covered in luscious, lemon-scented goblets, which you should put in pride of place in a simple silver cup on your table or desk.*

Stock
MATTHIOLA
Main entry: Summer Pink, page 123. *White stock (6) makes an invaluable scented mixer for any country bunch.*

Mock orange
PHILADELPHUS
Deciduous shrub Zones: 5–7
Height and spread: P. 'Dwarf Snowflake', 3–4ft (90cm–1.2m); P. 'Belle Etoile' 5ft × 5ft (1.5m × 1.5m); P. coronarius 10ft × 8ft (3m × 2.5m)
Good varieties for cutting *This family of floriferous, arching shrubs comes in many different shapes and sizes, each one with the most delicious scent. It is hard to choose between them. P. coronarius has the virtue of being among the earliest to flower – plant it to cascade forward from the back of the border. 'Dwarf Snowflake' is a good compact form for the small garden. But of all the philadelphus varieties, those producing white flowers with crimson hearts, like P. 'Belle Etoile' (8), are to me the loveliest. They merit arranging in a vase on their own, but can be cut short and mixed with pinks and deep plum roses to highlight their richly colored centers.*
Conditioning *Hammer the stem ends.*
Cultivation *Plant in sun or semi-shade in any fertile, well-drained soil. Prune shoots to within 1in (2.5cm) of the old wood*

❻ *Matthiola cultivar*
❼ *Phlox paniculata*
❽ *Philadelphus 'Belle Etoile'*
❾ *Rosa mulliganii*

SCALE
2in (5cm)

immediately after flowering. This lightens up the overall structure and encourages new shoots that will flower in one or two years' time. Propagate by layering, or from hard-wood cuttings (see pages 42 and 43).

PHLOX
Annual and perennial Zones: 4–8
Height: P. maculata 3ft (90cm); P. paniculata cultivars 4ft (1.2m)
Good varieties for cutting *The great honey-scented heads of perennial phlox look as if they were made to be waved by cheer-leaders. The slightly smaller, cylindrical-headed P. maculata forms come into flower as summer begins, while P. paniculata (7) varieties come into their own in mid-summer. Grow pure white P.p. 'White Admiral' or P.p. 'Fujiyama' to fill an arrangement of white 'Iceberg' roses, with green dill and deep purple lisianthus. Late-flowerers like 'Fujiyama' can be picked until the end of fall. The purple P. paniculata 'Amethyst' is good in bright resonant mixtures of bupleurum, yellow sunflowers, purple artichokes, scarlet*

lychnis, orange arctotis, and Euphorbia griffithii 'Fireglow'.
Conditioning *Though phlox are long-lasting, some blooms in the flower head will fade after a week. Give the stem a good shake to dislodge any aging flowers and clear the way for the smaller buds to open.*
Cultivation *Grow in full sun or light shade in a fertile, moisture-retentive soil. Stake the plants. Water in the morning to discourage mildew, and divide the clumps regularly. Propagate from softwood cuttings or division in early spring. Replant the divisions at once (see pages 37, 38, and 39).*

Rose
ROSA
Main entry: Summer Pink, page 124. *The climbing rose R. mulliganii (9) has a soft entrancing scent and lovely single flowers. Pale primrose-yellow buds open to clear white, backed by shiny, bottle-green foliage. This is the perfect rose for a simple pitcher in a table centerpiece; or use its lengthy stems for a summer globe (see pages 68–69).*

SCALE
2in (5cm)

Pink

Corncockle
AGROSTEMMA

Hardy annual
Height: 2–3ft (60–90cm)

Good varieties for cutting

The corncockle, A. githago, has delicate, saucer-shaped, pink flower on a tall spindly stem. Combine it in a sheaf or in a wide-necked vase with oats, wheat, or barley, grasses, blue cornflowers, viper's bugloss, scarlet poppies, and buttercups. A. githago 'Milas' (1) is an improved version with slightly larger, 2–3in (5–8cm), pink, saucer-shaped blooms. Mix it with the purple-red form A.g. 'Purple Queen'.

Conditioning *Strip the bottom leaves and give the stems a good long drink.*

Cultivation *Corncockle thrives in full sun in well-drained, not too fertile, soil. Do not fertilize. Always support with a network of sticks, because the fine stems are liable to collapse. Corncockle will self-seed. Propagate by seed sown in situ in spring or early fall. For a good supply do a second sowing two to three weeks later and thin to 6in (15cm).*

Cornflower, knapweed
CENTAUREA

Main entry: Summer Blue and Purple, page 131. *The perennial cornflower C. dealbata 'Steenbergii' (4) has large, Scotch-thistle-style flowers, and is lovely in vibrant multicolored mixtures with oranges, blues, and yellows, or in wild flower arrangements.*

Smokebush, smoke tree
COTINUS

Main entry: Fall Orange and Red, page 142. *The frothy, fluffy flowers of the smoke-bush, Cotinus coggyria (5), form a bright pink haze as they catch the light. Use it as a foliage flower to form a structure into which you can poke intense, saucer- or ball-headed flowers in contrasting colors.*

Pink, carnation, sweet William
DIANTHUS

Annual, biennial, and perennial Zones: 4–8 Height: old-fashioned and laced pinks and modern hybrids 9–12in (23–30cm); D. chinensis, clove carnations 10–14in (25–35cm); D. barbatus 18in (45cm)

Good varieties for cutting *It is difficult to know where to start with this huge genus of excellent cutting flowers, with their almost universal, rich clove scent and durability in water. The sweet Williams, D. barbatus, are the first to bloom. Grow them in jolly-colored panels of pink, white, and crimson, single and bicolored mixtures, with single or double flowers, or in groups of single colors. Of the biennial kinds, there is the small-flowered, highly scented, almost black D. barbatus Nigrescens Group (see pages 132 and 133). Grow also a rich crimson variety and a pure white. Add the deep rich reds to fragrant combinations of claret stocks and snapdragons, contrasted with deep blue anchusas and the velvety bells of white foxgloves. Use D.b. Nigrescens Group in a bedside bunch of sweet peas and roses (see page 70).*

From the huge range of perennial hybrid pinks, choose the taller, larger varieties, which combine well with other flowers or can be arranged on their own. The old-fashioned laced pinks will bloom only at

mid-summer, but there are some irresistible flowers in this group. Two of my favorites, with an intense clove scent, are the double-flowered, pale pink D.b. 'Alice' (2) and the rich crimson, pink-edged D. 'Laced Monarch' (3). For the best scent of all, it is worth growing some of the old clove carnations, which flower in late summer when the pinks are over.

Conditioning *Dianthus are among the longest-lasting cut flowers: they last up to two weeks in water. Just strip the bottom leaves.*

Cultivation *All dianthus like a sunny position, good drainage, and a reasonably alkaline soil. Sow the biennial sweet Williams inside in late spring to plant in a seed bed in summer. Alternatively, sow them directly in the seed bed in early summer and transplant to their flowering position in fall. Annual sweet Williams need sowing early for strong healthy plants.*

The perennial pinks all root easily from

cuttings. Put heeled cuttings into open ground with added sand, or in pots of sandy, cutting starter mix in early fall (see page 42).

Foxglove
DIGITALIS

Main entry: Summer White, page 119. *The D. Excelsior Group (6) contains some lovely, pale pink, plain and spotty foxgloves. Arrange seven to fifteen stems in an explosion of flowers for the centerpiece of a large table.*

GLADIOLUS

Main entry: Fall Orange and Red, page 143. *The carmine flowers of the species gladiolus G. communis subsp. byzantinus (7) are the color of a rich silk sari. For a*

❶ *Agrostemma githago* 'Milas'
❷ *Dianthus barbatus* 'Alice'
❸ *Dianthus* 'Laced Monarch'
❹ *Centaurea dealbata* 'Steenbergii'
❺ *Cotinus coggyria*

stunning contrast, mix with acid-green spurge and spikes of bells of Ireland, purple-blue anchusas, and lisianthus.

Honeysuckle
LONICERA
Evergreen and deciduous shrub and climber
Zones: L. splendida *9–10;*
L. periclymenum *5–9;* L. × brownii,
L. sempervirens *4–9*
Height: 13–20ft (4–6m)
Good varieties for cutting *The way honeysuckle twists and turns about an arrangement, disturbing symmetry and tidiness, is, in my view, reason enough to grow lots. Add to that the sweet spicy scent filling the evening or early-morning air and they are* irresistible. *If you have room, grow a selection of two or three scented varieties to flower at different times. Choose one of the yellows, one of the pinky reds, and perhaps one of the rich intense oranges. Avoid the most rampant (*L. japonica *or* L. henryi*), for the flowers will soon be out of reach of your nose and your pruners. Of the yellows, grow* L. periclymenum *'Graham Thomas' (see page 129). All the* periclymenum *varieties have the bonus of shiny red berries in the fall, along with a straggle of flowers.*

The deep carmine-pink and yellow L. periclymenum *'Serotina'* (**9**) *is the strongest scented of all the honeysuckles, and has a very long flowering season, from mid-summer to mid-fall. Combine it with* Cosmos pinnatus *'Versailles Carmine' and green dill for a light and fragrant bunch. During winter, the highly fragrant shrub honeysuckles such as* Lonicera × purpusii *come into their own (see page 157).*

Cultivation *Plant honeysuckles in sun or part shade. They are not fussy about soil, but, like clematis, they need a cool root-run. Enrich the soil with organic matter, keep it moist in summer, and give an annual mulch of leaf mold. On planting, it is worth shortening the main stems in order to promote early branching and ultimately create the maximum possible spread. Once this is achieved, regular pruning is not necessary, although it is worth periodically pruning out the flowered wood of the climbing forms. For summer-flowerers, do this after flowering; with plants that flower in fall, wait until early spring.*

Propagate by semi-ripe cuttings in summer, or by hardwood cuttings in late fall (see pages 38, 39, and 42).

Stock
MATTHIOLA
Annual, biennial, and perennial Zones 5–7
Height: M. incana *Brompton Group and white perennial matthiola 18in (45cm);*
M.i. *Giant Imperial Group and Giant Excelsior Group 24–30in (60–75cm)*
Good varieties for cutting *The heady, warm, clovelike scent of stocks* (**8**) *reminds me of balmy summer evenings. Plant them in clumps around a garden seat or by*

6 *Digitalis* Excelsior Group
7 *Gladiolus communis* subsp. *byzantinus*
8 *Matthiola* cultivar
9 *Lonicera periclymenum* 'Serotina'

your kitchen window so you can enjoy their wafting perfume, getting stronger and stronger into the night. The dark smoky purple-pink and rich wine-red varieties of annuals and biennials are the most striking for cutting. Mark the good color forms and collect seed from them for sowing the next year. Combine them with bright acid-greens and oranges for a rich glowing bunch of flowers (see page 70).

Grow, too, the pure white varieties in any of the giant forms, like the annual Giant Imperial or Giant Excelsior Groups. You can always cut down a tall stem but cannot elongate a short one. The bushy white perennial stock, with its white flowers held on short stems set against a mound of gray leaves, is useful for small scented bedside posies. Stocks are best in a mixture with other cut flowers, since their value is in their scent rather than their appearance.

Conditioning *Strip all leaves below the water line. These would taint the water quickly and exude a pungent smell.*

Cultivation *Plant stocks in sun or semi-shade in fertile, well-drained, ideally lime-rich soil. Sow seeds of annuals under glass in late winter or in situ outdoors in mid-spring. Sow biennials, like the Brompton stocks, in frames in high summer to flower the following spring. Sow seeds of perennials under glass in spring (see pages 32–34).*

SCALE
2in (5cm)

SCALE
2in (5cm)

Rose
ROSA

Deciduous and semi-evergreen shrub and climber Zones: 6–10 except: R. mulliganii 5–10; R. 'Souvenir du Docteur Jamain', 6–9; 'Cardinal de Richelieu', R. 'Charles de Mills', R. gallica 'Versicolor', R. moyesii 'Geranium', R. 'Nevada', R. 'Nuits de Young', R. 'Tuscany Superb', R. xanthina 'Canary Bird' 5–9; R. glauca 4–9

Height and spread: R. 'Iceberg' 3ft × 2ft (90cm × 60cm); R. 'Cardinal de Richelieu', R. 'Charles de Mills', R. 'Felicia', R. gallica 'Versicolor', R. 'Heritage', R. 'Nuits de Young', R. 'Tuscany Superb' 4ft × 4ft (1.2m × 1.2m); R. 'Fritz Nobis', R. 'Graham Thomas' 5ft × 4ft (1.5m × 1.2m); R. glauca, R. 'Nevada', R. xanthina 'Canary Bird', R. moyesii 'Geranium' 8ft × 6ft (2.5m × 1.8m) R. 'New Dawn', R. 'Souvenir du Docteur

❶ *Rosa* 'Charles de Mills'
❷ *Rosa* 'Fritz Nobis'
❸ *Rosa gallica* 'Versicolor'
❹ *Rosa* 'Nuits de Young'

Jamain', 10ft × 8ft (3m × 2.5m); R. mulliganii 15ft × 10ft (4.5m × 3m)

Good varieties for cutting *Choose roses that are irresistible to you on grounds of color or scent, but check that they will last in water. I would choose any of the deep rich chocolate-crimsons or deep purples, such as 'Cardinal de Richelieu', or even better those with golden-yellow centers and enveloping perfume, such as 'Nuits de Young' (**4**) or 'Tuscany Superb', which has the color and texture of the most luxurious, silk-velvet, gold-leaf brocaded curtain. Also grow a rich deep pink like the vibrant intense 'Charles de Mills' (**1**). 'Fritz Nobis' (**2**) is another wonderfully sumptuous rose, with more open flowers and less dense petals. I have a passion for the old-fashioned, striped, bi-colored roses. Grow R. gallica 'Versicolor' ('Rosa Mundi') (**3**), the oldest of all, with its carmine and pink dapples and stripes. It is excellent for cutting.*

Arrange any of these on their own in a shallow rose bowl, with a pin-holder for support, or combine them with other regal velvet beauties. Choose, too, some easy-to-grow, hard-working, scented roses, which flower over long periods. Pure white 'Iceberg' is a superb productive rose, which flowers from summer to winter.

There are three pale pink roses, 'New Dawn', 'Felicia', and the modern English rose 'Heritage', which fit into this category, too. They all pick well, flower from early summer until the first frost, require minimal care, and have good scent. For a similar, hard-working, yellow rose, try the modern English rose 'Graham Thomas' (see page 146). 'Souvenir du Docteur Jamain' is another good rose, and one of the most sumptuous in color and scent. It will flower for many months, well into fall.

If you have room, grow a vigorous, early-flowering rose for spring picking. The cream rose 'Nevada' and primrose-yellow R. xanthina 'Canary Bird' will both be in flower by mid- to late spring and are rampant enough to take some heavy picking. Fill a pitcher with several twisting and turning boughs and place it as the centerpiece on a large table.

If you have a wall or pergola, think of growing one of the summer-flowering, single Rambler roses. R. mulliganii, with its yellow buds and simple white flowers, is

ideal and not too rampant (see page 121). In fall R. moyesii 'Geranium' (see pages 144 and 145) and R. glauca are both excellent to cut for their elegant hips.

Conditioning *Always cut the stem ends of roses at a sharp angle, revealing more of the pithy stem center that absorbs water. This increases the surface area for drinking. Plunge the cut ends in boiling water for 20 seconds, before giving them a long drink in tepid water (see page 48).*

Cultivation *All the roses named above are easy to grow and will tolerate even the poorest soil. Most prefer full sun and all like a moist but well-drained position. If you buy bare-rooted plants, make sure that you dig a hole large enough to accommodate all the roots without cramping. Place the bush in the hole with the union (the point where the shoots join the rootstock) about 1in (2.5cm) below the soil level. Replace the soil in two or three stages, shaking it down and treading firmly with the heel each time. Top-dress with bonemeal. Avoid planting where roses have been grown before, since rose-specific diseases may be harbored in the soil.*

In late winter or early spring, apply a balanced fertilizer and a mulch of manure. Roses benefit from a monthly fertilizer in spring and summer. Deadhead repeat-flowerers. Propagate by semi-ripe cuttings in summer (see pages 38 and 39) or hardwood cuttings in winter (see page 43).

SCALE
2in (5cm)

Orange and Red

Peruvian lily
ALSTROEMERIA

Tuberous perennial Zones: 7–10
Height: A. ligtu hybrids 20–30in
(50–75cm); large-flowered A. aurea
hybrids 2–3ft (60–90cm)

Good varieties for cutting *When I
first started arranging flowers I used to avoid
alstroemerias, just because they are such a
common ingredient of florists' bunches. This
was misguided: they are popular for the good
reasons that they have a long flowering
season, come in a good medley of colors, and
last very well in water. They are well worth
growing. Start by selecting named varieties*

from among the listed, tall, large-flowered A.
aurea hybrids, which are raised for the cut-
flower trade. I would choose a deep resonant
orange for flamboyance and a white for
calmer, quieter bunches. The hardier A. ligtu
hybrids (**1**) have smaller flowers and shorter
stems but come in a range of rich deep pinks,
corals, oranges, buffs, and yellows.

Conditioning *Give them a good long
drink of tepid water.*

Cultivation *Alstroemerias may be
difficult to establish. Plant groups of three to
five in sites of rich, well-drained soil in full
sun. They spread by underground fleshy roots
and if happy may become invasive, so plant
them in a spot where you will not mind if
they run riot. In cold winters, protect the roots
with a good mulch of dry garden compost.*

*Propagate alstroemerias by division or if
possible by seed, since they do not enjoy
disturbance (some A. aurea hybrids do not
set seed, so must be propagated by division).*

Snapdragon
ANTIRRHINUM

*Perennial and semi-evergreen subshrub,
usually grown as an annual Zones: 5–9
Height: dwarf cultivars, e.g.* A. majus
*'Black Prince', 18in (45cm); tall cultivars,
e.g.* A. Forerunner Series, 36in (90cm)

Good varieties for cutting *The
cottage-garden snapdragon always reminds
me of old-fashioned English gardens. Antirrhinums can look handsome and regal, if the
right colors are chosen. Grow the aptly
named A. majus 'Black Prince' (**2**), with its
tall spikes of deep chocolate-crimson and
dark foliage. An arrangement of 15 to 20
stems on their own is an impressive sight,
but this snapdragon also combines well with
other rich and velvety flowers. The white
cultivar A.m. 'White Wonder' is another
fine one (see page 118). There are taller
varieties, but while many of these would be
good for cutting, they are rarely available as
single colors. The Rocket or Forerunner
Series antirrhinums, which reach 36in
(90cm), are excellent. Avoid the dwarf
forms, because the stems are too short to be
useful for cutting, and certainly avoid the
doubles, which confuse the lovely and simple
"snap" structure of the top and bottom lip.*

Conditioning *Strip the bottom leaves
and give the stems a long drink.*

Cultivation *Nurseries and garden centers
sell flats of snapdragons, but they are usually
of mixed colors. It is better to sow your own.
Treat them as half-hardy annuals and sow
under glass or in a plant incubator in late
winter (see pages 32–34). Don't pinch back
the main stems of your seedlings if you want
nice tall stems for cutting. Plant in pre-
fertilized ground once there is little risk of
frost: snapdragons need sun and rich, well-
drained soil. Plant closer than the seed
packet directs so that a little competition for
light helps the plants to maximize their
height. Water and pick antirrhinums regularly and they will flower well into fall. In a
sheltered spot they may come through the
winter, and you will have bigger, if woodier,
plants for next year. However, older snapdragons are more susceptible to rust fungus.*

Monarch of the veldt,
Namaqualand daisy
ARCTOTIS FASTUOSA

*Half-hardy annual and perennial
Zones: 9–10
Height: 24in (60cm)*

Good varieties for cutting *The
bright orange South African daisy A.
fastuosa (syn. Venidium fastuosum) is
like a marigold dolled up for a party, with
black markings on each petal and a deep
chocolate-brown-flecked, orange center (**3**).
As an extra bonus, it also has pretty gray-
tinged felted foliage. Arrange arctotis on their
own, 15 to 20 stems in a china pitcher for
your kitchen table, or with bupleurum and
the indigo-blue spires of gentian sage. They
last twice as long in water as the marigold.
Also grow the large-flowered, creamy white,
chocolate-centered A.f. 'Zulu Prince' (see
page 118).*

Conditioning *Strip the bottom leaves.*

Cultivation *Grow them in full sun in
very well-drained, ideally sandy soil. Plant
them creeping out over a path or lawn. The
stems tend to grow soft and floppy rather
than straight and upstanding, so they are
best suited to the front of the border. Water
and pick regularly and they will reward you
with flowers well into fall.*

1 *Alstroemeria ligtu* hybrid
2 *Antirrhinum majus* 'Black Prince'
3 *Arctotis fastuosa*
4 *Calendula* Art Shades Group

*Sow in early spring, under cover, with
some heat. Germination is usually excellent.
Thin when large enough to handle, and
plant once there is little risk of frost.*

Marigold
CALENDULA

*Hardy annual
Height: 24in (60cm)*

Good varieties for cutting *The
common-or-garden marigold is many people's
least favorite plant. It has an odd smell,
which you either like or hate, and it comes in
somewhat brash and brassy colors. I used
to be a subscriber to the anti-orange-and-
yellow-in-your-garden club. Since I started
arranging flowers regularly, I have joined the
opposite camp. The more easy-to-grow, jolly,
bright cottage-garden plants the better, and
now marigolds rank high on my list.*

*Pick one of the better mixtures, like the
double Art Shades Group (**4**), and you will
have the typical orange, plus yellows (see*

page 128), cream, buff, and apricot with dark chocolate centers. Of the single colors, 'Indian Prince' is one of the best, with a deep orange center and burnt-marmalade back. Avoid the dwarf varieties, which are too short for picking.

Arrange them all jumbled up together in a blue ceramic pitcher for the kitchen, or make up a tightly tied posy mixing the oranges with blue cornflowers. At the other end of the scale, their brightness, brilliance, and strong flower structure also make them a useful contrast in large and grand arrangements (see pages 70–71).

Conditioning Strip the bottom leaves. The flowers will last for a week.

Cultivation Grow in sun and any well-drained soil. Keep picking or deadheading to ensure flowers until the first frost. Sow directly in their flowering position in spring, and thin to 10–12in (25–30cm) apart. For very strong plants sow in situ in fall. Calendula will also self-seed.

CLEMATIS

Main entry: Spring White, page 99.
Of the summer clematis, I particularly like deep crimson-claret Viticellas 'Royal Velours' (1), 'Rouge Cardinal', and 'Jackmanii'. These are all much less vigorous than the anemone clematis, so rather than taking whole branches, I cut the flowering stems back to the wood.

COSMOS

Main entry: Summer White, page 118.
C. bipinnatus 'Versailles Carmine' (2) has a velvety color and texture that mix perfectly with 'Royal Velours' clematis, yellow and orange Iceland poppies, and green flowering tobacco for a head-turning wedding bouquet. Make matching headdresses for the bride and bridesmaids.

Sunflower
HELIANTHUS

Main entry: Summer Yellow, page 128.
For an exotic effect, try arranging a rich mahogany-red sunflower such as Helianthus annuus 'Velvet Queen' (4) one stem on its own in a tall decanter. The red sunflowers are also striking mixed with other warm colors (see pages 74–75).

IRIS

Main entry: Winter Blue and Purple, page 158. I grow the deep bronze-claret I. 'Ruby Mine' (5), a lovely long-flowering late Tall Bearded iris. 'Sultan's Palace' is another good red.

KNAUTIA MACEDONICA

Main entry: see Scabiosa, Summer Blue and Purple, page 135. The perennial K. macedonica blooms from the end of spring to mid-fall, producing a range of richly hued flowers to combine or contrast with almost any color scheme. It comes in whites, pinks, and mauves, but my favorite is the deep claret form (3). Its cultivation is as for scabious.

Lily
LILIUM

Main entry: Summer White, page 120.
The zingy rich orange lily 'Fire King' (6) looks wonderful with a clashing bunch of opposing colors and acid-greens.

SCALE 2in (5cm)

SCALE 2in (5cm)

1 Clematis 'Royal Velours'
2 Cosmos bipinnatus 'Versailles Carmine'
3 Knautia macedonica
4 Helianthus annuus 'Velvet Queen'
5 Iris 'Ruby Mine'

Jerusalem cross, Maltese cross
LYCHNIS

Annual, biennial, and perennial Zones: 4–8
Height and spread: L. × arkwrightii
'Vesuvius' 18in (45cm); L. chalcedonica
3–4ft × 12–18in (90cm–1.2m × 30–45cm)

Good varieties for cutting *You do
not get much brighter than the true scarlet
L. chalcedonica (**7**) and the shocking
brick-red-orange L. × arkwrightii 'Vesuvius'.
Both are colors for a fashion show. The neat,
star-shaped flowers, with their indented petals
like a snake's forked tongue, add to their
strength and beauty. The hybrid L. × a.
'Vesuvius' has a longer flowering season than
the species, and the intense flower color contrasts with deep purple-maroon foliage. Mix
them both with calming rich blue anchusas
and green artichoke buds, and flowering
tobacco (see page 73). Or use them as a com-
ponent of a zingy multicolored mix, with
lime-green bupleurum and dill, golden-yellow
sunflowers, and deep blue umbrellas of agapanthus. There is nothing subtle about these
reds, so have fun dreaming up the brashest
and most startling color collisions!*

Cultivation *Lychnis grows easily in good
moist soil in full sun in a sheltered position.
L. × arkwrightii is short-lived and best
treated as an annual. Sow singly in warmth
and plant out once there is minimal risk of
frost. Propagate L. chalcedonica by division or seed in fall or spring; it will flower
in the second year from seed.*

Poppy
PAPAVER

*Hardy annual, biennial, and perennial
Zones: 3–7*
*Height: P. commutatum 18in (45cm);
P. nudicaule 14–20in (35–50cm);
P. somniferum 'Danebrog', P. rhoeas
cultivars 18in–2ft (45–60cm); P. orientale
'Ladybird' 2–3ft (60–90cm)*

Good varieties for cutting *Many
people think poppies far too frail and fragile
to survive cutting. Think again. Poppies are
some of the best flowers you can grow in the
cutting garden. The biennial Iceland poppy,
P. nudicaule, is the most robust and long-
lasting in water. Once the stems have been
seared, the petals will emerge from tight*

*buds, and you will have a series of new
flowers for up to two weeks. What could be
better than a plain glass vase of 10 to 15
stems of the newly unraveled crinkly tissue-
paper flowers in their various whites, creams,
yellows, pinks, oranges, and brick-reds.*

*The best deep rich scarlet-orange forms,
P.n. 'Matador' (**8**) or 'Red Sail', are
marvelous mixed with the similarly colored
Lychnis × arkwrightii 'Vesuvius', green
Euphorbia palustris, and purple Salvia
× superba. Use them also in a flaglike
multicolored summer swag (see pages 64–67).*

*More frail, but perfect for a few days of
admiration, are all the corn poppy varieties.
Arrange the scarlet-red P. rhoeas (**10**), with
its elegant hanging hairy buds and stems, on
its own, or mix it in a medley from one of
the mixtures (P.r. Shirley Group or P.r.
Mother of Pearl Group) of whites, pinks,
mauves, doubles, and singles in an arrangement of great delicacy and grace. Just keep
the vase out of the wind and away from open
windows, or a gust of wind may destroy it,
scattering every petal on the table. Grow
some of the annual freaks, too, like the extra-
ordinary P. somniferum 'Danebrog' (syn.
P.s. 'Danish Flag') (**11**), with its huge
flowers with serrated petals in scarlet and
white. Also grow the red with black spotted
P. commutatum 'Ladybird'.*

*The perennial Oriental poppies,
P. orientale (**9**), will hold onto their petals
for several days if seared as soon as you pick
them. All are fabulous when cut, from the
white P.o. 'Perry's White' to the gray-crimson
'Patty's Plum'. Gray-green P. somniferum
seed heads and the blue-green seed heads of
P. orientale 'Patty's Plum' are also good cut.*

Conditioning *Plunge the cut ends into
boiling water for 20 seconds and then into
tepid water for a long drink (see page 48).
P. nudicaule buds may need helping out of
their tight glovelike calyces, which if torn in
one place will gradually unravel.*

Cultivation *These are easy plants to
grow and thrive if planted in sun or semi-
shade in a moist but well-drained soil. Plant
the annuals and biennials in generous clumps
in the border, at 10–12in (25–30cm) spac-
ings. Plant the perennials in groups of three,
18in (45cm) apart.*

*The hardy annuals can be sown in fall
or spring. They will not survive trans-
plantation, so must be sown in situ and then
thinned to 8–10in (20–25cm) in their
intended flowering position. The biennial
P. nudicaule varieties can be sown under
glass in late spring and planted in their
flowering position in fall. Or sow them in a
seed bed and thin to 10–12in (25–30cm).
P. orientale cultivars are best propagated by
root cuttings in winter (see page 43).*

6 *Lilium* 'Fire King'
7 *Lychnis chalcedonica*
8 *Papaver nudicaule* 'Matador'
9 *Papaver orientale*
10 *Papaver rhoeas*
11 *Papaver somniferum* 'Danebrog'

SCALE
2in (5 cm)

Yellow

Hollyhock
ALCEA

Annual, biennial, and short-lived perennial
Zones: 3–9
Height: 5–6½ft (1.5–2m)

Good varieties for cutting *Few arrangements could be more impressive than a collection of towering hollyhock spikes with their large, open, crinkled crêpe-paper flowers arranged all the way up the stem. Use their full height, and either several colors jumbled up together or many stems of a single color in a stately vase. Avoid the Powder Puff double varieties and any dwarf forms, but grow the pale yellow perennials A.* rugosa *and A.* pallida (**2**) *and the deep purple-black A.* rosea *'Nigra'. If you have a place for mixed colors, also grow the A.* rosea *white, pink, yellow, and red forms. These will all flower from late spring, producing new flower spikes until the end of fall.*

Conditioning *Sear the stem ends in boiling water for 20 seconds before giving them a deep cool drink.*

Cultivation *Plant hollyhocks 18in (45cm) apart, in groups of three to seven, depending on space. Easy to grow, they will thrive in full sun in fairly poor but well-drained soil. Of the single types, A.* rugosa *is the most resistant to rust. If rust occurs, cut off all the foliage and drench the plant with fungicide. If this inorganic treatment offends you, grow them as half-hardy annuals or biennials.*

Grow hollyhocks from seed. The annual varieties, if sown early in the year and planted out after the frost, will flower the same year. For larger finer plants, grow as biennials, sowing under glass in summer and planting out that fall to flower the following year. They self-seed freely.

Marigold
CALENDULA

Main entry: Summer Orange and Red, page 125. *Mix the bright buttercup-yellow marigold from the Art Shades Group (**1**) with other marigolds in orange, cream, and buff, or use it to highlight the middle of a bunch of roses and sweet peas (see page 70).*

Foxtail lily, king's spear
EREMURUS

Bulbous perennial Zones: E. robustus, E. *Ruiter Hybrid 6–9; E.* stenophyllus *subsp.* stenophyllus *5–9;* E. himalaicus *4–9*
Height: E. stenophyllus *3–4ft (90cm–1.2m); E.* Ruiter Hybrid *5ft (1.5m); E.* himalaicus, E. robustus *6–8ft (1.8–2.5m)*

Good varieties for cutting *These tapering towering spikes of small star-shaped flowers look more like the tail feathers of a giant exotic jungle parrot than a fox's brush – you can imagine them trailing down from a high branch of a mahogany tree, entirely surrounded by orchids and ferns and humid mossy smells.*

*They make luxurious and opulent cut flowers in white, cream, pink, orange, and bright yellow. Mix them in any great summer arrangement (see pages 70–71) or have them on their own, the colors jumbled like a collection of colored sparklers. For a mixture of colors and real statuesque height, grow the early-flowering Ruiter Hybrids (**4**). The earliest eremurus to flower, E. himalaicus, also tall, has immense pure white cylindrical spikes. E.* robustus, *in pale pink, is the next to flower and the shorter, more compact E.* stenophyllus (**3**), *with golden-yellow flowers, flowers last.*

Conditioning *As with other flower spikes, the bottom flowers die before the top blooms open. Cut when the bottom half is in flower and remove flowers as they wilt. The spike should last seven to ten days if kept out of strong heat.*

Cultivation *Buy in tuberous roots from a reliable supplier, making sure that you obtain freshly lifted crowns with succulent-looking roots. Plant 12–14in (30–35cm) apart into holes filled with course, sandy grit in a sheltered sunny position and you may have flowers the first year. Set the crown just below the surface. Mark each tuber with a stick so that you do not pierce the roots when you are planting around them. In a windy site support the stem with a stake.*

Eremurus are best propagated by division in early spring or fall (see page 37). Dig a wide circle around their radiating roots.

SCALE
2in (5cm)

❶ *Calendula* Art Shades Group
❷ *Alcea pallida*
❸ *Eremurus stenophyllus*
❹ *Eremurus* Ruiter Hybrid

Sunflower
HELIANTHUS

Hardy annual
Height: 3–10ft (1–3m)

Good varieties for cutting *The open, generous, cheery faces of the annual sunflowers, H.* annuus, *come in all shades of yellow, cream, and now rich maroon and mahogany. As a bonus, the petals often contrast with a lovely chocolatey center, matching the bumblebees that crawl all over them. If picked in bud or recently opened, the flowers will last in water, looking fresh and succulent, for over two weeks. Grow a rich red sunflower such as H.a. 'Velvet Queen' (page 126), the pale yellow H.a. 'Lemon Queen', and some of the classic bright golden-yellow forms, like H.a. 'Henry*

5 *Helianthus annuus* 'Henry Wilde'
6 *Lilium monadelphum*
7 *Helianthus annuus* 'Italian White'
8 *Lonicera periclymenum* 'Graham Thomas'
9 *Papaver nudicaule* Oregon Rainbow Group

SCALE
2in (5cm)

SCALE
2in (5cm)

SCALE
2in (5cm)

Wilde' (**5**) *and 'Valentine' and grow, too, some of the multicolored, cream, yellow, orange, crimson, and mahogany mixtures. The pale cream* H.a. *'Italian White'* (**7**) *flowers through summer and fall until the first hard frost.*

Conditioning *Put straight into water and keep them away from heat.*

Cultivation *Plant six to eight plants per square yard, in full sun, in a moist but well-drained soil. They will tolerate light shade, but remember that the flowers will always face the sun. Provide support, for the wind may catch the giant heavy heads.*

Sow them directly into their flowering position in spring. Place the large flat seeds in groups in the border or in lines in the cutting patch. Keep them well watered. Or sow early under cover in individual pots in a plant incubator or greenhouse, planting them once there is little risk of frost (see page 34).

Turkscap lily
LILIUM MONADELPHUM
Main entry: Summer White, page 120.
The elegant, golden-yellow turkscap lily L. monadelphum (**6**) *is beautiful arranged tall with blues and purples. Combine it with* bupleurum, *smokebush, larkspur, lupines, and* lisianthus. *Cut it short and use it to high-light the golden centers of crimson and claret roses* 'Tuscany Superb' *or* 'Nuits de Young'.

Honeysuckle
LONICERA
Main entry: Summer Pink, page 123.
The long-flowering, deciduous L. pericly-menum *'Graham Thomas'* (**8**) *is one of the best of the yellow honeysuckles. If pruned back in spring, it will flower continuously until late fall. Combine with its namesake* Rosa *'Graham Thomas' for a simple, pretty, fragrant posy.*

PAPAVER
Poppy
Main entry: Summer Orange and Red, page 127. *Iceland poppies come in all shades of yellow, cream, orange, and pink. The calm, pale yellow* P. nudicaule *Oregon Rainbow Group* (**9**) *with its crisp papery flowers is lovely in a tall glass on its own. Or arrange it with smoky purples: a few sprigs of purple sage and some sweet peas.*

Blue and Purple

African lily
AGAPANTHUS

Perennial, some evergreen
Zones: 8–10; A. Headbourne Hybrids 7–10
Height: most are 2–5ft (60cm–1.5m)

Good varieties for cutting *Grown in a row, these many-flowered blue pompons on their long straight stalks look like maces in an ecclesiastical procession. Arrange them in*

❶ Agapanthus Headbourne Hybrid
❷ Allium cernuum
❸ Allium cristophii
❹ Allium giganteum
❺ Anchusa azurea 'Royal Blue'

tall narrow vases on their own, or combined, in an explosion of flower color, with eremurus and alliums (see pages 70–71). Grow the hardiest, the Headbourne Hybrids (1), which come in a range of colors from deep blue to white. For the tall and stately, choose the purple-blue 'Storm Cloud' with 4ft (1.2m) flower spikes. 'Mood Indigo', 3ft (90cm), is a good dark purple. Grow, too, some of the smaller and more delicate varieties to mix with roses, phlox, and bupleurum for

a classic, traditional bunch. The deep blue 'Peter Pan' is a miniature only 18–24in (45–60cm) high.

The paler-colored, deciduous A. campanulatus varieties are almost completely hardy, too. Seek out the hardiest of all, A.c. subsp. patens and handsome A.c. var. albidus (see page 118). The angular agapanthus seed heads are lovely in fall arrangements (see page 136).

Conditioning *Pick when there are still many unopened flowers, and remove dead florets as they age.*

Cultivation *To get the best color forms, choose your agapanthus plants when in flower. Plant generous clumps of three to five, depending on their size. These are sun-loving plants which thrive in a fertile soil that is moist but well drained, particularly during the winter months. They do best with the shelter of a sunny wall. Protect the crowns in winter with a good layer of mulch (see page 37). Clumps increase slowly, but after some years can be divided in spring.*

ALLIUM

Bulb Zones: Triteleia laxa 7–10; Allium giganteum, A narcissiflorum 7–10; Triteleia hyacintha 5–10; Allium aflatunense, A. cristophii, Nectaroscordum siculum 4–10; Allium flavum, A. 'Globemaster', 3–9; A. cernuum, A. sphaerocephalon 3–8
Height: A. narcissiflorum to 12in (30cm); Triteleia laxa 12–20in (30–50cm); Allium cernuum, A. cristophii, A. flavum 12–28in (30–70cm); A. sphaerocephalon to 3ft (90cm); A. 'Globemaster' 3–4ft (90cm–1.2m); Triteleia hyacintha, Nectaroscordum siculum 4ft (1.2m); Allium aflatunense 5ft (1.5m); A. giganteum 6½ft (2m)

Good varieties for cutting *There are so many excellent alliums for cutting that it is impossible to mention them all. The ones to go for are those that look like starry explosions of spectacular fireworks, spreading a globe of cascading flowers in all directions.*

A. cristophii (3), with its green-centered, spiny stars, A. giganteum (4), and A. 'Globemaster' are the largest and most impressive. Grow these for combining in

giant arrangements with lilies, lupines, and eremurus spikes (see pages 70–71). Heavy-headed, deliciously scented white lilies like L. 'Casa Blanca' are especially good with A. giganteum, because they counteract the indisputably oniony smell of the allium as it ages. What is more, both flowers continue to look good for 10 to 14 days, without any rearranging. Just change the water every other day. For similar, slightly smaller flowers, which will be produced up to six weeks earlier, plant A. aflatunense.

Among the shorter-stemmed and smaller-headed varieties, grow A. sphaerocephalon. Its magenta-purple, shuttlecock-shaped heads are beautiful with whites and greens, or in a mixture of hotter colors. The rosy-purple A. cernuum (2) and lemon-yellow A. flavum provide more fireworks.

Grow also the less hardy, related Triteleia (syn. Brodiaea) with six-petaled, starry blooms like a twice-magnified allium flower. T. hyacintha is a pretty white flower flushed with pink. It looks like wild garlic but without the smell. T. laxa is a good mid-blue (see pages 134 and 135). Another impressive plant related to the alliums is Nectaroscordum siculum subsp. bulgaricum. The pendant, bell-shaped, early-summer flowers in white flushed with purple and green are followed by angular, agapanthus-style seed heads.

Conditioning *Change the water of the larger varieties regularly to minimize their onion smell.*

Cultivation *Alliums are easy to grow in an open sunny situation with good drainage. Plant generous quantities in the fall, 5in (13cm) deep. Left undisturbed, most alliums quickly form clumps. These can be divided: the spring-flowering varieties in late summer, the summer-flowering forms in spring (see pages 37 and 41). Alliums can be grown from seed – most will self-seed all over the garden, so be careful where you put them.*

ANCHUSA

Annual, biennial, and perennial, some evergreen Zones: 4–8
Height and spread: A. azurea cultivars 4ft × 2ft (1.2m × 60cm); A. capensis varieties 8–18in × 8in (20–45cm × 20cm)

Good varieties for cutting

A. azurea *(syn.* A. italica*) flower spikes remind me of a circus clown balancing 30 or 40 plates on a series of stakes. Each of the anchusa's blooms has a clear white center and a wide, rich blue surround. They make robust, long-lasting, graceful, and elegant cut flowers. Of the short-lived perennials, grow the deepest and richest,* A. azurea *'Loddon Royalist' with indigo-blue, almost purple, flowers, and the gentian-blue* A.a. *'Royal Blue'* (**5**). *Combine either with rich scarlets and oranges for a strong contrasting arrangement (see page 73). Avoid the pinks and whites, which look washed out.*

A. capensis, *the bushy South African biennial, usually grown as a half-hardy annual, is good for smaller bunches.* A.c. *'Blue Angel' is too small, except for the tiniest posies, but the pretty 'Blue Bird' reaches nearly 24in (60cm), and is well worth growing as a filler at the front of a border in the cutting garden.*

Conditioning *Dislodge any aging flowers by turning the stem upside-down and giving it a good shake.*

Cultivation *This is a flower of Mediterranean origin, so it needs sun and very well-drained soil, without too much winter wet. Plant perennials 18in (45cm) apart in clumps of three to five. Stake the tall flower spikes. If you keep picking anchusas to stop them from going to seed, they will flower from the beginning of summer to mid-fall.*

You can propagate perennials easily from root cuttings in winter. A. azurea *varieties can also be successfully grown as biennials, sown in late spring and transplanted to rows in a seed bed for summer. Plant into their flowering position in fall, and they will be in bloom by late spring the following year. Propagate half-hardy annuals, such as* A. capensis, *from a spring sowing under cover with heat, planting once there is little risk of frost (see pages 32–34 and 35). They all self-seed freely and are easily transplanted.*

Bellflower
CAMPANULA

Annual, biennial, and perennial, some evergreen Zones: 3–8; C. pyramidalis *7–8 Height:* C. *'G.F. Wilson' 3–4in (8–10cm);*

C. portenschlagiana *6in (15cm);* C. glomerata, C. persicifolia *2½–3ft (75–90cm);* C. lactiflora, C. pyramidalis *5–6½ft (1.5–2m)*

Good varieties for cutting

Campanulas, with their simple silhouettes of hanging bells, seem to me the most serene of flowers. Grow the simple bellflower, C. persicifolia (**6**), *in blue and white (see page 118), and mix it with lady's mantle, snapdragons, roses, and other cottage-garden-type plants. It is a robust cut flower and also good for using in florist's oasis to fill out a summer swag. Avoid the double forms of* C. persicifolia, *'Fleur de Neige' and 'Pride of Exmouth'; the flower's charm lies in its simplicity. Grow also the long-flowering, tall and stately spikes of the biennial* C. pyramidalis *in blue and white and the other magnificent, giant, late-summer-flowering* C. lactiflora *'Superba'. Arrange these on their own in a huge ceramic pitcher as the centerpiece on a large table, or mix them simply with boughs of roses. Right at the other end of the scale, grow the tiny delicate-looking* C. *'G.F. Wilson' or more vigorous* C. portenschlagiana *for your small posies.*

The stronger, richer-colored and quickly spreading C. glomerata *'Superba' has a more cultivated feel, but is also excellent for cutting. Mix this with intense oranges and scarlets, all contrasted with lime-greens.*

Conditioning *Plunge the cut ends of* C. lactiflora *cultivars in boiling water for 20 seconds.*

Cultivation *Campanulas are easy and unfussy plants to grow, and thrive in sun or partial shade. They like a moist but well-drained soil. The more vigorous varieties, like* C. glomerata, *should be dug up and replanted regularly or the centers of the ever-expanding clumps will begin to die off. The tall* C. pyramidalis *and* C. lactiflora *need staking (see page 37).*

Propagate the perennials by softwood or basal cuttings in summer (see pages 36, 38, and 39), or by division in fall or spring (see pages 37 and 41). Use this method for good color forms and named varieties. They are also easy to grow from seed. Sow the biennial C. pyramidalis *under cover in late spring, planting it in a seed bed for summer.*

Cornflower, knapweed
CENTAUREA

Annual and perennial Zones: 4–8 Height: C. moschata *cultivars (correctly Amberboa moschata)* 18–24in (45–60cm); C. cyanus *vars 1–3ft (30–90cm);* C. dealbata, C. macrocephala *3ft (90cm)*

Good varieties for cutting *The bright thistlelike heads of the clear blue*

cornflower C. cyanus *combine well with any color. Grow the improved and larger-flowered* C.c. *'Blue Diadem'* (**8**) *for a more showy variety. Use it in an informal bunch of country-garden flowers with sweet Williams, snapdragons, and love-in-a-mist. Try the almost black cornflower* C.c. *'Black Ball'* (**7**) *with the very dark sweet pea 'Pageantry', contrasted with the orange-scarlet* Lychnis × arkwrightii *'Vesuvius'.*

SCALE
2in (5cm)

6 *Campanula persicifolia*
7 *Centaurea cyanus 'Black Ball'*
8 *Centaurea cyanus 'Blue Diadem'*

SCALE
2 in (5cm)

Avoid the dwarf varieties, which are less useful for cutting. Many of the perennial centaureas also make good cut flowers. The pink C. dealbata varieties like 'Steenbergii' (see page 122) are also excellent for cutting.

Conditioning *Pick cornflowers when the flowers are half-open, and strip the bottom leaves. They will last four to five days.*

Cultivation *Cornflowers will grow in even quite poor soil in full sun. If you want really bumper-sized flowers you can strip the buds from the young plants, but this seems unnecessary to me; lots of slightly smaller flowers are just as nice as fewer giant ones. If you do not pick very regularly, remove the bleached flowers before they set seed. They may suffer from powdery mildew in hot summers.*

Sow the hardy annual forms in situ in spring and thin to 4–6in (10–15cm). Even better, sow in early fall so they can build up large rosettes and good energy stores before they have to produce a flower spike. Grow the perennial forms from seed, division, or root cuttings (see pages 32–34, 37, 43).

CLEMATIS
Main entry: Spring White, page 99.

I like to arrange a few velvety heads of the herbaceous blue-purple C. × durandii (1) on its own, for the middle of a table. In late summer and fall I mix its feathery, spiraling seed heads with honeysuckle berries and roses like the pink English Rose 'Heritage'.

Cardoon, globe artichoke
CYNARA
Perennial Zones: 7–9
Height and spread: C. cardunculus 6–8ft × 3ft (2–2.5m × 90cm); C.c. Scolymus Group 3–4ft × 2ft (90cm–1.2m × 60cm)

Good varieties for cutting *This genus, which includes both cardoons and globe artichokes, is excellent for huge arrangements in tall vases or party urns. Pick leaves of the cardoon, C. cardunculus (5), to combine with bright blue delphiniums and eremurus, cutting them so they stand about 3ft (90cm) tall. The young leaves of the globe artichoke, C.c. Scolymus Group, are also lovely in spring, mixed with* Helleborus orientalis *seedlings (see pages 56–58). Cut artichoke and cardoon flowers both in bud and in full flower. While still green, they provide perfect strong architectural stems for mixing with startling scarlets and oranges (see page 73). When they have opened and are showing their rich purple plumes, combine them with sunflowers and acanthus, or simply arrange them on their own.*

Conditioning *Strip the bottom leaves on the flowering spikes and change the water regularly because it may turn brown.*

Cultivation *Plant a good clump of three to five artichokes and, if you have room, at least one cardoon. Plant in spring, in a warm, well-drained, sunny site. Cut your artichokes down in late fall and protect the crowns with a thick mulch of straw or leaves. Stake the cardoon flower spikes when they reach their giant height. Propagate by division or from seed in spring.*

DELPHINIUM and CONSOLIDA
Annual and perennial Zones: Delphinium grandiflorum 4–9; D. Belladonna Group 3–9; large-flowered hybrids 2–8
Height: D. grandiflorum *18in (45cm); dwarf, large-flowered hybrids,* Consolida regalis, D. Belladonna Group *3–5ft (90cm–1.5m); large-flowered hybrids 5–6ft (1.5–1.8m)*

Good varieties for cutting
Delphiniums make a graceful addition to any bunch of flowers and to the flower border. They come in blues, white, and pink, and more recently, yellows, reds, and creams have

been developed. From among the large-flowered delphiniums, such as the Pacific Giant hybrids, choose a rich violet-blue. Put it at the back of the border beside a stately cardoon and pick them together for a 5ft (1.5m) display of flowers and foliage. Grow also a bright royal blue delphinium – to combine with oranges and yellows – a white, and perhaps a cream.

Many of the species and old hybrid delphiniums are also excellent cut. D. Belladonna Group is a delicate branched variety with lovely, single, open-winged flowers in a deep rich blue with a white eye. Try also D. grandiflorum (often listed as D. chinense), which is a short-lived perennial usually grown as an annual. D.g. 'Blue Butterfly' has large, rich, royal blue flowers and is well worth growing.

Others invaluable for cutting are the annual delphiniums, Consolida regalis, or larkspur. Grow the deep rich purple-blues like C. (Exquisite Series) 'Blue Spire' (3) and the pure white 'White King', from the Giant Imperial type. Avoid the pinks, which tend to be either powder-pink or a deep gray-pink, both difficult colors to mix.

Conditioning *Pick delphiniums when most of the flowers on the spike are open. They are very sensitive to ethylene gas, which is emitted as fruit ripens, so do not put them near a bowl of fruit.*

Cultivation *Delphiniums grow vigorously on most types of soil with good drainage. Most prefer full sun, although some can be planted in part shade. All need ample water and fertilizer and should be kept weed-free. Mulch in spring with organic material and apply fertilizer at regular intervals during the flowering season.*

Plant perennials 24in (60cm) apart, in groups of three to five. Plant annuals closer, in blocks in the border or lines in your cutting patch. Adequate spacing to allow a

good air-flow through the foliage is important, since both perennial and annual delphiniums have a problem with mildew, particularly in late summer. Regular cutting of delphiniums will promote the development of lateral shoots and prolong the flowering season. The taller varieties need staking (see page 37).

Annuals can be sown either under cover in early spring, to be planted once there is little risk of frost, or in situ in early fall or spring (see pages 32–34 and 35). If late-summer mildew is a problem it is well worth sowing in fall for earlier flowering, so that they will give of their best before it strikes. Named cultivars of perennial delphiniums and D. Belladonna Group should be propa-gated from basal cuttings of young shoots in spring. Take them, 2–3in (5–8cm) long, when the shoots first emerge in early spring, before they develop a hollow center. Put them in individual 3in (8cm) pots and allow them to develop roots (see pages 34 and 36).

1 *Clematis × durandii*
2 *Dianthus barbatus* Nigrescens Group
3 *Consolida* (Exquisite Series) 'Blue Spire'
4 *Eustoma grandiflorum* F₁ Hybrid

SCALE
2in (5cm)

Sweet William
DIANTHUS BARBATUS
Main entry: Summer Pink, page 122.
D.b. *Nigrescens Group* (**2**) *has black-purple flowers that complement pink roses or sweet peas in a rich-scented bouquet (see page 70).*

Viper's bugloss
ECHIUM
Annual and biennial
Zones: E. vulgare *4–8*
Height: E. plantagineum *'Blue Bedder' 12in (30cm);* E. vulgare *24in (60cm)*
Good varieties for cutting *The biennial species of echium,* E. vulgare (**7**), *is a wild flower that grows around rocky coasts. Its blue, pink, and purple flowers surrounded by a hairy spiky calyx look lovely mixed with anchusas and contrasted with acid-green dill, claret stocks, and sweet Williams. Use the spike to break up the symmetry of a bunch.* E. plantagineum *'Blue Bedder' is the best and most widely available of the hardy annual varieties.*
Conditioning *Strip the bottom leaves.*
Cultivation *Grow them in clumps of five, in a sunny, well-drained, even stony site.* E. vulgare *is best grown as a biennial, sown under cover in late spring, planted outdoors for summer, and transplanted to its flowering position (see page 38). It can also be treated as a hardy annual, but it will produce smaller plants.* E.p. *'Blue Bedder' should be grown in the same way. Both self-seed freely and can be transplanted.*

Sea holly
ERYNGIUM
Main entry: Summer Green and Silver, page 116. *Mix the indigo-blue, spiky flower of* E. × zabelii *'Violetta'* (**8**) *with poppy seed heads, bupleurum, alstroemerias, and eremurus spikes, and contrast them with the sumptuous, deep purple lisianthus.*

Lisianthus, prairie gentian, Texas bluebell
EUSTOMA
Hardy perennial grown as half-hardy annual
Height: 18–24in (45–60cm)
Good varieties for cutting *The deep purple lisianthus* E. grandiflorum *(syn.*

Lisianthus russellianus*) (**4**) *is one of the most richly textured and colored of all annuals. Lisianthus make long-lasting and robust cut flowers. Grow lots for mixing and enriching any bunch – combine them with oranges, blues, and greens for a luxurious, hot, exotic display. Or mix them with whites and greens for a bride's wedding bouquet. Grow the* E.g. *Yodel Series, which are improved* F_1 *hybrids. The pure white and cream forms are well worth growing to take center stage in any calming, cool-colored bunch. Their open tubular flowers are like large poppies. Avoid the ruched double forms.*

⑤ *Cynara cardunculus*
⑥ *Delphinium 'Nobility'*
⑦ *Echium vulgare*
⑧ *Eryngium* x *zabelii 'Violetta'*
⑨ *Iris* 'Jane Phillips'

Conditioning *Recut the stem ends, removing at least 1in (2.5cm). Do not allow the flowers to get wet; they will become transparent and brown quickly.*
Cultivation *This is a difficult annual to grow, although well worth the effort. Sow seed under cover in winter, when it is fresh (see pages 32–34). Plant in a well-drained site in full sun. Pinch back the growing points for maximum flowers on branching plants.*

IRIS
Main entry: Winter Blue and Purple, page 158. *The mid-season, soft violet-blue Tall Bearded iris 'Jane Phillips'* (**9**) *is a stunning sculptural flower with a sweet, rather exotic smell. It lasts for over a week in water. 'Titan's Glory' is another good blue.*

SCALE
2in (5cm)

SCALE
2in (5cm)

Sweet pea
LATHYRUS ODORATUS
Main entry: Summer White, page 120.

The deep claret-black L.o. 'Pageantry' (1) is beautiful mixed with the bicolored purple and carmine L.o. 'Matucana' (2). They can be grown in the main part of the garden in an elegant combination with deep purple climbing green beans, and arranged on their own or combined in a fragrant mixture of clarets and reds with roses, stocks, and sweet Williams (see page 70).

Lavender
LAVANDULA
Evergreen shrub Zones: L. stoechas 8–9; L. angustifolia varieties 5–9
Height and spread: both 2–3ft (60–90cm)

Good varieties for cutting *Although deliciously scented, lavender can appear unimpressive as a cut flower. You need to mass several stems together before you get much of a show. Both L.a. 'Munstead' (3), a mauve-purple, and L.a. 'Hidcote', a deeper violet, are worth growing and cutting. On the whole, though, it is the tender lavenders with large showy bracts that win the day in the cutting garden. L. stoechas subsp. pedunculata is a superb flower for cutting (see page 113). If you are worried about its*

hardiness in your area, grow it in large terracotta pots so that you can bring the plants in for winter.

Conditioning *To preserve the scent, pick flowers for drying at mid-morning and dry them in a cool dry room, not in the sun.*

Cultivation *For a good flower crop, plant lavender in full sun on well-drained, preferably lime-rich soil. Lavenders do not like boggy clay. Prune well after flowering in late summer, but do not cut into old wood. Lavender is easily propagated by semi-ripe cuttings in summer (see pages 38 and 39).*

Lupine
LUPINUS
Annual, perennial, and semi-evergreen shrub
Zones: 3–7
Height: all 3–5ft (90cm–1.5m) except: L. luteus, L. varius 18–24in (45–60cm); L. mutabilis var. cruckshanksii 'Sunrise' 3ft (90cm)

❶ *Lathyrus odoratus 'Pageantry'*
❷ *Lathyrus odoratus 'Matucana'*
❸ *Lavandula angustifolia 'Munstead'*
❹ *Salvia x superba*
❺ *Triteleia laxa*

Good varieties for cutting *I love lupine flower spikes, which look like the tail feathers of an exotic parrot or tropical pheasant (6). There are many good color forms, which are best grown clumped together. Grow the indigo-blue L. polyphyllus and the white and blue cultivar L. 'The Governor'. The Russell lupines are also excellent, and have the added bonus of being long-flowering. The white lupine L. Noble Maiden Group is an exotic beauty and a good mixer (see pages 120 and 121).*

Lupines also look spectacular grown in a great jumble of different colors, if you can provide the right self-contained spot. Plant L. 'The Page' in shades of carmine next to L. 'Chandelier' in many shades of yellow. Put in some reds, pinks, and purples for good measure. You could also try one of the better mixtures, like the L. Band of Nobles Series. For a spectacular display, cut and arrange

them as they come, in a huge pitcher of clashing, contrasting colors.

There are some annual lupines that are also worth growing. The hardy, and scented, L. mutabilis var. cruckshanksii 'Sunrise', with its white, egg-yolk yellow and blue flowers, is a good one. The half-hardy, exceptionally bright yellow L. luteus and deep blue-black L. varius also make lovely cut flowers. Avoid the dwarf varieties, which are not much use for cutting.

Conditioning *To prevent the flower spikes from bending up toward the sun, plunge them in a pail of water right away. They tend to drop their pealike flowers after four or five days, even sooner in a warm room.*

Cultivation *Lupines thrive in sun or part shade in ordinary, lime-free soil (L. polyphyllus particularly hates lime), but they need good drainage and do best in sandy soil. Picking the flower spikes will encourage the development of laterals and a longer flowering season. It also prevents them from setting seed, which weakens the plant. Mildew can be a problem on the foliage in late summer. To avoid this, treat lupines as biennials and remove them when they finish flowering.*

The perennial lupines can be propagated by spring cuttings (see pages 38 and 39). Most can also be grown from seed sown in mid-spring. They will flower in the second year. Rub the large seeds briefly with sandpaper and then soak them until they have plumped up. This may take a day or two. Sow them individually about ¼in (5mm) deep, in 3in (8cm) pots. Move to the garden when they have three or four true leaves.

Hardy annual L. mutabilis var. cruckshanksii 'Sunrise' is easily grown from seed. It must be sown where it is to flower. The half-hardy annuals are best sown in fall, so they have time to thicken up before flowering.

Stock
MATTHIOLA
Main entry: Summer Pink, page 123.

This smoky purple stock (7) is dramatic mixed with bupleurum and moluccella; any of the dark-colored forms are good for adding richness and scent to summer arrangements.

SCALE
2in (5cm)

Love-in-a-mist
NIGELLA

Hardy annual
Height: N. damascena cultivars,
N. hispanica 14–18in (35–45cm);
N. damascena 'Oxford Blue',
N. hispanica 'Curiosity' 30in (75cm)

Good varieties for cutting *Both the*
blooms, like a Tudor ruff, and the purselike
seed pods of love-in-a-mist make excellent
cut flowers. Grow it as a filler for the front
of your cutting borders and to mix in
country-style bunches for the house. Make
hand-tied posies of the seed pods and pretty
feathery foliage. Grow the showiest variety,
N. hispanica, with its large, deep blue
flowers and pronounced black and maroon
stamens. Or try the tallest, richest blue form
of N. damascena, 'Oxford Blue' (8),
which has striking dark-striped seed heads.
There are also fine pink and white forms of
N. damascena and good colored mixtures,
like Persian Jewel Group. N. orientalis is
also well worth growing.

Conditioning *Strip the bottom leaves.*

Cultivation *Love-in-a-mist grows best in*
sun in fertile, well-drained soil. Keep
picking, but leave a few flowers to form seed
pods for mixing with later flowers. Sow in
situ, scattering the seed in the flowering posi-
tion. This annual hates being transplanted.
For large, early-flowering plants sow in early
fall in preference to mid-spring. The seeds
germinate quickly and will need thinning to
about 4in (10cm). Love-in-a-mist self-seeds
freely in all nooks and crannies, and if not
weeded will become self perpetuating.

SALVIA

Main entry: Fall Blue and Purple, page
147. *The rich purple S. × superba (4), one*
of the earliest salvias to flower, is good mixed
in borders and in arrangements with deep
orange 'Matador' Iceland poppies, Lychnis
× arkwrightii 'Vesuvius', and the green and
orange, unripe seed cases of Chinese lanterns.

Scabious, pincushion flower
SCABIOSA

Hardy annual and perennial Zones: 4–8
Height: S. caucasica cultivars 24in (60cm);
Double Mixed S. atropurpurea 3ft (90cm)

Good varieties for cutting *The*
mauves, dark oranges, whites, and pinks of
the annual mixture Double Mixed S. atro-
purpurea (9) are pretty for informal
bunches, but it is the deep crimson form that
I like best. The large-domed, dark flowers on
their long stems make a fine duo with
Zinnia 'Envy' and mix well with crimson
stocks, sweet Williams, and snapdragons,
contrasted with viper's bugloss and anchusas.
The perennials include many handsome,
large-flowered varieties in pale blue, mauve,
and white. Grow the long-flowering S.
caucasica 'Fama', a strong, bright mauve,
to mix with flowering teasels, love-in-a-mist
seed pods, and dill. Pinkish-mauve
S.c. 'Clive Greaves' (10) mixes well with
acid-green and orange. I use the white S.c.
'Perfecta Alba' or cream 'Miss Willmott' in
bridal and bridesmaids' bouquets.

Conditioning *Give them a good drink*
before arranging.

Cultivation *Scabious thrives in sun in*
fertile, well-drained, alkaline soil. Plant a
good clump of three to five plants of each
perennial variety, since one plant will not
have an enormous number of flowers at one
time. They will, however, flower for many
months, particularly if you keep picking and
prevent them from setting seed. Support
scabious with a network of thread and twigs
for each clump (see page 37). If you keep
picking, they will flower until the first frost.

Grow the annuals from seed sown in situ
or under cover in spring. They can also be
sown under cover in early fall for an earlier
start to flowering. Overwinter them in a cold
frame and plant them in mid-spring. Pinch
back growing points from seedlings to
encourage branching.

Grow the perennials from young basal
cuttings in summer, from seed in fall, or
from division in early spring as growth begins.

TRITELEIA LAXA

Main entry: see Allium, page 130.
T. laxa (5), a mauve-blue allium relative, is
one of the longest-lasting cut flowers. Use it
in a bright mix with alstroemerias, poppies,
and bupleurum.

SCALE
2in (5cm)

6 *Lupinus*
7 *Matthiola cultivar*
8 *Nigella damascena*
'Oxford Blue'
9 *Scabiosa atropurpurea*
10 *Scabiosa caucasica*
'Clive Greaves'

Fall

Once fall arrives, it is time to create wild, ragged vases of leaves turning with the season, seed heads, berries, and hips. As the outdoor light fades, bring inside the hot, clashing colors of the rich velvety dahlias, gladioli, and zinnias that are now flowering.

Silver, Green, and Brown

African lily
AGAPANTHUS
Main entry: Summer Blue and Purple, page 130. *Tall and statuesque agapanthus*

seed heads (1), *their droplets of jade held on delicate stems, look like Fabergé jewels. Mix them with richly colored dahlias, Chinese lanterns, and late sunflowers.*

Love-lies-bleeding
AMARANTHUS CAUDATUS
Half-hardy annual
Height: 3–4ft (90cm–1.2m)
Good varieties for cutting *The bright green version of love-lies-bleeding, A.caudatus 'Viridis' (2), makes an invaluable addition to any large fall bunch. This late-maturing annual mixes well with whites and blues, and contrasts dramatically with the oranges, crimsons, browns, and scarlets of berries and turning leaves. Arrange it or the more usual, red-tasseled form (see page 22) to look tall and stately, the tassels hanging in a staggered curtain, like icicles in a frozen waterfall. Some of the more upright*

amaranthus, like 'Green Thumb' and 'Pygmy Torch', are too pert and unrelaxed for my liking. Keep to the tall, laid-back, hanging varieties and you won't go wrong.
Conditioning *Remove the lower leaves and sear the stem ends in boiling water for 20 seconds before giving them a long drink.*
Cultivation *Plant out at 18–24in (45–60cm) intervals (amaranthus become large plants). Choose a site in full sun with fertile, well-drained soil. They will not reach full height and maturity until late summer or early fall but will continue to flower until the early part of the winter – these are among the last flowers to be picked. Fertilize them well and you may produce 5ft (1.5m) giants.*

Amaranthus are easy to grow from an early-spring sowing under cover. The tiny seeds produce little spindly seedlings, which should be thinned at the one or two true-leaf stage (see page 34). They also self-seed.

Wormwood
ARTEMISIA
Perennial and deciduous or semi-evergreen shrub or subshrub Zones: A. arborescens 'Faith Raven', A. 'Powis Castle' 7–10; A. pontica 5–10; A. absinthium 'Lambrook Silver' 4–10
Height and spread: A. pontica 24in × 8in (60cm × 20cm); A. absinthium 'Lambrook Silver' 32in × 20in (80cm × 50cm); A. 'Powis Castle' 2–3ft × 3–4ft (60–90cm × 90cm–1.2m); A. arborescens varieties 3–4ft × 3ft (90cm–1.2m × 90cm)
Good varieties for cutting *The bright silver-filigree foliage of many aromatic artemisias provides excellent contrast to the hot and intense colors that are so common in the garden at this time of year. It enlivens and lightens what can become a cloying richness when the oranges, reds, and ochers are left on their own. While it is pretty combined with nigella, bishop's flower, and roses in summer, in fall it becomes invaluable.*

A. arborescens 'Faith Raven' (4) was named after my mother, who found this variety on top of a mountain in Rhodes. It will quickly form a brilliant silver mound; if you pick carefully around its underskirts, you will leave no sign of your harvest. Like the similar 'Powis Castle', it retains its compact, domelike structure because it flowers little in colder climates. More delicate in appearance are A. absinthium 'Lambrook Silver' (3), with widely spaced, feathery foliage, and the very upright, elegant A. pontica, perfect for poking into a small, intense-colored, hand-tied bunch. They all mix well with salvias, dahlias, and asters (see page 78).
Conditioning *Artemisias flop easily. Sear the cut end of the stems (see page 48), then give them a cool drink overnight.*
Cultivation *These Mediterranean plants thrive in open, sunny, well-drained sites. Neaten established shrubs and subshrubs with a hard prune in spring to encourage a neat hummocky shape. They will quickly*

SCALE
2in (5cm)

❶ *Agapanthus* (seed head)
❷ *Amaranthus caudatus* 'Viridis'
❸ *Artemisia absinthium*
   'Lambrook Silver'
❹ *Artemisia arborescens* 'Faith Raven'

SCALE
2in (5cm)

refurbish themselves from their woody basal shoots. Pinch back the tips of young plants to encourage a bushy habit, and subsequently pinch any wayward long shoots.

Propagate the suckering A. pontica by division in spring or fall (see pages 37 and 41). The shrubs and subshrubs are easily propagated from softwood or semi-ripe cuttings in summer (see pages 38 and 39).

CLEMATIS

Main entry: Spring White, page 99.
The wispy seed heads of C. *'Bill Mackenzie'* (**5**), *like those of* C. × durandii *and* C. tangutica, *have an elegantly disheveled look. Team them with* Cosmos pinnatus *'Versailles Carmine' and tithonia.*

Papyrus, galingale
CYPERUS

Evergreen perennial Zones: 4–8
Height: C. albostriatus *24in (60cm)*
Good varieties for cutting *Most of the papyrus family, like* C. involucratus *and* C. papyrus, *are tender greenhouse plants. This is a great loss because they are excellent for cutting and add real spice and interest to any bunch.* C. albostriatus (**6**), *however, will grow happily in a cold climate and is invaluable in fall, providing bright lime-green foliage at a time when the euphorbias are mostly over, and annual foliage plants such as bupleurum are at an end.*

Try it with asters, dahlias, and the seed heads of Iris foetidissima *(see pages 76–78), or with zingy pink nerines.*
Cultivation *Cyperus will grow in almost any soil in sun or shade. It needs little care or maintenance. Propagate by division in spring or fall. It self-seeds freely.*

Spurge, milkweed
EUPHORBIA

Main entry: Spring Green and Silver, page 96. *The pretty gray-green annual* E. marginata *with white-striped margins comes into its own in late summer and fall. Mix it with 'Iceberg' roses, trailing hops, and crinum lilies for a cool and fresh-looking table centerpiece for a party.*

Hop
HUMULUS LUPULUS

Deciduous twining climber Zones: 3–9
Height and spread: 3–6m/10–20ft
Good varieties for cutting *The twisting and twirling stems of the hop are one of the real boons of fall, with their crop of bright green, heavily scented fruit that follows the flowers of the female plant. Cut them long or short for arranging around the house. Use them trailing for a hand-tied bunch, or make a medallion (see pages 78–79); a series of these hung for a party will intoxicate the guests as they arrive. The ordinary, dark green-leaved form,*

H. lupulus (**7**), *is still commercially grown in parts of England for flavoring bitter beer.* H.l. *'Aureus' flowers and fruits less freely, but its bright yellow-green foliage is more ornamental.*
Conditioning *Hang hops immediately, so that they dry quickly without becoming mildewed or musty. Spray the entire structure with odorless hair spray to hold seed heads in place and slow the inevitable molting.*
Cultivation *Grow hops in sun or semi-shade in any well-drained soil; they thrive in a warm, sheltered position. Hops need some support to clamber over.* H.l. *'Aureus' is best grown in full sun in a soil that doesn't dry out. Propagate by division in early spring.*

Shoo-fly plant
NICANDRA PHYSALODES

Hardy annual
Height: 3ft (90cm)
Good varieties for cutting *The bright green or green-and-black fruit calyces of the shoo-fly plant (**9**) make elegant additions to a bunch of almost black dahlias or bright pink, orange, and yellow zinnias, providing a balance to these vigorous colors. Look out for the large-flowered variety, which has bell-shaped sky-blue and white flowers and sculptural fruit calyces. The flowers make pretty fillers for an immature garden, but keep in mind that they last only a day or so when picked (see pages 78–79).*
Conditioning *Remove some or all of the leaves, since the seed cases last much longer.*
Cultivation *An easy annual to grow, the shoo-fly plant likes full sun and rich, well-drained soil. Sow under cover in early spring and plant out after the frosts have finished. It can also be sown directly into the ground as the soil warms up in mid-spring.*

Feather-top
PENNISETUM

Herbaceous perennial
Zones: P. alopecuroides 7–10;
P. villosum *5–10;* P. orientale *5–6*
Height: P. alopecuroides 24in (60cm);
P. orientale *30in (75cm);* P. villosum *36in (90cm)*
Good varieties for cutting *The fluffy squirrel-tail grasses with their green centers*

and pink-white, hairy outlines make good fall foliage. Grow both the brown-pink P. orientale *and the lighter* P. villosum (**I**, page 138) *and cut either one to stand up above a dome of bright rich salvias and asters (see pages 76–78), or deep crimson dahlias and Zinnia 'Envy'. Place on a windowsill, so the light enhances their radiant halo. The free-flowering* P. alopecuroides, *with its indigo bottle-brush appearance, is another good variety.*
Cultivation *Grow pennisetums in any well-drained but not too fertile soil, but choose a warm open site in full sun. If you fertilize pennisetums too generously, you will*

5 *Clematis* 'Bill Mackenzie'
6 *Cyperus albostriatus*
7 *Humulus lupulus*
8 *Euphorbia marginata*
9 *Nicandra physalodes* (seed pods)

SCALE
2in (5cm)

① Pennisetum villosum
② Rubus lasiostylus var.
   hupehensis
③ Rubus fruticosus
④ Typha latifolia
⑤ Zinnia 'Envy'

SCALE
2in (5cm)

promote soft growth, which can lead to death
in winter. All pennisetums, however, need a
good mulch to protect them in a cold winter.

Propagate by division in late spring or
fall. Keep recent offsets in the cold frame
during winter. P. orientale, in particular,
is not reliably hardy, and this way you will
have a fall-back stock to rely on.

Blackberry, raspberry, wineberry
RUBUS
Deciduous shrub Zones: 6–9
*Height: R. fruticosus, R. idaeus 3–6ft
(90cm–1.8m); R. lasiostylus var. hupehensis,
R. phoenicolasius 6–8ft (1.8–2.5m)*
Good varieties for cutting *A bough
of red or black berries is often the making
of a late-summer or early-fall arrangement.
The luscious and shiny berries stand in
contrast with brilliant reds, yellows, and*

oranges, mixing perfectly with red or yellow
chilis, zinnias, and deep red snapdragons.
You should definitely have a blackberry,
R. fruticosus (**3**). R.f. 'Loch Ness' is a
thornless variety. The bright red, fuzzy-stemmed
Japanese wineberry, R. phoenicolasius, with
its packed branches of long-lasting berries, is
also excellent when cut.

In summer, mix the acid-green leaves of
fruiting raspberry canes, R. idaeus, and the
contrasting fruit with boughs of pink roses or
white 'Casa Blanca' lilies. R. lasiostylus
var. hupehensis (**2**) will fit comfortably
into a small garden, and its white stems are
striking in a sculptural arrangement in late
fall or winter.
Conditioning *Invest in a pair of thorn-
proof gloves for picking rubus. Keep fruiting
varieties as cool as you can since mildew can
become a problem.*
Cultivation *Most rubus are best planted
in fall in a deep, rich, well-drained but
moist soil in sun. Cut the fruited stems of
raspberries and blackberries to the ground.
Cut out about one-third of the stems of R.
phoenicolasius and R. lasiostylus each
spring to encourage new growth. Mulch all
rubus with manure in late fall and in spring.
Give raspberries a high-potassium fertilizer
and keep them well watered when they fruit.*

*Propagate by semi-ripe cuttings in
summer (see pages 38 and 39) or by division in fall. R. phoenicolasius is also
easily grown from seed. Blackberries are best
propagated by layering tips in summer or by
transplanting suckers in fall.*

Cattails
TYPHA
Deciduous perennial Zones: 3–9
Height: 6–8ft (1.8–2.5m)
Good varieties for cutting *The
cylindrical brown frankfurter that we think
of as a cattail flower is the seed case
produced from the female part of the flower.
Grow T. latifolia (**4**) or the slightly smaller
T. angustifolia. Make a dramatic arrangement by mixing them in a vase with many
stems of white crinum lilies, or use them as
the vertical addition to a pitcher of dahlias,
salvias, leaves turning color, and hips (see
pages 82–83).*

④

SCALE
2in (5cm)

Conditioning *Do not keep cattails too
long in the house; after two or three weeks
the seed heads will disintegrate and seeds
will pour out like bubbles from a newly
opened champagne bottle.*
Cultivation *Grow cattails in sun or
shade, in the shallows of a pond edge, or in
a damp swampy area. They are invasive
plants, so take care where you plant them.*
Propagate in spring by seed or division.

ZINNIA
Half-hardy annual
Height: 12–36in (30–90cm)
Good varieties for cutting *This huge
family ranges from Las Vegas to Venetian
silks, from Manhattan blare to Old World
richness. The best of all is the double lime-
green 'Envy' (**5**). Mix it with contrasting deep
crimsons and reds, or arrange one or two
stems simply on their own, to appreciate the
sophisticated bitterness of the dramatic color.
But don't stop there: pick zinnias in each and
every color and enjoy their brassy brightness in
the time of shortening days and deepening chill.*
Conditioning *Just strip the bottom
leaves. These long-lived cut flowers should
look good for at least two weeks.*
Cultivation *Plant zinnias out in full sun
in fertile, well-drained soil. Pick them regularly from the moment they start flowering
and they will continue to flower until winter.
They do best in baking hot summers, but be
careful not to overwater them once they are in
the ground; they can suffer from mildew.
Propagate from seed sown under cover in late
spring. Thin the seedlings and plant them in
pots, taking care not to overwater.*

⑤

SCALE
2in (5cm)

White

Japanese anemone
ANEMONE x HYBRIDA
Main entry: Spring White, page 98.
The clear white, saucer-shaped flowers of
A. x h. 'Honorine Jobert' (1), with their
crisp yellow and green centers, make a
perfect foil to intense hot colors. Use tall
in big pitchers or cut short in delicate
arrangements of fall crocus and colchicums.

Crinum lily
CRINUM x POWELLII
Bulb Zones: 7–10
Height: 4ft (1.2m)
Good varieties for cutting *When*
your lilies are over, crinums will do more
than merely replace them. The pure white
trumpets of C. x p. 'Album' (2) are beau-
tiful to behold. The five to seven buds held
on each tall stem will open in succession,
while their scent pulses out in great bursts.
Seven or nine stems arranged on their own
with their scent suffusing the air will give a
feeling of rare luxury. Or mix them with the
variegated annual Euphorbia marginata
and heavy-headed white roses as the glam-
orous stars of a table for an evening party.
Crinum lilies also come in pink. The
deep pink C. x p. 'Krelagei' and 'Ellen
Bosanquet' are both attractive; try mixing
them with white crinums, or combining them
with Euphorbia schillingii and Rosa
'New Dawn' for a pretty and fragrant vase.
Cultivation *Plant crinums in a sunny,*
well-drained site with the bulb necks above
ground. They like a rich, deep soil, with
adequate moisture. Mulch thickly with
manure every second year. Buy five to ten
bulbs from a good wholesaler. You can
propagate by offsets in spring, but they
take several years to flower.

Flowering tobacco
NICOTIANA
Half-hardy annual, and perennial grown as
an annual
Height: N. alata 24in (60cm);
N. langsdorffii, N. sylvestris 5ft (1.5m)
Good varieties for cutting *Many*
of the flowering tobacco plants with their

elegant tubular flowers and powerful evening
fragrance make excellent cut flowers. The
giant N. sylvestris (3) is dramatic in the
fall garden and arranged on its own (see
page 82). Or combine it with the tassels
of Amaranthus caudatus *'Viridis' and*
the purple and white Dahlia *'Edinburgh'.*
For summer and fall picking, grow the
bright velvety annual N. 'Lime Green' (see
page 117). Another pretty lime-green
tobacco is N. langsdorffii, with its ball-
dress-shaped small flowers.
Conditioning *Nicotianas last well in*
water. Give them a good drink before
arranging and remove fading flowers.
Cultivation *Grow in full sun or part*
shade in a fertile, well-drained soil. Picking
the flowers will encourage lateral growth and
prolong flowering. Flowering tobacco can be
grown from seed sown under cover in early
spring (see pages 32–34). Plant out after the
last frost. N. sylvestris readily self-seeds.

❶ Anemone x *hybrida* 'Honorine Jobert'
❷ Crinum x *powellii* 'Album'
❸ Nicotiana sylvestris
❹ Rosa 'Iceberg'

Rose
ROSA
Main entry: Summer Pink, page 124.
Whether grown as a standard or a shrub,
Rosa 'Iceberg' (4) is a must for even the
smallest cutting garden. It will continue to
flower, producing faintly scented but generous
bosomy white roses, from early summer right
up until the really cold weather of late fall.

SCALE
2in (5cm)

Pink

Daisy, Michaelmas daisy
ASTER

Herbaceous perennial Zones: 5–10
Height: A. amellus *12in (30cm);*
A. × frikartii *'Mönch', 36in (90cm);*
A. novi-belgii *3–4ft (90cm–1.2m)*

Good varieties for cutting *These
frothy single and double daisies come in a
full range of blue, purple, mauve, and white.
I especially like the long-flowering pale
mauve* A. × frikartii *'Mönch' with its
yellow center, and the richer purple-with-
yellow* A. amellus *'Rudolf Goethe'. The
various forms of* A. novi-belgii *(4) are
good, too: try* A. n.-b. *'Crimson Brocade'
and the mid-purple* A. n.-b. *'Sailor Boy'.
Mix bright asters in a brilliant color
jamboree with salvias and dahlias (see
pages 76–78).*

Conditioning *Strip the bottom leaves,
give them a drink overnight, and the flowers
will last up to two weeks in water.*

Cultivation *Grow asters in sun or
partial shade, in a rich but well-drained
soil, with adequate moisture throughout the
summer. Taller varieties may need staking.
The* novi-belgii *cultivars in particular may
need regular spraying against mildew.*

*These plants are easy to grow from
softwood cuttings or division in spring.*

COLCHICUM

Bulb Zones: 6–8
Height: C. autumnale *4–6in (10–15cm);*
C. speciosum, C. *'The Giant' 6–8in
(15–20cm)*

Good varieties for cutting *The large
goblet-shaped flowers of colchicums are like
robust and strapping crocuses. Arrange many
stems on their own, or mixed only with the
fresh green grass in which they grow. Grow
the classic* C. autumnale *(1). Try also the
chunky, large-flowered, white-based violet or
pink 'The Giant' (2), handsome in a
shallow colored glass on its own or mixed
with* C. autumnale *'Album' or a purple
variety of* C. speciosum.

Cultivation *Order corms from a bulb
wholesaler in late winter for late-summer
delivery and planting. Colchicums do best in*
*a dry, well-drained soil in full sun or light
shade. They are perfect for planting under
fruit trees. Cut a hole in the turf, plant them
2–3in (5–8cm) below the surface, and
replace the sod. As the buds emerge, place
slug pellets around each clump, or you will
have no more than a few ragged scraps left.
Slugs or colchicums, that's your choice.*

*Propagate established colchicums by
division immediately after flowering.*

CYCLAMEN

Main entry: Winter Pink, page 153.
The delicate pink C. hederifolium *(3) is
lovely arranged on its own, many stems in
a cup placed on a windowsill or in the pool
of light from a table lamp. Mix it, too, with
its own leaves and its white color form.*

DAHLIA

Main entry: Fall Orange and Red, page
143. *The handsome, long-stemmed*
D. *'Edinburgh' (5), with its great pompon
heads of rich purple-pink with white tips,
makes a fabulous cutting plant. Arrange it
with boughs of acorns or mix it with fall
leaves, hips, and berries (see pages 82–83).*

NERINE

Bulb Zones: 8–10
Height: 18–24in (45–60cm)

Good varieties for cutting *I used to
have an aversion to nerines. The hardiest, the
harsh nail-polish pink* N. bowdenii, *can
shout too loudly from their sunny flower bed.*

SCALE
2in (5cm)

1 *Colchicum autumnale*
2 *Colchicum 'The Giant'*
3 *Cyclamen hederifolium*
4 *Aster novi-belgii*
5 *Dahlia 'Edinburgh'*
6 *Penstemon*
7 *Rosa 'New Dawn'*
8 *Schizostylis coccinea 'Major'*
9 *Nerine bowdenii*
10 *Phlox paniculata*

SCALE
2in (5cm)

I like them better since discovering that you can have fun with them. Place them on their own in a turquoise ceramic vase for a modern still-life, or mix them with bright green cyperus, shrubby bupleurum, and sky-blue Salvia uliginosa. *The even more brazen salmon-orange-pink color forms are fabulous with crimson-black dahlias and Chinese lanterns. If you want a more subtle effect, try the white or deeper pink cultivars (9).*

Conditioning *Give them a good drink and they will last for over a week in water.*

Cultivation *Plant the hardy varieties in late summer or after flowering, with the noses of the bulbs showing above the soil. Choose a sheltered site, in full sun, preferably with the shelter and warmth of a sunny wall. They do best on a light sandy soil. Grow the more tender forms in a greenhouse and plant out after the frosts.*

The leaves appear after the flower spike and disappear by summer. To get the best flowers, water until the leaves die down, then let them dry off. Protect with a good mulch through winter. Nerines dislike being disturbed, but as they become congested, lift and replant every four to five years in fall or when the leaves die down. They can also be grown from seed sown when it is fresh.

Beard tongue
PENSTEMON

Evergreen herbaceous perennial and subshrub
Zones: 8–10
Height and spread: 18–36in × 12–24in (45–90cm × 30–60cm)

Good varieties for cutting *The lovely flower spikes of the large-flowered border penstemon hybrids with their many tubular flowers arranged on the stem like*

an array of trumpets are a real mainstay of the fall cutting garden. Their velvety colors range from white to pink, and bright scarlet to purples and reds so dark they are nearly black (**6**). I like to mix dark penstemons such as 'Blackbird', 'Sour Grapes', or 'Midnight' with orange and yellow red-hot pokers and Chinese lanterns (see pages 80–81). For paler pinks and mauves choose the lovely P. campanulatus hybrids.

Conditioning *Some penstemons droop after cutting. Strip the bottom leaves and sear the stem before soaking overnight.*

Cultivation *Plant penstemons in full sun in a fertile, well-drained soil, facing south or west and well sheltered from wind. If you pick or deadhead regularly, you will have three or four months of flowering well into the fall. They are best treated as half-hardy perennials with stock replenished from cuttings in late summer to early fall. Over-winter away from frost in a cool greenhouse or a cold frame. The parent plant can be potted up and kept in frost-free conditions. Cut it right back in late winter and by the time it can be planted out after the last frost it will be covered in new leaves and shoots.*

PHLOX

Main entry: Summer White, page 121.
*Many of the pink forms of P. paniculata (**10**) are good late-flowerers to combine with white Japanese anemones and 'Iceberg' roses.*

Rose
ROSA

Main entry: Summer Pink, page 124.
*It is well worth growing some bosomy pink roses for picking right through the summer and into the colder autumn months. The climber 'New Dawn' (**7**) is a very free- and long-flowering pale pink rose with a pretty, open flower and gentle scent. R. 'Heritage' is another fine long-flowering variety.*

SCHIZOSTYLIS COCCINEA

Bulb Zones: 6–9
Height: 24in (60cm)

Good varieties for cutting *Pick a generous bunch of the miniature, gladiolus-like pink and red flowers of S. coccinea. The delicate flower spikes with neat, cup-shaped*

SCALE 2in (5cm)

SCALE 2in (5cm)

blooms held on thin stems look best en masse. When they are fully open in sun, the darker colors shine as if cut from the finest iridescent silk. These slightly tender bulbs will provide a strong splash of color even after the first frosts have finished off almost everything else. Grow the rich scarlet-pink S. coccinea 'Major' (**8**) or white S.c. var. alba, and the salmon-pink 'Sunrise'.

Cultivation *These bulbs do well in full sun in almost any soil, but need a lot of moisture during the summer to enable them to throw up good flower spikes in fall.*

The thick matting roots become rapidly congested. To keep up good flower production, they should be divided every few years and moved to a fresh place.

SCALE 2in (5cm)

Orange and Red

ABUTILON

Herbaceous perennial and deciduous shrub
Zones: 9–10
Height and spread: A. 'Clementine', 'Yellow
Belle' 3–6ft × 18in–3ft (90cm–1.8m ×
45–90cm); A. × suntense cultivars, A.
vitifolium 6–10ft × 3ft (1.8–3m × 90cm)
Good varieties for cutting *With*
generous, open, saucer- and bell-shaped
flowers in rich reds, yellows, oranges,
purples, and whites, abutilons make stat-
uesque additions to any bunch and are also
perfect as single stems for a desk or bedside
table. 'Clementine' (2), with its papery, deep
orange-red flowers and pale green calyx, will

SCALE 2in (5cm)

flower from summer right through to the first
frosts. 'Yellow Belle' is an excellent, clear
vibrant yellow form of similar habit. For
summer flowering, the lovely pale mauve
A. vitifolium 'Veronica Tennant' has huge,
disk-shaped flowers with brilliant golden
anthers. Look out, too, for the pure white
A.v. var. album. Best of all these earlier
flowerers for a sheltered spot is the rich dark
blue-purple A. × suntense 'Violetta'.
Conditioning *Strip most of the leaves,*
which tend to flop. Sear the stems in boiling
water for 20 seconds.
Cultivation *Grow the more tender vari-*
eties such as 'Clementine' and 'Canary Bird'
in large pots so that they can be moved inside
during winter. They like moist but not wet
soil. Fertilize them well for a good long
flowering season. Cut them to the ground
in winter and they will be covered in new
growth and leaves by mid-spring.

A. vitifolium and A. × suntense are
best grown against a warm wall, or as free-
standing specimens in a sheltered, sunny site.
They do well in any average, fairly dry soil.
Pick small sprigs, cutting back lightly to
avoid spoiling the shrub's elegant form.
To be safe, cover them in a frost-protective
netting during winter.

Propagate from semi-ripe cuttings taken
in mid- to late summer. A. vitifolium also
grows quickly from seed and self-seeds abun-
dantly around the parent plant.

Butterfly weed, silkweed
ASCLEPIAS TUBEROSA

Tuberous perennial Zones: 4–9
Height: 18–24in (45–60cm)
Good varieties for cutting *I long*
believed that the rather waxy, exotic-looking
asclepias had to be grown in a greenhouse.
There are indeed some tender varieties, but
others are fully frost-hardy and do well in
temperate climates. The North American

① *Asclepias tuberosa*
② *Abutilon 'Clementine'*
③ *Cosmos atrosanguineus*
④ *Dahlia 'Arabian Night'*
⑤ *Dahlia 'Bishop of Llandaff'*
⑥ *Dahlia 'Queen Fabiola'*

native A. tuberosa (1) is an excellent plant
that flowers for many weeks in late summer
and early fall. Its light and airy flowers com-
bine well with tithonias and contrast with
acid-green dill, bupleurum, and purple
lisianthus. For a truly stunning combination
mix it with red crabapples and add pale
yellow sunflowers.
Conditioning *Remove the bottom leaves*
and sear the stems in boiling water immedi-
ately after picking. Like euphorbias, the cut
stems exude a sticky sap, which will block
water uptake.
Cultivation *Plant the wandering fleshy*
roots 4in (10cm) deep. A. tuberosa thrives
in shelter and full sun in a deep, sandy, dry
soil where the roots can make a good run.

Propagate by division in spring. A.
tuberosa germinates freely and easily from
fresh seed, but seeds from a packet produce
unreliable results.

COSMOS

Main entry: Summer White, page 118.
C. atrosanguineus (3), a chocolate-red
ruby of a flower, exudes a scent you might
imagine wafting from the seraglio in Istanbul
as the Sultan's chef concocted his latest and
richest chocolate pudding: exotic, dense,
magical, altogether alluring! The flowers are
best on their own or grouped with other
single flowers (see pages 78–79).

Smokebush, smoke tree
COTINUS

Deciduous shrub and tree Zones: 5–8
Height and spread: C. coggygria 8–13ft ×
8–13ft (2.5–4m × 2.5–4m); C. obovatus
20ft × 15ft (6m × 4.5m)
Good varieties for cutting *The*
smokebush, C. coggygria, is a large plant
for the average-sized cutting garden, but its
summer foliage and flowers (see page 122)
and its vibrant orange, pink, red, and purple
leaves in fall are spectacular for cutting.
Grow the claret-colored C.c. 'Royal Purple'
(7) or 'Notcutt's Variety', or, if you have
room for an even bigger shrub, the American
smoke tree, C. obovatus (see pages 82–83),
which has larger leaves in a mix of crimson,
deep carmine-pink, golden-yellow, tangerine-
orange, and flame-red.
Conditioning *Hammer the stem ends.*
Cultivation *These are easily grown*
shrubs, which will thrive in any reasonably
drained soil. Too fertile a soil can inhibit
the development of fall colors and make the
shrubs coarse and sappy. They do best and
color most dramatically in full sun; the
purple-leaved varieties tend to revert to green
in shade. Prune to remove dead wood in
spring. If you cut them back hard, you will
not get the feathery haze of summer flowers,
which are produced on wood three years old
or more; you will, however, get larger leaves.

DAHLIA

Tuberous perennial Zones: 9–10
Height: 3–7ft (90cm–2m)

Good varieties for cutting *Dahlias are the most exuberant and dramatic of fall flowers. I love them in nearly all their shapes, forms, and colors. You can grow tall, voluptuous herbaceous dahlias, like 'Edinburgh' (see page 140), or jazzy, rich burnt-orange ones such as 'Glow', deep crimsons like 'Queen Fabiola' (6), or almost black 'Natal' or 'Arabian Night' (4). More subtle varieties include 'Bishop of Llandaff' (5) with its scarlet petals and central ruff and its exotic dark crimson foliage. This combines effectively with lime-green Zinnia 'Envy'.*

Conditioning *Only pick dahlias in full flower. The buds tend to wither and die without opening. Recut the hollow stem ends under water to avoid airlocks.*

Cultivation *Select tubers in flower at a good nursery, or from a reliably illustrated list; color descriptions are always misleading. Start them into growth in spring and they will have formed good plants by early summer, when you can plant them out in a sunny position in well-drained soil. Add a handful of bonemeal to the planting hole and plant the tubers 4in (10cm) below the surface. When they are growing strongly, pinch back the tip of the main stem to encourage bushy growth. Stake the taller varieties. Keep the plants well watered in summer and, if you are not picking them, deadhead them as the flowers fade. After flowering, lift the tubers and store them in a frost-free place. Propagate dahlias from basal cuttings (see page 36).*

Spurge, milkweed
EUPHORBIA

Main entry: Spring Green and Silver, page 96. *The vibrant* E. griffithii *(8), the color of tomato soup in spring and summer, turns a mixture of reds and yellows in fall, and adds vim and zest to any fall arrangement (see pages 82–83).*

GLADIOLUS

Corm Zones: G. communis *subsp.* byzantinus *6–9; Guildhall hybrids 9–10*
Height: 3–5ft (90cm–1.5m)

Good varieties for cutting *The reputation of gladioli has been tarnished by the sickly pinks, pale butterscotch-oranges, and washed-out yellows that you inevitably find in funeral wreaths and floral tributes. Poor flowers! They can be so much better than this. There are sumptuous crimson, violet, lime-green, burnt-orange, and nearly black gladiolus hybrids, not to mention the head-turning, deep carmine-pink G. communis subsp. byzantinus (see pages 122–23). Try 'Green Woodpecker' with its crimson throat and good, sulfurous-green flowers, mixed with the lovely rich red-purple 'Plum Tart'. Another of my favorite gladioli is the deep red 'Black Lash' (9). This is perfect when used as a strong spike with huge sunflowers, thistles, and dahlias to break up any neatness and symmetry in a hanging globe (see pages 74–75).*

Conditioning *Remove the bottom leaves. Some people cut off the top 2in (5cm) of the flower spike to make sure the lower flowers all come out; I think this a shame, since the twists and turns of the spike end are an integral part of the plant's appeal.*

Cultivation *Choose gladioli when in flower, or order corms from a well-illustrated list of a good bulb wholesaler to make sure you get the best colors. Plant out summer- and autumn-flowerers after the last spring frosts, and stagger the planting at 10-day intervals from mid-spring to mid-summer, to prolong the season. Choose a site in full sun with light soil rich in organic material. Plant them 4in (10cm) deep and 4–6in (10–15cm) apart in clumps or lines in the cutting garden. Water regularly and plentifully during the growing season, and stake the taller varieties. Lift your corms after the first frost, cut off*

⑦ *Cotinus coggygria* 'Royal Purple'
⑧ *Euphorbia griffithii*
⑨ *Gladiolus* 'Black Lash'
⑩ *Helenium* 'Moerheim Beauty'
   (see page 144)

SCALE
2in (5cm)

❶ *Iris foetidissima*
(seed heads)
❷ *Leonotis ocymifolia*
❸ *Physalis alkekengi*
var. *franchetii*
❹ *Rosa moyesii*
'Geranium' (hips)

SCALE
2in (5cm)

their stems, dry and clean them, and rigor-ously discard any that have signs of disease. Dust them with fungicide and store them in a frost-free, cool, airy place for next year. Plant the spring-flowerers, such as G.c. subsp. byzantinus, in fall.

Propagate by removing young cormlets from the parent plant after lifting in fall. Be patient; they will flower in one or two years.

Sneezeweed
HELENIUM

Herbaceous perennial Zones: 4–8
Height: 3–5ft (90cm–1.5m)
Good varieties for cutting *The petals of these big-boned, daisylike flowers fold back from the fuzzy central hub, almost like the wings of an insect. The heleniums have an air that somehow combines the obvious with the delicate; they do everything that an aster does, but more so. My favorite is the rich orange-brown 'Moerheim Beauty' (10, page 143) with its bumblebee center and its ring of jagged, crinkled petals. Combine it in a tightly tied bunch with orange and green Chinese lanterns and nutmeg rudbeckias, all contrasted with rich purple*

gladioli and acid-green bupleurum. Or mix it simply with deep blue salvias.
Conditioning *This is a very reliable plant. Strip the bottom leaves and they will last over a week in water.*
Cultivation *Plant in full sun. These tolerant, easily grown plants will survive in any soil short of a bog. Support the heavy flowering stems with a network of hazel sticks. The clumps quickly get congested and thrive on regular division (see pages 37 and 41) in spring or fall. If you buy just one plant, you will soon have a good-sized colony for a minimal price.*

IRIS
Main entry: Winter Blue and Purple, page 158. *The fruits of* I. foetidissima, *whether picked unripe with their angular, green pods or bursting open with glistening, pomegranatelike seeds (I), make a colorful and spicy addition to any fall bunch (see pages 76–78).*

Lion's ear
LEONOTIS OCYMIFOLIA

Semi-evergreen shrub Zones: 7–9
Height and spread: 5ft × 30in (1.5m × 75cm)
Good varieties for cutting *The tall spikes of leonotis (2) carry whorls of rich orange flowers divided by expanses of empty stem; they always remind me of those one or two brightly lit floors in a high-rise. Use their vibrant color to contrast with purple Dahlia 'Edinburgh' in an arrangement with cattails and fall leaves (see pages 82–83), or mix them with crimson gladioli and russet-red sunflowers.*
Conditioning *Sear the bottom 1in (2.5cm) of the stems and give them a long drink.*
Cultivation *This tender plant will not survive winter in any but the mildest climate. Dig it up, cut it back hard, and pot it in a well-drained potting mix to overwinter in the greenhouse. It will start into life again in late spring, and you can plant it out after the last frost. It will not flower until late summer or early fall. Choose a sunny posi-tion with well-drained, fertile soil.*

Propagate from seed sown in spring or from softwood cuttings taken in late summer and overwintered under glass.

Chinese lantern
PHYSALIS ALKEKENGI

Herbaceous perennial Zones: 5–8
Height: 24in (60cm)
Good varieties for cutting *P.a. var. franchetii (3), with its fragile green or orange fruits like hanging lights made from*

colored paper, is a glamorous fall foliage plant. The lanterns are light at the top and dark at the bottom, almost as if they were lit from inside. The stems twist and turn, and the whole effect is like a particularly delicate sort of Christmas decoration. Look out, too, for the showier P.a. 'Gigantea' with larger leaves and bigger, more impressive, pointed lanterns. Combine them with deep crimson

SCALE
2in (5cm)

penstemons, red-hot pokers, and chestnut, mahogany, and orange rudbeckias (see pages 80–81). Or simply mix them with rich royal blue gentians. During summer the unripe green pods make fine foliage to contrast with the rich cardinal colors of cosmos, roses, or snapdragons.

Conditioning *Remove the leaves because they flop within a week or so. The lanterns continue to look as good as new for months.*

Cultivation *Physalis is invaluable for filling in awkward corners, since it will thrive in sun or shade and is not fussy about soil. But when you choose the site do keep in mind that the running roots of physalis can become invasive, so they should be kept well away from your more delicate plants. The tall stems tend to flop but can be held up by a network of sticks and thin twine or thread (see page 37).*

Propagate by division in fall or spring, planting the tendrillike roots 3in (8cm) deep, or sow seed in early spring. It will fruit in the fall of the same year.

❺ *Rudbeckia 'Nutmeg'*
❻ *Tithonia rotundifolia*
❼ and **❽** *Viburnum opulus*
❾ *Zinnia Scabious-flowered Group*
❿ *Zinnia Giant Cactus Group*

Rose
ROSA
Main entry: Summer Pink, page 124.
For long-lasting hips, grow R. moyesii and R. glauca. R.m. 'Geranium' forms tall, long-limbed bushes, which have lovely single silk-scarlet flowers in summer, followed by bright scarlet hips which last for several weeks without aging, even out of water. I make collections of these hips to mix with fallen leaves and anything else I can find in the garden, to fill bowls and vases around the house. Try them with stems of cotinus and red oak, cattails, and snowberry berries (see pages 82–83), or with clematis seed heads, acorns, and filberts. Add any flowers there are around, and make generous, billowing arrangements.

The pretty but discreet flowers of R. glauca are followed by shiny red balloon-shaped hips that look beautiful against the fine gray foliage. The branches are elegant enough to be arranged on their own.

Many of the Rugosa roses also have wonderful hips – shiny red balls the size of crabapples. Growing on shorter stems, they are especially useful for smaller posies.

Coneflower, gloriosa daisy
RUDBECKIA
Main entry: Fall Yellow, page 146.
*The large-flowered gloriosa daisy R. 'Nutmeg' (**5**) comes in a variety of rich oranges and browns. Any of them look appealing in a large pitcher on the kitchen table. I like to pick out the most chocolate-colored flowers and mix them in a tightly tied bunch with russet sunflowers.*

Mexican sunflower
TITHONIA ROTUNDIFOLIA
Half-hardy annual
Height and spread: 4ft × 2ft (1.2m × 60cm)
Good varieties for cutting *Think of the sort of sofa that Liberace would have lounged in: velvet, cushioned, full, and plush. That is the tithonia: as comfortable as flowers get. Whether you grow a vibrant orange tithonia (**6**), or a less blatant form, mix them with luxurious velvety blue salvias, deep crimson dahlias, and gladioli.*

Conditioning *Tithonia flower heads have hollow, bulbous bases, which easily bend and break, so handle them carefully after picking.*

Cultivation. *Plant tithonia out in full sun in well-drained soil 12in (30cm) apart, or to fill gaps left by early-summer flowers.*

To propagate, sow under cover in late spring. Keep seedlings protected from cold breezes or they will yellow and die.

VIBURNUM
Main entry: Winter Pink, page 154.
*The glistening berries of the European guelder rose, V. opulus (**7** and **8**), come in red, orange, and yellow (V.o. 'Xanthocarpum'). Pick them while they are still bright and succulent. They are perfect fillers for a fall bunch (see pages 80–81). In early fall V. lantanoides has red and green berries.*

ZINNIA
Main entry: Fall Silver, Green, and Brown, page 138. *The shaggy Giant Cactus Group zinnias (**10**) look like the sort of hat fashionable women of the 1950's wore to society weddings, while the altogether more sharp-edged zinnias of the Scabious-flowered Group (**9**) have a ring of pointed petals around a central hub.*

SCALE
2in (5cm)

❶ *Capsicum annuum*
❷ *Helenium* 'Butterpat'
❸ *Kniphofia* 'Yellow Hammer'
❹ *Rosa* 'Graham Thomas'
❺ *Rudbeckia hirta* 'Green Eyes'

SCALE
2in (5cm)

Yellow

Chili pepper
CAPSICUM ANNUUM

Half-hardy annual
Height: 18in (45cm)

Good varieties for cutting *Chili peppers come in oranges, reds, and yellows (1), and when unripe they are a deep bottle-green. Mix the ripe fruits with blackberries, sloes, and Chinese lanterns, or use them to brighten any fall bunch.*

Conditioning *Strip all the leaves, and the fruit will last for well over a month in water before beginning to age. You can also hang them upside-down in a warm, well-ventilated place, and use them dried.*

Cultivation *Sow under cover in early spring. Thin. Keep in the greenhouse until there is no risk of frost, then plant against a sunny wall or in some other sheltered spot.*

Sneezeweed
HELENIUM

Main entry: Fall Orange and Red, page 144. *One of the brightest heleniums is yellow 'Butterpat' (2). Cut it 3ft (90cm) tall to mix with sunflowers and boughs of green and red crabapples; or include it in a multicolored jamboree with gentians, salvias, and dahlias.*

Red-hot poker, torch lily
KNIPHOFIA

Perennial, some evergreen Zones: 5–9
Height: 3–4ft (90cm–1.2m)

Good varieties for cutting *The bottlebrush flowers of the kniphofia cultivars come in a variety of bright and brilliant colors. Try the more delicate, slender dwarf hybrids, which have the majority of flowers on each spike at their peak at the same time. Grow the dazzling yellow-flowered, green-budded 'Yellow Hammer' (3) to contrast with deep red penstemons or mix with nutmeg and yellow rudbeckias and orange* Viburnum opulus *berries (see pages 80–81). Or try the paler yellow K. citrina or 'Primrose Beauty', which are lovely mixed with turquoise* Salvia uliginosa.

Conditioning *If the bottom two or three whorls of flowers are fading, pull them off.*

Cultivation *Plant in full sun in sandy soil that does not dry out in summer. Winter wet is the kniphofia's main enemy, so drainage must be excellent. In colder regions, give them a heavy mulch in late fall.*

Propagate by division in spring (see page 37). Remember, though, that clumps are slow to increase and it may be several years before they are ready for division. Kniphofias set seed freely, but a motley crew of offspring usually results.

Rose
ROSA

Main entry: Summer Pink, page 124. *The new English rose R. 'Graham Thomas' (4) has huge cabbage flowers the color of pale yellow butterscotch and is an unbelievably productive performer, pumping out flowers from mid-summer to late fall and, in temperate climates, even into winter.*

Coneflower, gloriosa daisy
RUDBECKIA

Half-hardy annual and herbaceous perennial
Zones: 4–9 Height: 24–36in (60–90cm)

Good varieties for cutting *In your florist's shop, you will probably find that the rudbeckias have been stripped down to their bald central heads. The petals are stripped because they last only three to four days and would look wilted before they reached the customer. All the more reason to grow your own, for rudbeckias come in a sumptuous mix of mahogany, nutmeg, yellow, and burnt-marmalade colors. Grow the annual gloriosa daisies with 7in (18cm) diameter flowers: R.* hirta *'Green Eyes' (5) is bright yellow with a contrasting green center, and R. 'Nutmeg' (see page 145) comes in a wide range of browns.*

Conditioning *Pick these flowers regularly, use, and throw away. Strip the leaves and give them a long drink.*

Cultivation *Plant in sun, shade, wet, dry – anywhere, short of a bog. Keep cutting and they'll keep coming. Propagate perennials by division in spring (see page 37) and annuals by a mid-spring sowing under cover. Plant out to replace your early-summer cutting plants such as sweet Williams, cornflowers, and wallflowers.*

❶ *Ampelopsis glandulosa*
   var. brevipedunculata
❷ *Salvia viridis*
❸ *Salvia patens*

Blue and Purple

AMPELOPSIS

Deciduous climber Zones: 5–8
Height: 16ft (5m)

Good varieties for cutting A. glandulosa *var.* brevipedunculata (**1**), *with its three- or five-lobed, hoplike leaves, is covered with porcelain-blue berries in fall. Arrange them on their own, leaves stripped to reveal the fruits better, with the stems writhing here, there, and everywhere, or use them as foliage with* Salvia uliginosa, *orange zinnias, and late marigolds. Look out for the pretty and less vigorous cultivar* A.g. var. b. 'Elegans', *with small leaves delicately splashed with pink. You sometimes see it for sale in a flower shop as a house plant.*

Cultivation Ampelopsis, *a fast-growing, self-clinging plant, needs plenty of room, so pick your site with care. Grow on a hot, sunny wall in poor soil for the most fruit. Propagate by semi-ripe cuttings in mid-summer (see pages 38 and 39), by layering (see page 42), or from seed.*

Globe thistle
ECHINOPS

Herbaceous perennial Zones: 3–9
Height: 4–6ft (1.2–1.8m)

Good varieties for cutting *The gray-blue, fluffy spheres of* Echinops ritro 'Veitch's Blue' (**4**) *look like the pompons on top of children's stocking caps. Pick it in spiny, silver bud or in full flower when its dense clustered heads, as weighty and substantial as wrought-iron balls, lend authority to any arrangement, underpinning the frothier flowers. They look beautiful mixed simply with orange marigolds in a pitcher for the kitchen, or cut them long to arrange with sunflowers in a large vase.*

Conditioning *Just strip the slightly prickly lower leaves.*

Cultivation *Ideally plant in full sun, though* E. ritro *varieties will flower in partial shade. These plants do best in poor soil, so omit them when you are fertilizing the garden. They otherwise become lank and leggy. Propagate by division in fall or by root cuttings in winter (see pages 41 and 43).*

Gentian, willow gentian
GENTIANA

Herbaceous or alpine perennial Zones: 6–9
Height: G. triflora var. japonica 32in (80cm); G. asclepiadea 36in (90cm)

Good varieties for cutting *The taller gentians are a must for fall arrangements. The flowers of* G. triflora *var.* japonica (**5**), *set in pairs up long spikes, are the true blue of Moroccan tiles. A few stems will bring any bunch to life. Contrast this gentian powerfully with orange dahlias and butterfly weed or, even better, in a multi-colored arrangement with pink and orange zinnias, orange and yellow rudbeckias, and deep rich-colored asters and dahlias. Also excellent is the slightly paler blue* G. asclepiadea, *or willow gentian, and a less showy, white form,* G.a. var. alba.

Conditioning *Strip the bottom leaves and give an overnight drink before arranging. They like a bright warm place to open fully.*

Cultivation G. asclepiadea *and* G. triflora *do best in acidic soil but will tolerate lime.* G. triflora *likes a moist, peaty, well-drained soil in full sun or partial shade.* G. asclepiadea, *a woodland plant, needs a moist soil in shade with lots of humus.*

Propagate in fall from ripe seed. To help germination, stand the containers where frost can reach them. Do not cover the seed. G. asclepiadea *self-seeds freely.*

Sage
SALVIA

Annual, tender perennial, and evergreen and semi-evergreen shrub Zones: S. patens 9–10; S. uliginosa 8–9; S. × superba 5–9
Height: S. patens, S. × superba 30in (75cm); S. uliginosa to 5ft (1.5m)

Good varieties for cutting *The huge sage family, with its simple, double-lipped flowers in resonant colors and soft, tempting textures, is vital in fall. Throughout summer and fall* S. patens *in all its color forms is excellent for cutting. Best of all is the deep, luxurious royal blue (**3**), which is good with scarlets and reds (see page 73), but there are also pretty pale blue and pale mauve forms. Another must is* S. uliginosa (**6**), *with sky-blue spikes. Grow, too, the early-flowering* S. × superba *with warm purple flowers, and* S. guaranitica *in the darkest purple-blue. I also cut bright red* S. elegans *and* S. fulgens *to mix with oranges and ochers. Of the many good annual salvias, look out for* S. viridis (**2**), *with green-veined bracts of purple, blue, or pink and* S. farinacea 'Victoria', *with its deep violet flowers; both are 18in (45cm) tall.*

Conditioning *Strip the bottom leaves of* S. patens. *For the others, sear the bottom 1in (2.5cm) of stem and give a cool drink.*

Cultivation *Plant sages in a sunny, well-protected site to get the maximum number of flowers. Most like plenty of moisture during summer, and the tender varieties especially need well-drained soil. Stake the tallest forms. Protect the underground roots of* S. uliginosa *in winter with straw.*

Propagate more tender varieties from cuttings taken in late summer and over-wintered in a frost-free cold frame or cool greenhouse (see pages 38, 39). Dig up the parent plant, allow it to die down in winter, and it will shoot again in spring. Plant out once there is little risk of frost. For robust plants, treat S. patens *as a half-hardy annual and sow every year.* S. uliginosa *and* S. × superba *are best propagated by division. Sow seed of the annuals directly in the ground in mid-spring (see pages 34, 35).*

❹ *Echinops ritro* 'Veitch's Blue'
❺ *Gentiana triflora* var. *japonica*
❻ *Salvia uliginosa*

SCALE
2in (5cm)

SCALE
2in (5cm)

Winter

Few people grow flowers to pick for arrangements during the winter, yet many winter-flowering plants are among the most fragrant of all. They are powerfully scented to attract the few insects still around for pollination – think of the exotic perfume of the winter honeysuckles or the sweet-scented daphnes.

Winter flowers in particular have a delicacy and elegance that are best appreciated when they are displayed in small bunches or as solitary stems. The fine, spidery flowers of the witch hazels are best in a vase on their own, and I always prefer to have the subtly different varieties of *Iris unguicularis* arranged singly, each in a narrow, tall, colored glass.

I always pot some spring bulbs for early forcing, and amaryllis, which is a winter indoor bulb. They are easy to grow inside and provide a welcome boost to the flower arranger's reper-toire in the garden's least productive season. I was married on New Year's Eve in Scotland, and my husband filled every room for the wedding party with nothing but the fragrant Tazetta narcisi 'Paper White' and 'Soleil d'Or'. They covered all the tables, the window ledges, and the mantels. These and other white flowers look beautiful with ivory candles (see pages 84–86).

Green and Silver

Cuckoo pint, lords and ladies
ARUM
Tuberous perennial Zones: 7–9
Height: 8–12in (20–30cm)
Good varieties for cutting *For elegant and interesting winter foliage, choose Italian arum, A. italicum 'Marmoratum' (1), the cultivated variety of the wild southern European A. italicum. While almost all other plants are dying back in fall, this, along with cyclamen, behaves in reverse and*

its leaves begin to appear. Then they go right through winter and spring and even into the early summer before they fade.

A.i. 'Marmoratum' has arrow-shaped, cream-veined, glossy, bright green leaves with bending and curling edges. Mix them with cyclamen leaves, scented narcissi, and winter honeysuckle for a pretty and fragrant arrangement (see pages 84–86). I also like to pick them to form a green and white marbled ruff around a tight bunch of flowers. In winter I mix them with snowdrops and aconites, tying the flowers tightly in a posy with a frill of arum foliage around the edge. The white-veined marbling of the leaves, picked out by the white of the snowdrop bells, looks fresh and inviting. Later I use them to frame spring and early summer flowers.

Rarely available but even more dramatic is A. nigrum, with deep purple-brown-black spathes in summer. (It always seems a great pity that the velvet purple-black dragon arum, Dracunculus vulgaris, smells of rotting meat – it would otherwise be sensa-tional in arrangements!)

Cultivation *Plant in fall or spring in a sunny or lightly shaded spot. A. italicum 'Marmoratum' is easy to grow in a moist, well-drained soil. Protect it with a covering of leaves if a hard frost is expected.*

Increase your stock from seed or by division in fall (see pages 36–37). When digging for division, remember that the tubers go deep into the soil. Once established, A.i. 'Marmoratum' seeds itself freely.

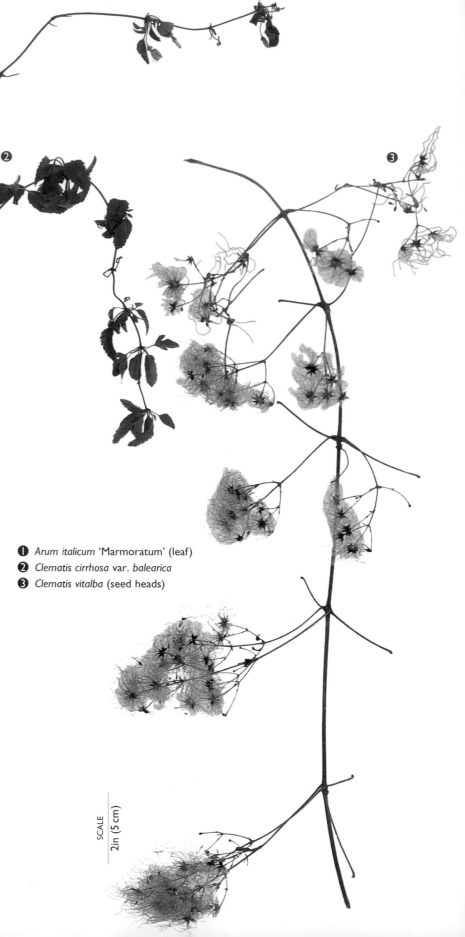

SCALE
2in (5 cm)

❶ *Arum italicum* 'Marmoratum' (leaf)
❷ *Clematis cirrhosa* var. *balearica*
❸ *Clematis vitalba* (seed heads)

SCALE
2in (5 cm)

❹ *Daphne laureola*
❺ *Helleborus argutifolius*
❻ *Helleborus foetidus*
❼ *Helleborus orientalis*

SCALE
2in (5 cm)

CLEMATIS

Main entry: Spring White, page 99.

*Among my absolute mainstays for winter arrangements are great fluffy boughs of old man's beard, the seed heads of the wild C. vitalba (**3**). (See pages 84–86 and 88–89.) Less rampant and better for the garden, with pretty yellow bell-flowers in fall, are C. tangutica and C. 'Bill Mackenzie', which always add an interesting twist and turn to any arrangement (see page 137). Their seed heads seem to stay intact better than those of old man's beard. I also cut the green and freckled flowers of C. cirrhosa var. balearica (**2**) or C.c. 'Freckles'. I love almost all green-flowered plants, and this is a great winter favorite – especially because it is so surprising that it pumps its flowers out at this time of year.*

No special conditioning is needed, but it is worth spraying the delicate seed heads with odorless hair spray if you want them to last. This makes them hold better, and so you won't end up with bare branches while all the fluffy stuff scatters over the floor.

DAPHNE

Main entry: Winter Pink, page 153.

*D. laureola (**4**) is a handsome plant for winter picking and is most scented in the evening. Strip the lower, larger leaves from the stem to reveal the cool green flowers. Combine with hellebores and snowdrops in a small arrangement or with willow and clematis stems in a looser display (see pages 84–86).*

Corsican hellebore, Lenten rose, stinking hellebore
HELLEBORUS

Herbaceous perennial
Zones: H. argutifolius, H. foetidus 6–9; H. orientalis 4–8
Height and spread: 18–24in × 12–24in (45–60cm × 30–60cm)

Good varieties for cutting *All of them! Hellebores, with their fascinating forms and subtle green, pink, and cloudy purple hues, are stars of the winter garden and in arrangements (see pages 84–86, 92).*

*The Lenten rose, H. orientalis (**7**), bears cuplike flowers in various tones of green, pink (see page 154), claret, white, and almost black (see page 158). Some have beautiful freckling all over their faces. Choose plants when they are in flower to make sure you get your favorite colors, and select cultivars that hold their flower heads horizontally, not modestly bowed with their faces hidden. These are better for arranging.*

*The Corsican hellebore, H. argutifolius (**5**), is the most vigorous. This serrated-leaved evergreen has open, clear green flowers from mid-winter to mid-spring, and the angular, geometric-shaped seed pods make a sculptural addition to any large late winter or spring arrangement.*

*The stinking hellebore, H. foetidus (**6**), has lovely, hanging, green, bell-shaped flowers that look as if the petal edge has been dipped in a deep purple dye. The unpleasant odor recorded in its name should not present any problem, since it is released only when leaves are crushed between the fingers.*

Conditioning *Immediately after cutting, put the bottom 1in (2.5cm) of the stem in boiling water for about twenty seconds, then plunge it into deep cold water. Given this treatment, hellebores should stay fresh for three or four days, or even longer. If the flower heads still droop, re-cut the stems, repeat the searing process, and they should pick up again. They do not last well in florist's oasis.*

Cultivation *All these hellebores are easy to grow. They like cool conditions with light shade and a heavy, rich soil that stays moist in summer. This makes them an ideal choice for a well-drained, shady border. Plant them in fall or early spring in well-manured soil and then leave them alone: none likes to be moved. The different varieties will interbreed, so keep them separated unless you wish gradually to develop a new colony of mixed hybrids. Mulch with well-decayed manure or garden compost in mid-spring and apply a liquid manure through the summer. Fertilize again with bonemeal in the fall. Water freely in very dry weather.*

H. argutifolius likes protection from strong winds and the worst frosts. Cut back all hellebore leaves and spent flowering stems in spring. This will minimize any problem with leaf spot, make room for new growth, and allow more light in for any young seedlings around the parents' skirts.

Propagate by division in early spring, or dig up seedlings from your own garden, or from a friend's. Clear the area around the parent plants as they flower to encourage seedling growth. Transplant the offspring in early summer when they are still small and relatively tolerant of being moved.

Hellebores can also be grown from seed, sown ⅛in (3mm) deep in shallow flats of sandy seed starter mix in a cold frame in summer. Transplant the seedlings outdoors when they are a year old. They will flower the following year. Most hellebores will then self-seed freely.

Willow
SALIX

Deciduous tree and shrub

Zones: 5–9

Height and spread: S. daphnoides 25ft × 25ft (7.5m × 7.5m); S. caprea 30ft × 25ft (9m × 7.5m); S. alba varieties 50ft × 25ft (15m × 7.5m); S. × sepulcralis var. chrysocoma *40ft × 40ft (12m × 12m)*

Good varieties for cutting *I prize willows mainly for their catkins, but they have other excellent features that are equally valuable for the flower arranger. Their pliable young branches (up to two years old) can be used to form the base for wreaths, globes, and medallions (see pages 88–89). Their color and habit can also be exploited: the brightly colored stems of species such as* S. alba var. vitellina *(golden-yellow) and* S.a. var. v. 'Britzensis' *(scarlet-orange), both of which are upright in form, mix well with the golden weeping willow,* S. × sepul-cralis var. chrysocoma, *which is more flowing in habit. They make an eye-catching combination in a simple tall glass vase. The pussy willow,* S. caprea (**1**), *bears catkins from late winter; females are silky gray and the males are gray with yellow anthers. The giant pussy willow,* S. acutifolia, *has silvery catkins up to 3in (8cm) long.*

The smaller violet willow, S. daph-noides (**2**), *is my favorite willow in winter for its catkins, and* S.d. 'Aglaia' *is its best form. This is a loose-growing willow with elegantly twisting branches and a fluid shape which makes for relaxed arrangements. It mixes beautifully with amaryllis and filberts (see page 87).*

If you cut a branch of pussy willow in early winter, you will have to remove the female catkins' black glovelike coverings. As the winter goes on, they split open naturally. Then the bright, plump pussy willows look from a distance like silver-white blossom, those of S.d. 'Aglaia' *contrasting dramati-cally with its plum-purple branches.*

Cultivation *Willows are mostly as tough as old boots and will grow anywhere with some moisture (exceptions are* S. daph-noides *and* S. caprea, *which do not need damp conditions). Left alone, most willows will become large trees, but you can coppice them and so restrict their growth. Do this by allowing them to become established for a couple of years and then cut the stems where you want new growth to break at the begin-ning of spring, just before the sap starts to rise. This will give brighter-colored branches, but if done every year will reduce the number of catkins, which are best on wood that is at least two years old. Compromise and remove half the stems each year rather than cutting them all to the ground, and you will always have vivid stems and some flowers.*

All varieties of willow root easily from semi-ripe cuttings. Insert the cuttings with at least half their length below ground in a damp place, or even in a bottle of water, in the summer. If you cannot push them into the ground easily, it is not damp enough and not the right time to be planting.

If you plant hardwood cuttings of young branches 3-6ft (0.9-1.8m) long in late fall or early spring (again, push half their length into the ground), by spring they will be in leaf and growing as young trees.

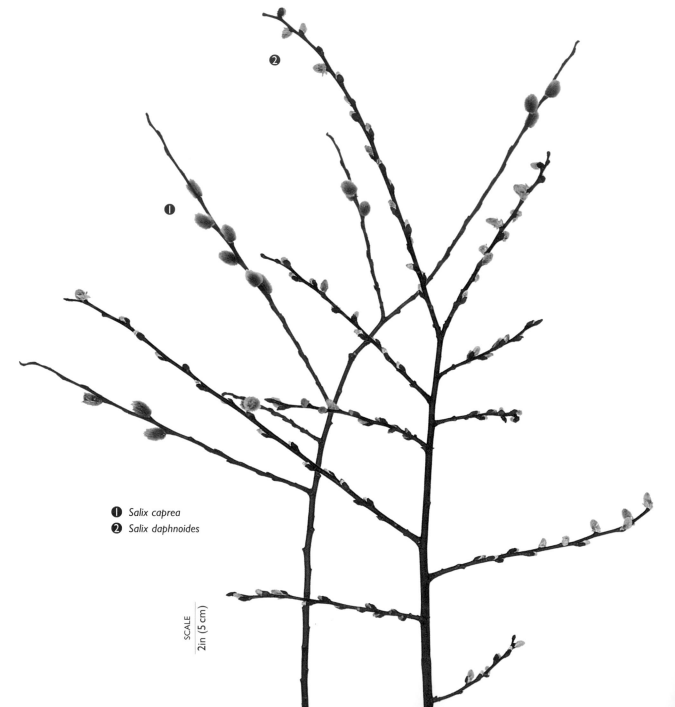

❶ *Salix caprea*
❷ *Salix daphnoides*

SCALE
2in (5 cm)

① *Camellia japonica* 'Alba Simplex'
② *Chaenomeles speciosa* 'Nivalis'
③ *Galanthus nivalis* 'Flore Pleno'
④ *Galanthus* 'S. Arnott'

SCALE 2in (5 cm)

White

CAMELLIA

Evergreen shrub and tree Zones: C.
japonica *and* C. × williamsii *7–10
Height and spread:* C. × williamsii *4ft
× 8ft (1.2m × 2.5m);* C. japonica *10ft
× 26ft (3m × 8m)*

Good varieties for cutting *I like
best the pure white single varieties such as
C. japonica 'Alba Simplex' (1) or C.j.
'Devonia', and, at the other end of the spec-
trum, the flamboyant raspberry-ripple
semi-double ones such as C.j. 'Tricolor'.
C. japonica varieties may be shy to flower
at first, but will be covered with blooms after
four or five years. I am less keen on the solid
red and pink camellias, but if you like these
colors, go for C. × williamsii varieties.
These, the easiest to grow, are the most reliable and hardy and drop their flowers as
they brown and die; with some C. japonica
varieties you have to remove the browning
flowers by hand.*

Conditioning *All camellias last a long
time in water; even the tightest buds will
come into flower three weeks after picking.
Just slit the stem ends before immersing in
cold water.*

Cultivation *Camellias grow well in a
lime-free (pH4–6.5), moist soil with good*

drainage and plenty of organic matter.
*Although they can cope with occasional
windy blasts, they suffer if they are
constantly in a draft. They are ideally suited
to sheltered, shady spots such as walls that
get little sun. Do not put them where they get
early morning sun or the frozen flowers will
thaw too quickly and turn brown.*

*Plant during fall or spring. Dig a large
hole twice the diameter plus the depth of the
pot and part-fill the hole with peat (in the
case of acid-loving plants, there is no alternative to using peat). Put in the root ball
and back fill with soil mixed with leaf
mulch or peat. This will give your plant a
good start, and you will not lose your flowers.*

*In mid-spring, scatter blood, fish, and
bonemeal on the soil around the roots and
then work in leaf mulch. For a good flower
crop, it is vital to keep plants well watered
between mid-summer and early fall when the
flower buds are produced. Otherwise they
will drop without opening.*

*You can propagate camellias by semi-ripe
or hardwood cuttings from summer to early
winter (see pages 38, 39, and 43).*

Japonica, flowering quince
CHAENOMELES

*Deciduous shrub Zones: 5–9
Height and spread: 8ft × 15ft (2.5m × 5m)*

Good varieties for cutting *The
C. speciosa cultivars are among the earliest
to flower, from late winter to mid-spring.
My favorites are the pure white, large-
flowered varieties such as C.s. 'Nivalis' (2).
The blossom appears all over the bare
branches. Trained on a high wall, the startling, plump flowers jut out directly from the
main branches as if they have been stuck
there to cheer up the winter scene. The
flowers are followed by sweet-smelling,
yellow fruits.*

Cultivation *Plant japonicas in a well-
drained soil in a sheltered, warm position.
Prevent sparrows and starlings from stripping the fat blossom buds, to which they are
very partial, by covering the entire plant with
a fine black cotton mesh. Cut back side
shoots, or those growing away from the wall
in wall-trained plants, to two or three buds
immediately after flowering. This promotes
strong new growth to provide next year's
flowering branches. Propagate by softwood
cuttings in summer (see pages 34–35).*

CROCUS

Main entry: see Winter Yellow,
page 156. *One of the loveliest winter
crocuses is the see-through white C. versicolor 'Picturatus' (5) with its feathery purple
veins and contrasting orange center.*

Snowdrop
GALANTHUS

*Bulb Zones: 2–9
Height: 4–6in (10–15cm)*

Good varieties for cutting *All
snowdrops look fresh and pretty when cut.
They are often best displayed in a clump of
flowers rather than individual heads scattered
through an arrangement. A single flower on*

its own may easily be overwhelmed. Snowdrops look lovely teamed simply with ivy.
G. nivalis *is the delicate species form.
G. 'S. Arnott'* (4) *has broad outer petals and
is fragrant and long-flowering. The showy
double G.n. 'Flore Pleno'* (3), *with its
flowers like ballroom dance dresses with all
their netting, lasts very well in water. All of
these appear in the depths of winter, cheering
up the garden and the house.*

Cultivation *These hardy winter and
early spring-flowering bulbs need cold to
make them flower, and thus are ideally
suited to places where the winter is severe.
Find them a shady and damp, but not
boggy, site, in a humus-rich, heavy soil, and
be careful not to let bulbs dry out excessively
in the ground. Snowdrops do not do well if
planted as dry bulbs, so if you are starting
from scratch, persuade a friend to let you
divide their clump, or buy some in pots from
a nursery. They increase rapidly once they
are established, quickly forming a carpet, so
you will soon be able to divide your own
clumps. Always divide when the plants are
"in the green," that is, just after flowering
and before the leaves start yellowing, usually
in late winter or early spring. Use a spade to
dig deep under large clumps and lift them,
split them by hand into smaller clumps, and
replant these at the same depth.*

⑤ *Crocus versicolor* 'Picturatus'
⑥ *Muscari azureum* 'Album'
(see page152)

SCALE 2in (5 cm)

SCALE
2in (5 cm)

① *Hyacinthus orientalis* 'Sneeuwwitje'
② *Pulmonaria officinalis* 'Sissinghurst White'

Hellebore, Lenten rose
HELLEBORUS
Main entry: Winter Green and Silver, page 149. *White varieties of the Lenten rose,* H. orientalis, *are commonly available. This one (3) has the creamy white flowers and yellow anthers of the Christmas rose (*H. niger*), but is more free-flowering.*

Amaryllis
HIPPEASTRUM
Main entry: Winter Orange and Red, page 155.
The lovely white amaryllis 'White Dazzler' (4) and 'Wedding Dance' look like winter lilies. Arrange on their own, or mix with a few handsome lichened branches or catkins.

Hyacinth
HYACINTHUS
Main entry: Spring White, page 101.
The Fairy or Roman hyacinths, such as Hyacinthus orientalis *'Sneeuwwitje' (1), have a lovely natural look.*

Grape hyacinth
MUSCARI
Bulb Zones: M. armeniacum, M. azureum *4–9;* M. macrocarpum *7–10 Height: 6–8in (15–20 cm)*
Good varieties for cutting
M. azureum *'Album' (6, page 151), the white form of grape hyacinth, looks lovely in a color jamboree with other early bulbs. Of the deep blue forms, choose* M. armeniacum *with intense, compact flowerheads (see page 159). If planted in a sunny spot, they often start appearing when snow is still on the ground. Mix them with any of the miniature daffodils, like 'Tête-à-Tête', for bright late winter table arrangements or arrange them tightly in a bobbly blue dome on their own.*

Daffodil, jonquil, narcissus
NARCISSUS
Main entry: Spring Yellow, page 109.
'Paper White' jonquils (5) are one of the joys of winter. Pot them at two-week intervals from early fall, and you can have highly scented, fresh flowers through winter. Keep these bulbs cold but frost-free while they form their leaves and flower buds.

Lungwort
PULMONARIA
Main entry: Winter Blue and Purple, page 159.
P. officinalis *'Sissinghurst White' (2) is a striking pure white variety with bright, faintly dappled leaves. It mixes well with snowdrops and other early bulbs (see page 93).*

Cultivation
Plant bulbs in fall, 2–3in (5–8cm) deep and 3–4in (8–10cm) apart, in clumps of fifteen to twenty. They rapidly form good patches, and you will be able to divide them by the second fall. They thrive in full sun, in a well-drained soil.

Christmas box, sweet box
SARCOCOCCA
Evergreen shrub Zones: 6–8 Height and spread: S. humilis *2ft (60cm);* S. hookeriana *var.* digyna *(page 154) 2–3ft × 3ft (60–90cm × 90cm)*
Good varieties for cutting
At first sight, sarcococcas are insignificant – only when you pick a piece and smell the tiny flowers will you discover their sensational scent. S. humilis *(6) has glossy, belt-shaped leaves and little white spiky flowers followed by large black berries in spring. Combine sarcococca with pink hellebores.*
Cultivation
Plant in fall or spring in a fertile, not too dry soil, in sun or shade. Sarcococcas thrive under trees. Propagate by semi-ripe cuttings taken in summer or early fall and planted in sandy soil in a cold frame.

VIBURNUM
Main entry: Winter Pink, page 154.
Use the evergreen laurustinus, V. tinus *(7), with its flat white to pink flower heads, as a background for large or small arrangements.*

③ *Helleborus orientalis*
④ *Hippeastrum* 'White Dazzler'
⑤ *Narcissus* 'Paper White'
⑥ *Sarcococca humilis*
⑦ *Viburnum tinus*

SCALE
2in (5 cm)

Pink

Cuckoo flower, lady's smock
CARDAMINE

Main entry: Spring Pink, page 104.

The very early flowering C. quinquefolia *(1) is a welcome surprise at this time of year. Arrange on its own or mix its clear pinkish-mauve flowers with early anemones or with deep blue pulmonarias.*

Japonica, flowering quince
CHAENOMELES

Main entry: Winter White, page 151.

The pale pink forms of the flowering quince, C. speciosa *(2), are among the prettiest of all. Like the harsher red forms, they can look impressive in minimalist, Japanese-style arrangements, with just a few sprigs displayed on their own. Or you could cut the short branches off individually and float them in a shallow saucer.*

❶ *Cardamine quinquefolia*
❷ *Chaenomeles speciosa*
❸ *Daphne odora 'Aureomarginata'*
❹ *Cyclamen coum*
❺ *Cyclamen hederifolium (leaf)*

CYCLAMEN

Corm Zones: C. coum *6–9;* C. repandum *7;* C. hederifolium *5*
Height: 4in (10cm)

Good varieties for cutting *The rich deep pink forms of the late-winter-flowering* C. coum *(4) are my favorites for cutting at this time of year, until the similar, carmine-colored* C. repandum *with its honey-scented flowers takes over in spring. Both look pretty and intense contrasted with bright orange or purple crocuses and purple and blue pulmonarias in tiny bunches.*

With their scalloped edges and white, lacy veining, the leaves of C. hederifolium *(5)*

SCALE
2in (5cm)

appear after the pink or white fall flowers and are excellent for winter cutting.

Cultivation *Cyclamen do well in rich, well-drained, crumbly soil containing plenty of leaf mulch. Dry, shaded nooks and crannies under trees or among rocks are ideal except for* C. coum, *which prefers moist sun or half-shade. Provide protection against hard frost in winter for* C. repandum. *Top-dress with manure or garden compost*

annually after the leaves die down (rake last year's mulch away first). Do this in early summer for C. hederifolium *and in the fall for* C. coum *and* C. repandum. *Take care not to bury the corms too deeply.*

Cyclamen are great self-seeders, so it is easiest to buy a few corms and leave them to spread naturally. Plant the corms in late summer or early fall, 2-3in (5-8cm) apart and 1in (2.5cm) deep, with the flattest side down and the tops visible at soil level.

DAPHNE

Evergreen shrub Zones: D. odora *8–9;* D. mezereum *3–7*
Height and spread:
D. mezereum *2ft × 2ft (60cm × 60cm);*
D. laureola *3ft × 3ft (90cm × 90cm);*
D. odora *5ft × 5ft (1.5m × 1.5m)*

Good varieties for cutting D. odora *and its cultivars have a fragrance that is a perfect mix of sharp citrus with spicy incense and ginger. Three sprigs by your bedside are enough to scent the whole room for up to two weeks. It is a compact, modest shrub with deep pink buds and paler flowers grouped above a whorl of mid-green leaves.* D.o. *'Aureomarginata' (3), which is hardier than the species, has a cream edge to the leaf, which makes it more interesting when not in flower.* D. mezereum *has striking, bright carmine-pink flowers and is also scented, but with less of a punch.* D. × burkwoodii *'Somerset' is also lovely (see page 104).*

SCALE
2in (5cm)

Cultivation *Daphnes do not like being disturbed, so plant them when they are young, preferably in groups of three because one plant will not tolerate excessive cutting. They thrive on fertile, well-drained but not over-dry soil; both* D. mezereum *and* D. laureola *do well on limestone. Most like full sun, although* D. laureola *prefers a cool, shaded spot. Provide them with some shelter and protect* D. odora *from severe frost. Keep them well fertilized with regular topdressings. They are easy to propagate from semi-ripe cuttings in summer or from fresh seed. Many daphnes tend to be short-lived, so it makes good sense to nurture the offspring as replacements.*

Hellebore, Lenten rose
HELLEBORUS
Main entry: Winter Green and Silver, page 149.
The Lenten rose, Helleborus orientalis (1), *has some lovely pink forms. Some, like 'Zodiac', have been specifically developed for their smattering of freckles whereas other marked forms are chance seedlings.*

Hyacinth
HYACINTHUS
Main entry: Spring White, page 101.
The zany pink H. orientalis *'Jan Bos'* (2) *is startling in the garden and even more eye-catching arranged in a lime-green cup.*

Polyanthus, primrose
PRIMULA
Main entry: Spring Yellow, page 110.
A pretty pink or carmine primrose (4) *mixes well with bulbs in a cheering winter posy.*

Christmas box, sweet box
SARCOCOCCA
Main entry: Winter White, page 152.
The heavily perfumed S. hookeriana *var.* digyna (3) *has a red stem and pink petals.*

Laurustinus
VIBURNUM
Deciduous and evergreen shrub
Zones: V. tinus 8–9 ; V. × bodnantense 7–8; V. farreri, V. fragrans 6–8; V. carlesii, V. × burkwoodii, V. opulus cultivars 5–8

Height and spread: V. opulus *'Compactum'* 5ft × 5ft (1.5m × 1.5m); V. × burkwoodii *varieties* 8ft × 8ft (2.5m × 2.5m); V. × bodnantense *varieties* 10ft × 7ft (3m × 2.2m); V. tinus, V. sargentii 10ft × 10ft (3m × 3m)

Good varieties for cutting *As a family, the viburnums are in my top 10 for year-round picking. Of the winter-flowering viburnums, the evergreen laurustinus,* V. tinus, *with its white or pink flower heads, is good in arrangements of any size. For smaller bunches, though, I tend to strip some of the leaves, otherwise the overall effect may be too dense, overwhelming other flowers. Metallic blue berries, left over from the previous year of flowering, are a bonus of this handsome shrub, and the pale pink 'Gwenllian' has the best berries of all.*

Highly recommended for larger gardens are varieties of the winter-flowering V. × bodnantense *such as 'Dawn'* (5) *with deep pink buds and paler pink flowers, and 'Deben' with white flowers tinted pink. Both last well cut, and their clumps of white or* pale pink flowers on bare branches are ideal at the bedside – you can wake to enjoy their gentle scent. V. farerri (syn. V. fragrans) does not last so well, and its flowers tend to drop. Varieties of the late winter- and spring-flowering V. × burkwoodii (6) and of V. carlesii are also pretty and scented. Later in spring and early summer V. opulus 'Roseum' comes into its own, and in fall the wild form of V. opulus with its red, orange, or yellow berries is a must (see page 145).

Cultivation *All viburnums enjoy fertile, moist soil, and most grow happily on alkaline soils. Plant them in late fall in sun or semi-shade and mulch in late winter. In general viburnums do not need pruning, but when you cut branches for the house keep in mind the resulting shape of the bush. With big shrubs like these, I recommend buying one good specimen. It takes years before you can pick from newly propagated plants. However, if you are patient, you can take softwood cuttings from deciduous plants and semi-ripe cuttings from evergreens in summer, and insert them in a sandy mix. V. tinus can also be layered (see page 42).*

SCALE 2in (5cm)

❶ *Helleborus orientalis*
❷ *Hyacinthus orientalis* 'Jan Bos'
❸ *Sarcococca hookeriana* var. *digyna*
❹ *Primula variety*
❺ *Viburnum* × *bodnantense* 'Dawn'
❻ *Viburnum* × *burkwoodii*

Orange and Red

Witch hazel
HAMAMELIS

Main entry: Winter Yellow, page 157.
Hamamelis × intermedia *'Diane'* bears
*flowers of a rich burnt copper with a deeper
red calyx. H. × i. 'Jelena'* (**1**)*, the most
vigorous of the witch hazels, grows 15–20ft
(4.5–6m) high and has more delicate,
orange-red flowers with the petal tips fading
out to a buttercup-yellow. Both have vivid
fall leaves in hot orange, red, and scarlet.*

Amaryllis
HIPPEASTRUM

Indoor bulb
Minimum temperature: 55°F (13°C)
Height: 12–20in (30–50cm)

Good varieties for cutting *All the
chunky indoor amaryllis are excellent for
cutting. I love the deep rich red shades (**2**, **3**)
and the delicate pale green variety 'Lemons
and Lime'. The pure white varieties and the
white veined with red or green, with their
huge open flowers and overlapping petals, are
also favorites. The larger blooms, which may
be up to 6–8in (15–20cm) across, look*

*glamorous with a few simple branches of
filbert or willow (see page 87); or make
them the focus of a tight, vibrantly colored
arrangement with Narcissus 'Soleil d'Or'.
The smaller blooms look best on their own.*

Conditioning *Always cut and arrange
them while still in bud and then leave them
alone. The large flower heads bruise easily
and lose the density of their color where they
are damaged. They last for up to three
weeks, but their stems often collapse much
earlier because of their length and the weight
of the flower. Avoid this by inserting a stick
into the hollow stem and blocking it in with
a cotton ball. The bases of the flower stems
have a tendency to split and roll upwards in
water after a few days. Prevent this from*

*happening by securing the stem end with a
rubber band.*

Cultivation *These are bulbs for indoor or
greenhouse growing. Buy them from a wholesaler rather than a garden center so you can*

1 *Hamamelis × intermedia* 'Jelena'
2 *Hippeastrum*
3 *Hippeastrum*
4 *Pulmonaria rubra* 'Redstart'

SCALE
2in (5 cm)

*afford lots, and then plant them in groups of
nine or more at different times. Each group
will give you enough flowers for one
wonderful arrangement (see page 87).*

*The best soil mix for these bulbs is one
part well-rotted manure, one part sand, and
two parts leaf mulch. Put some pottery
shards (they need good drainage) in a pot
2in (5cm) wider than the diameter of the
bulb and plant them half-in and half-out of
the soil. Do not water much initially. Keep
bulbs in a warm place near a heat source
until they have made a growth of 4in
(10cm); they can then be moved somewhere
cooler, in full sun or partial shade.*

*Apply liquid fertilizer until one week
before flowering. After flowering, fertilize
every 10 days. Cut the foliage in the summer
and leave dormant without water until the
buds begin to show again. When they do,
give the pot a topdressing to a depth of 2in
(5cm). Repot only every three to four years.*

*If you are prepared to wait for three years
for flowers, you can propagate from seed
sown in spring or from offsets planted in fall.
I lack the patience for this and simply buy
bulbs every year.*

Lungwort
PULMONARIA

Main entry: Winter Blue and Purple,
page 159. P. rubra *'Redstart'* (**4**) *is the
most upright of the red forms of pulmonaria.
The flowers have a slightly muddy redness to
them but brighten when they are mixed with
P. 'Sissinghurst White' or white crocus.*

Yellow

Mimosa, wattle
ACACIA
*Evergreen shrub and small tree Zone: 9–10
Height and spread: A. dealbata and
A. longifolia 25ft × 25ft (7.5m × 7.5m)
(twice this height in Mediterranean-type
climates)*

Good varieties for cutting *Not
many of us will have a spot sheltered enough
for an acacia tree, but I include it for the
fortunate few who have. Mimosa makes a
staggering sight in full, fluffy, primrose-
yellow flower in the depths of winter, so
grow it if you can. Quantities of it arranged
on its own in a huge pitcher brighten gloomy
winter days, looking and smelling lovely. A.
dealbata has feathery, gray-green leaves and
pompon flowers. A. longifolia (1) has belt-
shaped leaves and long strands of flowers.*

Conditioning *Strip the bottom leaves.*

Cultivation *In temperate climates, plant
in full sun in a sheltered site away from
winds. Most acacias prefer a moist, acidic
soil although A. longifolia can tolerate some
lime and drought. They may be harmed by
long and severe frost, but often come again
from the base. Unless you start with a
reasonably mature plant, you will have
several years to wait before you can cut
much. Acacias are fast growers though, so
you can increase your stock by semi-ripe
cuttings in summer (see page 38–39).*

Dogwood
CORNUS
*Mainly deciduous shrub and tree
Zones: 2–8 (C. mas 5–8)
Height and spread: C.a. 'Elegantissima' to
7ft × 7ft (2.2m × 2.2m); C. alba 'Sibirica'
and C. stolonifera 'Flaviramea' to 6ft ×
13ft (1.8m × 4m); C. mas to 18ft ×18ft
(5.5m × 5.5m)*

Good varieties for cutting *One of
my favorite dogwoods for cutting is the
Cornelian cherry, C. mas (2), with its
starry, bright yellow flowers in late winter.
A few sprigs cut and arranged on their own
look lovely; or mix them with hamamelis. If
you have space, it is also worth planting a
small clump of C. stolonifera 'Flaviramea',*

*with green-yellow stems. Cut the bare winter
branches for a huge arrangement in a simple
glass vase or use them to make the basis of
wreaths and globes at any time of year. The
stems, like those of willow, are pliable and
soft when newly cut. On into late spring and
summer, there is no better foliage than variegated C. alba 'Elegantissima' as the base of
a large, white-and-green arrangement.*

Conditioning *Branches cut for foliage
should have the bottom 1in (2.5cm) of stem
plunged in boiling water for a minute, before
having a good soak in deep, cold water.
Otherwise they have a tendency to droop.*

Cultivation *Most dogwoods are tough
plants and thrive almost anywhere. The
exception is C. mas, which prefers a sunny,
sheltered position against a wall. Plant
dogwoods in early winter.*

*If left to their own devices, all dogwoods
become large shrubs or small trees. Like
willows, their size can be kept in check by
cutting back hard in late winter. If you are
growing them for their winter stems, delay
cutting back until early spring. It is the new
growth that provides the bright color. You
can take softwood cuttings in summer or
hardwood cuttings in fall or winter.*

Filbert, cobnut
CORYLUS AVELLANA
*Deciduous shrub and tree Zones: 3–8
Height and spread: C. avellana 13ft
× 20ft (4m × 6m); C.a. 'Contorta' both
18ft (5.5m)*

Good varieties for cutting *Good
throughout the winter as a source of lovely
boughs of catkins which gradually elongate
while still on the tree, the filbert, C. avellana
(3), reaches its resplendent climax toward the
end of the season when the pollen emerges.
Dazzling displays of yellow male catkins
radiate from woods and hedges all around
where I live in southeastern England. Even
before the catkins are smothered with pollen,
they look glamorous teamed with violet
willow and amaryllis (see page 87). Harry
Lauder's walking stick, C.a. 'Contorta', is
a more rarefied plant with deep brown,
twisting stems and 2in (5cm) long yellow
catkins, which look dramatic in the garden
as well as in a vase.*

Cultivation *Group filberts 10ft (3m)
apart. They will thrive in sun or partial
shade and look wonderful underplanted with
wood anemones and violets. Prune in early
spring, cutting back to the base shoots that
are more than two years old. The tree will
then provide catkin-laden branches for the
next winter. Grow filberts from seeds (nuts)
planted 2in (5cm) deep in the open ground
and transplant the seedlings two years later.
Alternatively, take suckers, with some root
attached, from the parent plant in mid-fall.*

CROCUS
*Corm Zones: C. tommasinianus, C.
versicolor 'Picturatus' 5–9; C. chrysanthus varieties 4–9; C. vernus varieties 3–9*

*Height: C. chrysanthus varieties 2–3in
(5–8cm); C. tommasinianus, C. versicolor 'Picturatus' 2¼–3in (6–8cm);
C. vernus, larger-flowering varieties
3½–4in (9-10cm)*

Good varieties for cutting *Crocuses
always seem bright and optimistic, and these
qualities are to be enjoyed indoors and out.
As soon as there is any sun, they open so
wide that their petals double right back,
echoing one's own feelings about the sun at
the end of a long winter. All of the smaller-
flowered C. chrysanthus varieties, the first
to come into flower, are good for winter*

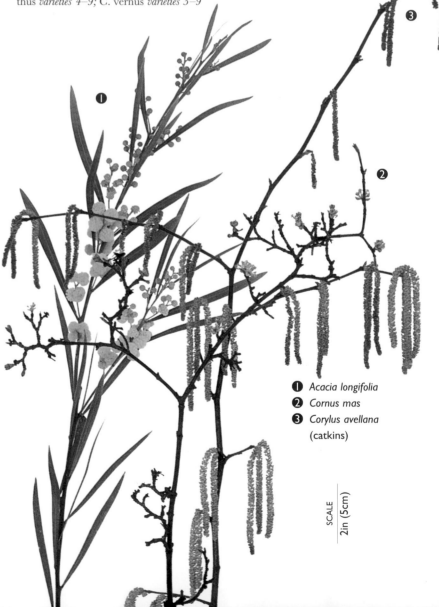

1 *Acacia longifolia*
2 *Cornus mas*
3 *Corylus avellana*
  (catkins)

SCALE
2in (5cm)

SCALE
2in (5 cm)

picking. Try C.c. 'Ladykiller': the outside of its petals are a deep purple-violet, the inside a pale white lilac. I also like the bright, brassy orange ones (**4**), and the larger-flowering varieties such as purple C. vernus 'Remembrance' (see page 158).

The delicate and dainty species crocuses are lovely arranged in a small glass on their own to have near you, perhaps on a desk or bedside table, where you can inspect their brilliant saffron-yellow and orange stamens, anthers, and pollen. I also love C. versi-color 'Picturatus' (see page 151) and the straight C. tommasinianus with its chalky mauve exterior and richer inside. All the larger-flowered crocuses look good combined with other late winter flowers or floating on their own in a shallow glass bowl as a table centerpiece. They last only two to three days when cut, but the pleasure they bring is as intense as it is brief.

Cultivation Plant fall-flowering crocus varieties in late summer, and winter- and spring-flowering varieties in late summer or fall. Plant them 2in (5cm) deep and about 3in (8cm) apart in well-drained soil or short grass and in full sun.

I simply buy crocus bulbs and let them spread. You can also propagate in early fall by seed or by division, if clumps of bulbs have formed.

Winter aconite
ERANTHIS

Tuberous perennial Zones: 4–7
Height: 2–4in (5–10cm)

Good varieties for cutting *These buttercup-yellow flowers with their green ruff of leaves look best on their own either in a short glass or floated in a shallow bowl. Choose* Eranthis hyemalis *Tubergenii Group 'Guinea Gold', which is a good large-flowered variety (***5***).*

Cultivation *Like snowdrops, aconites are best divided and planted while still "in the green," so beg a clump from a friend. Plant in a heavy, reasonably fertile, moist but well-drained soil. They do best in alkaline conditions, under deciduous trees and shrubs.*

Witch hazel
HAMAMELIS

Deciduous shrub Zones: 5–9
Height and spread: 8–10ft × 8ft (2.5–3m × 2.5m)

Good varieties for cutting *All the witch hazels with their spidery, frost-proof flowers, like the tentacles of a sea anemone, are lovely cut and last up to two weeks in water. Arrange simply, three branches to a vase and put where you can enjoy their faint but delicious scent. H. × intermedia 'Pallida' (***7***) is an excellent yellow-flowered*

form. H. × intermedia 'Jelena' has a more delicate flower (see page 155).

Cultivation *Plant in moist but well-drained, preferably neutral to acidic soil. Most like a sunny, open site, though H. × intermedia thrives in semi-shade. They are slow growers, but you can propagate by layering in the fall.*

IRIS

Main entry: Winter Blue and Purple, page 158. *The little reticulata iris I. danfordiae (***6***) with green spots on its falls, flowers in late winter.*

Honeysuckle
LONICERA

Main entry: Summer Pink, page 123. Lonicera × purpusii (**8**) *is another winter flower with an exotic scent. It outdoes both its parents,* L. fragrantissima *and* L. stan-dishii, *by more continuous flowering. Strip some of the leaves to show the flowers better.*

Daffodil, jonquil, narcissus
NARCISSUS

Main entry: Spring Yellow, page 109. *Put a few stems of the pretty, little, bright yellow N. 'Tête-à-Tête' (***10***) in a jug as the centerpiece of the kitchen table, or mix it with double snowdrops and ivy. 'Topolino' (***9***) is a similar narcissus to 'Soleil d'Or'.*

4 Crocus chrysanthus
5 Eranthis hyemalis
6 Iris danfordiae
7 Hamamelis × intermedia 'Pallida'
8 Lonicera × purpusii
9 Narcissus 'Topolino'
10 Narcissus 'Tête-à-Tête'

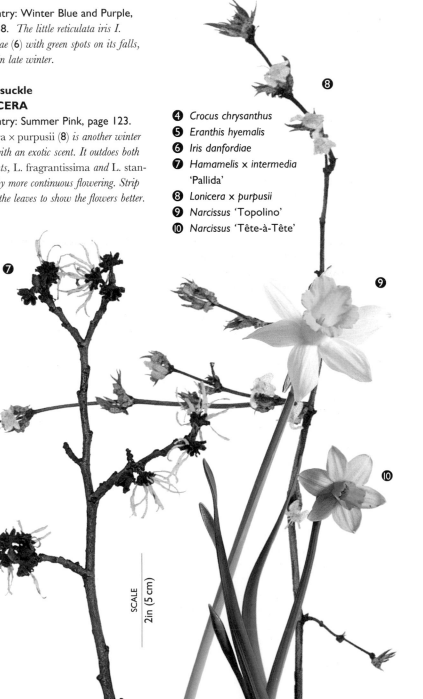

SCALE
2in (5 cm)

Blue and Purple

CROCUS

Main entry: Winter Yellow, page 156.
Large-flowered C. vernus *'Remembrance'* (**1**) *fits well in a multicolored late winter posy.*

Hellebore, Lenten rose
HELLEBORUS

Main entry: Winter Green and Silver, page 149. *I love the purple-black varieties of* H. orientalis (**2**). *Try 'Queen of the Night' or 'Philip Ballard'.*

IRIS

*Rhizomatous perennial and bulb, some ever-green Zones: 4–9 (*I. unguicularis *8–9) Height:* I. reticulata *4–6in (10–15cm);* I. unguicularis *8in (20cm); Bearded irises: 16–28in (40–70cm);* I. foetidissima *12in–3ft (30–90cm);* I. sibirica *20in–4ft (50cm–1.2m)*

Good varieties for cutting *The winter irises are an essential of the cutting garden.* I. unguicularis *in all its color forms produces flower after exquisite, fresh-looking*

SCALE
2in (5 cm)

flower to provide regular bunches for the bedside or your desk. Grow clumps of plush purple-velvet I. unguicularis *'Mary Barnard'* (**5**) *to mix with a few sprigs of* Cornus mas *or* hamamelis. *Grow, too, the scented, pale lilac* I. unguicularis *'Walter Butt', which looks best in a glass on its own.* I. lazica (**4**), *a more robust version of* I. unguicularis, *flowers from late winter through the spring. Even more delicate is the deep purple, yellow-veined* I. reticulata (**3**) *that appears toward the end of winter. An early spring iris relative is* Hermodactylus tuberosus *with its green and bumblebee brown flowers. In spring and early summer I would not be without the aristocratic Tall Bearded irises. Choose a selection of early, mid-season, and late flowers, from the Intermediate or Tall groups, including at least one white, one violet-blue ('Jane Phillips' or 'Titan's Glory'), one red 'Ruby Mine' or 'Sultan's Palace'), one black ('Superstition'), and one purple variety. Darkest indigo-violet* I. chrysographes *is also stunning. Grow* I. foetidissima *for its fall seed heads (see page 144).*

Conditioning *Stand in deep water after cutting. Remove fading flowers of bearded irises, and buds will continue to emerge.*

Cultivation *Except for* I. foetidissima, *all irises grow best in full sun. The beardless Siberian irises (*I. sibirica) *need moist but not waterlogged conditions, succeeding best in humus-rich moist open sunny sites.* I. unguic-ularis *prefers a sheltered site and thrives in poor, well-drained, even gravelly soil. Do not fertilize or mulch these irises, or you will have lovely lush leaves and no flowers.*

Unlike most perennials, irises benefit from summer planting. Bearded irises, I. unguicularis, *and* I. reticulata *all like their rhizomes to be baked by the sun. When planting, dig out a wide shallow hole and make a low mound in the middle, like an earth castle surrounded by its moat. Rest the iris rhizome on this, spreading out the roots into the moat. Plant 5in (12cm) apart, with their leaves and buds facing south to get maximum sunlight. Cover the roots and lower part of the rhizome with soil and firm it down. The central ridge of the rhizome should show above the soil.*

SCALE
2in (5 cm)

1 *Crocus vernus* 'Remembrance'
2 *Helleborus orientalis*
3 *Iris reticulata*
4 *Iris lazica*
5 *Iris unguicularis* 'Mary Barnard'

Irises will produce more flowers if dug up, divided, and replanted every three years. Both after planting and after flowering, cut the leaves to 6in (15cm) to prevent the rhizome from being dislodged by wind.

Propagate rhizomatous irises by division of the rhizomes after flowering in late summer. Dig up the whole clump, inserting the fork well away from the plant to avoid damaging the rhizomes. Split it into manageable 3–4in (8–10cm) pieces. Discard any old rhizomes, detach the young parts from the clump, and trim off the ends. Dust with fungicide. Trim long roots by one-third and cut the leaves. Replant, firm in, and water.

Propagate bulbous species, like the reticulatas, by division after flowering in spring.

Grape hyacinth
MUSCARI
Main entry: Winter White, page 152
M. armeniacum (**6**) is a lovely, deep blue, scented grape hyacinth. Pick ten to twenty heads to mix with snowdrops in a shallow vase, or use it in a late winter combination with other tiny gems (see page 93).

Lungwort
PULMONARIA
Herbaceous perennial Zones: 3–8
Height: 8–16in (20–40cm)
Good varieties for cutting Showy pulmonaria cultivars are far more interesting than the wild species lungworts with their slightly muted blue and pink. Most have the characteristic pretty, spotted white and green leaves, hairy stalks, and cowsliplike flowers. Since many of the most attractive are unnamed hybrids, it is best, as with hellebores, to buy them in flower. Look for the deep resonant blue and purple forms with large flowers and long stems (**7**, **8**, **9**). P. longifolia is good. P. 'Frühlingshimmel' is pale mauve-blue. Red forms include P. rubra 'Redstart' (page 155), and for white there is P. officinalis 'Sissinghurst White' (page 152). All pulmonarias look pretty arranged on their own in a small vase.
Cultivation Pulmonarias thrive in shade. Keep them moist and they will soon self-seed in your darkest corner.

Rosemary
ROSMARINUS
Evergreen shrub Zones: 6–9
Height and spread: 6½ft × 6½ft (2m × 2m)
Good varieties for cutting I pick rosemary throughout the year to use as foliage in many smaller bunches, but it is at its best in late winter and through the spring when covered with a haze of blue flowers. With its fragrant and robust leaves, it is a good addition to any table centerpiece or in a bedside arrangement. Grow the deep blue forms like R. officinalis 'Sissinghurst Blue' (**10**). Use its highly branched structure as your main

6 Muscari armeniacum
7 8 9 Pulmonaria (hybrid blue)
10 Rosmarinus officinalis 'Sissinghurst Blue'
11 Scilla siberica 'Spring Beauty'
12 Chionodoxa forbesii

foliage to mix with fresh whites, yellows, blues, and greens or in a brightly colored bunch with tulips and anemones.

Use the very hardy upward-growing R.o. 'Miss Jessopp's Upright' for a hedge around your garden. With its tall, nonbranching, twisted and turning stems, it is excellent to add as the final vertical emphasis in a bunch of flowers, to break up any symmetry and neatness. When the flowers are over, the green-blue foliage makes a pretty and aromatic combination with lavender and honeysuckle, or you could mix a few sprigs with a handful of sweet peas.
Conditioning Strip leaves that will be below the water line and crush woody stems.
Cultivation Rosemary is a slightly tender shrub, so needs a position in full sun, or against a sunny, protective wall, with a dry, well-drained soil. If a shrub is frost damaged, cut it back to healthy wood in the spring. If you have a straggly old plant, cut back hard in spring. It is good practice to prune shoots to half their length in spring. Rosemary is easily propagated from semiripe cuttings in summer (see pages 38, 39).

Squill
SCILLA and CHIONODOXA
Bulb Zones: 3–9
Height: 4–10in (10–25cm)
Good varieties for cutting These two very similar-looking families of bulbs are both ideal for late winter and early spring cutting. Their clear, azure-blue starry flowers are perfect for tiny mixed posies (see page 93). It is always better to choose the brighter, more intense color forms, such as Scilla siberica 'Spring Beauty' (**11**) and Chionodoxa forbesii (**12**), not the washed-out pale blue varieties. Pink and white forms include C.f. 'Pink Giant' with white petals flushed soft pink.

To tell the two genera apart, check the placing of the petals. If they are separate all the way down, the plant is a chionodoxa. If the petals are fused as they emerge from the center, it is a scilla.
Cultivation These are inexpensive bulbs and are quickly established. Plant them 2-3in (5-8cm) deep, in a site that does not completely dry out in summer. The scillas prefer full sun, except for S. siberica which does well in shade. The chionodoxas all thrive in sun or part shade. Top-dress with leaf mulch or garden compost in the fall.

Propagate both scillas and chionodoxas by division in late summer or fall.

SCALE
2in (5cm)

Year-round foliage, trees, and shrubs

Many of the foliage plants here are used as structural stems in starting arrangements. Then there are a few beauty queens, such as callicarpa and spindle berries, to use on their own. Evergreens provide material all year round, but be careful to avoid the deadening greens, such as laurel.

Maple
ACER PLATANOIDES

A. platanoides (1) *and* A.p. *'Crimson King'* (2) *are bright and fresh with their acid-green and yellow flowers and red or bright green newly emerging leaves. Mix with spring bulbs or anemones. The red and yellow colors of* A.p. *'Crimson King' are the perfect complement to bright Parrot tulips (see page 59).*

European horse chestnut
AESCULUS HIPPOCASTANUM

The sticky buds of the horse chestnut tree (3) emerge from tight bud into luscious green new leaves. Cut boughs to watch them emerging on their own, or mix them with strong and flamboyant flowers such as the Parrot tulips, which parade their huge, frilly flowers at the same time in spring.

Alder
ALNUS

During late winter, the elongating rich brown-purple catkins and small cones of A. cordata (4) *make a lovely structure for any big vase. Mix with sumptuous amaryllis or simply*

with a great haze of pussy willow. The crinkly bright green leaves emerge from bare branches to appear suddenly one morning when you come down for breakfast.

CALLICARPA

The tiny pinhead purple berries of C. bodinieri (5) *have a brightness and beauty that make them look like a peculiar, poisonous sort of medicine. They are at their best in late fall when the leaves are shed, with only the brilliant violet berries remaining on their slim branches. The*

berries look good on their own in a bright and contrasting orange or turquoise vase, but they also mix spectacularly with orange dahlias. They will last for over a month before wrinkling.

European hornbeam
CARPINUS BETULUS

Hornbeam provides exciting and unusual foliage to add to any arrangement, first in spring, with its early catkins, and then in the summer when its seed cases hang from the tree like upside-down pagodas (6). The tall, elegant branches will enhance any large vase; or cut them short and mix the bright lime-green seed cases with poppies, cornflowers, and lavender in a multicolored summer swag (see pages 64–67).

Mexican orange blossom
CHOISYA

Both the ordinary luscious shiny bottle-green variety of Mexican orange blossom, C. ternata (8), and the bright yellow-green-leaved C.t. 'Sundance' (7) have excellent long-lasting foliage. Pick them in spring for their scented flowers, too.

Tatarian dogwood
CORNUS ALBA

Cornus is an invaluable shrub for the cutting garden. C. alba colors up beautifully in fall (10), and you can use its bright bare branches in winter, too. The fresh white-bordered leaves of C.a. 'Elegantissima' (9) are excellent in summer for mixing in a white and green arrangement.

Teasel
DIPSACUS

The great spiny spikes of common teasel, D. fullonum (syn. D. sylvestris) either in green bud (11) or with whorls of pale mauve (12) are impressively sculptural on their own or mixed with luscious bunches of lilies.

Russian olive, silverberry
ELAEAGNUS

The silver-leaved deciduous Russian olive, E. angustifolia, and the silverberry, E. commutata (13), make an elegant addition to summer or fall arrangements. They go particularly well with my favorite crimsons, lapis-lazuli or sky-blues, and oranges.

SCALE
2in (5cm)

SCALE
2in (5cm)

SCALE
2in (5cm)

Gumtree
EUCALYPTUS

*The many varieties of eucalyptus (*1*) provide invaluable foliage through the winter. Use sprigs of eucalyptus to lighten an arrangement of green and white. Cut larger stems to arrange on their own.*

European euonymus
EUONYMUS

*The European euonymus, E. europaeus (*2*) has pink fruits in fall. As the fruits ripen, the hanging purses open to reveal the wonderful contrasting orange seeds contained in their vibrant pink fleshy carapace. Arrange*

the branches simply on their own in a pitcher, or use them as foliage with other pinks and greens.

Ivy
HEDERA

*The delicate bird's foot ivy, H. helix 'Pedata' (*5*), is my favorite among the ivy family. Trail it across the table for a winter dinner or arrange it twisting and turning out from a tied bunch. In the fall the black shiny berries of the wild form of H. helix make a useful addition to an arrangement.*

Privet
LIGUSTRUM

*Ordinary privet, L. vulgare, is unremarkable except in the fall, when it is covered in shiny black berries. For the rest of the year, more interesting foliage is provided by the golden variety, L. ovalifolium 'Aureum' (*3*) and silver L.o. 'Argenteum', which are both good in large arrangements (see pages 74–75).*

Apple, crabapple
MALUS

*The white-flushed pink blossom of the apple M. 'Ribston Pippin' (*6*) is to me a symbol of spring. Cut a few of its gnarled and knotted branches to have on their own. Crabapple M. 'John Downie' is another beauty, providing pure white blossoms. In late summer and fall, this fruit tree family comes into its own again – any of the crabapples such as 'Golden Hornet' (*7*) or even the smaller apples are fine companions to the flowers of early fall.*

SCALE
2in (5cm)

Buckthorn
RHAMNUS

The white-margined evergreen R. alaternus *'Argenteovariegata' (9) is unusual in its tolerance of shade and is an invaluable filler for winter and early-spring bunches.*

Rue
RUTA GRAVEOLENS

Rue (10) is almost alone in its delicacy among the evergreen plants which can provide foliage at the leaner times of year. Its deeply divided little blue-gray leaves and fine stems are lovely mixed with daphne or pulmonarias. Rue can cause skin allergies, so always wear rubber gloves when cutting and arranging it, particularly on a hot, sunny day.

Whitebeam mountain ash
SORBUS ARIA

The chiseled, deeply veined, silver-gray leaves of S.a. *'Lutescens' (16) are perfect to lighten up any mixed spring vase. Pick them in bud to open out gradually, revealing their fresh gray upper surface and silver underside.*

Snowberry
SYMPHORICARPOS ALBUS

The snowberry (11) has milky white berries, often flushed with pink, hanging at the end of narrow pliable twigs. Pick them through fall and into the winter to freshen heavy hot colors (see pages 82–83).

PITTOSPORUM

P. tenuifolium, *with its small, wrinkle-edged gray-green leaves and* P. *'Garnettii' (4), a variegated hybrid with white-flushed-pink margins around the leaves, are a great source of foliage throughout the winter. The deep crimson cultivar* P.t. *'Purpureum' is a perfect background plant to zingy oranges and acid greens at any time of year.*

Cherry, plum, blackthorn, sloe
PRUNUS

P. *'Taihaku' (8), my favorite tree for spring cutting, is a must if you have room for it. Its huge white saucer-shaped flowers drop a dense cloud of white confetti like a snow storm in spring. The species* P. avium *with its smaller denser collections of flowers (12) is a lovely companion for any spring flower you care to name. The blackthorn,* P. spinosa, *also has a pretty Japanese-style blossom that is light on the eye. This doubly earns its keep, for in fall the black-smeared-blue sloes are set against the panther-blue-black of the spiny stems (13). Combine this with the rich chocolate, oranges, and yellows of rudbeckias, sunflowers, and dahlias.*

Oak, red oak
QUERCUS

The copper, brown, and ocher leaves of oak trees are excellent as a base for fall vases (see pages 82–83). The red oak, Q. rubra *(14), with its mixture of green, chestnut-brown,* orange, and red leaves, is enough arranged on its own in a vase in the fall, or use it as your foliage for a great dahlia, salvia, and gladioli arrangement. I mix the bright green acorns of Q. robur (15) with crabapples and sun-flowers for a glamorous yet relaxed vase (see page 55).*

SCALE
2in (5cm)

Index of Plants

Page numbers in *italic type* refer to plans, photographs or their captions. Numbers in **bold type** indicate main entries.

Author's Acknowledgments

I have many people to thank for helping me in the writing and making of this book. First of all I want to thank Za Sturgis and Anna Ben for getting married. It was at their wedding that my husband Adam Nicolson cornered Frances Lincoln and suggested that, if she wanted someone to write a book about growing and arranging cut flowers, I might be the person she was looking for.

I also want to thank several people for being very generous with plants from their gardens. My mother, Faith Raven, supplied me with the bulk, particularly for the plant portrait section. I also want to thank Robert and Jane Sackville-West, Simon and Antonia Johnson, and Peter, Ian and Tony at Baker and Duguid in Nine Elms Market. Thompson and Morgan and Chiltern Seeds supplied me with the seeds for my annuals. I must not forget Nipper Keeley who made the much admired blue onions on top of the gondola posts in the cutting garden.

There are several people who allowed us to take photographs in their houses. Again I thank my mother, Faith Raven, my father-in-law, Nigel Nicolson, and the former administrator at Sissinghurst, Paul Wood. Hugh Raven, Jane Stuart-Smith, and Pia Tryde also allowed us to invade their privacy.

There are many people who have, over the time I was writing the book, been a fount of gardening information. My mother and my sister Anna Raven have taught me a lot, as have Christine and Andrew Banbury, David Aitcheson, and Sarah Cook, but perhaps most of all I owe thanks to Montagu Don.

There has also been a great team working on the look, the words and the accuracy of this book. Tony Lord has checked the plant nomenclature and hopefully ironed out most of my ignorance. Sally Cracknell, Trish Going, Akio Morishima, and Caroline Hillier have made it look so beautiful. Caroline came and held my hand at every one of the photography shoots and, without her and Pia, there would have been many flops. Erica Hunningher, Jo Christian, Alison Freegard, Tristram Holland, and Sarah Mitchell have done equal magic with the words. I always write too much. I am also very grateful to Penny Hobhouse for agreeing to write the Foreword.

There have been many friends and members of my family who have helped out in the crises along the way, with support and advice or help with the children and cooking when I was late on the delivery of a batch of text. Patricia Howie, Alex and Marion Kelsey, Chris Aston (who was the midwife for my daughter Molly), my agent Sarah Lutyens, my partner in "Garlic and Sapphire" Louise Farman, and of course close friends, Pots and Ivan Samarine, Aurea and Andrew Palmer, and Sarah and Montagu Don.

Perhaps at the top of the list are those that are here from day to day, taking the home and garden pressure off me so I can concentrate on writing. Adam, my twin sister Jane Raven, Ken Weekes, Peter, Will, and Feo Clark, and Anna and the entire Cheney family are all owed a huge debt of gratitude.

Sarah Raven
Perch Hill, July 1996

Publisher's Acknowledgments

The publishers thank Valerie Hill for the watercolor plans and illustrations on pages 16–21, 24–25 and 28–29, and Andrew Lawson for the photographs on pages 10, 22, 26–27, 31, 118 (1, 4), 119 (6, 7), 121 (7), 122 (1, 2, 3, 5), 125 (2, 3), 126 (4), 127 (11), 128 (2), 129 (5), 131 (6, 7, 8), 132 (3), 133 (5, 8), 135 (9), 136 (2), 137 (9), 142 (4, 5), 145 (7, 9, 10), 147 (4). They are also grateful to the following people for their help in producing this book: Joanna Chisholm, Jonathan Folland, Celia Levett, Anne Kilborn, Maggi McCormick, Annabel Morgan, Peggy Sadler, Richard Schofield, and Caroline Taylor. Special thanks are owed to Coleen O'Shea and Diane Lemonides for their advice and support, and to Akio Morishima for the initial design.

Editors Jo Christian, Alison Freegard
Art Editor Sally Cracknell
Horticultural Consultants Tony Lord, John Elsley
Index Penny David
Production Jennifer Cohen
Editorial Director Erica Hunningher
Art Director Caroline Hillier
Head of Pictures Anne Fraser

PLANT ZONES

The Hardiness Zones for each plant represent the range of zones, according to the USDA system, in which the plant may be successfully grown in North America. The lower figure gives the coldest zone in which the plant will be hardy without protection, the higher shows the limit of its tolerance of hot summer weather. The chart below indicates the average annual minimum temperature of each zone.

Remember that zoning data can only be a rough guide. Plant hardiness depends on a great many factors, and within any one zone particular regions may be endowed with more or less favorable conditions, just as on a smaller scale in any one garden plants can be positioned in individual situations that will suit their needs to a greater or lesser extent.

CELSIUS	ZONES	°FAHRENHEIT
below -45	1	below -50
-45 to -40	2	-50 to -40
-40 to -34	3	-40 to -30
-34 to -29	4	-30 to -20
-29 to -23	5	-20 to -10
-23 to -18	6	-10 to 0
-18 to -12	7	0 to 10
-12 to -7	8	10 to 20
-7 to -1	9	20 to 30
-1 to 4	10	30 to 40